Military History's
Most Wanted

Related Titles from Brassey's

Military History's Most Wanted

The Top 10 Book of Improbable
Victories, Unlikely Heroes, and
Other Martial Oddities

M. Evan Brooks

Brassey's, Inc.

WASHINGTON, D.C.

Library of Congress Cataloging-in-Publication Data

Brooks, M. Evan.
   Military history's most wanted : the top 10 book of improbable victories, unlikely heroes, and other martial oddities / M. Evan Brooks.— 1st ed.
      p.   cm. — (Brassey's most wanted series)
   Includes bibliographical references and index.
   ISBN 1-57488-509-X
   1. Generals—Biography. 2. Admirals—Biography.
   3. Military biography. 4. Naval biography. 5. Military history. 6. Naval history. I. Title. II. Series.

U51 .B66 2002
355'.0092'2—dc21

                                    2002003952

Printed in Canada
paper that meets the American National Standards
Institute Z39-48 Standard

Brassey's, Inc.
22841 Quicksilver Drive
Dulles, Virginia 20166

Designed by Pen & Palette Unlimited.

First Edition

10 9 8 7 6 5 4 3 2 1

Dedication

In loving memory

Eugene Irwin Brooks, CPT, VC, AUS
(April 14, 1921–August 27, 1996)

Audentes Fortuna Juvat

Contents

BATTLES AND MANEUVERS

Photographs

All photos courtesy of the National Archives and
Records Administration

Acknowledgments

I would like to thank the following persons for their assistance, suggestions, and advice concerning this book (of course, any errors are entirely my own):

My agent and friend, Fritz Heinzen, whose lively discussions concerning the inclusion and exclusion of particular personages were always interesting and hopefully added to the usefulness of this book;

My editor, Rick Russell, who was responsible for the concept, and whose appreciation, encouragement, and suggestions were most appreciated;

Michael Markowitz, Center for Naval Analyses, for his willingness to share his esoteric knowledge of Byzantine and other neglected areas of history;

Dr. Peter Perla, Center for Naval Analyses, for his willingness to act as a sounding board;

Samuel Wallace Kent Miller, III, CW4 (USARNG, Ret.), for his suggestions in American military history;

Matthew B. Caffrey, Lieutenant Colonel, United States Air Force, Air Command and Staff College, Maxwell Air Force Base, Montgomery, Alabama, for his assistance on air force history, gaming, and general history;

Flint Dille, *Ground Zero Productions,* for his interest in providing alternate hypotheses;

Nancy Ehlke and the rest of the staff at the George Mason Regional Library, Fairfax County Public Library System, Virginia, for their assistance in verifying facts and data;

Barbara L. Krieger, Dartmouth University, who, unlike most representatives of the Ivy League institutions, proved capable of providing willing and generous assistance;

My wife, Suzanne, who was willing to offer suggestions and criticisms about what people would and would not know;

My son, Jason, who was willing to offer some criticism and occasional support;

And to my daughter, Jessica, who insisted that I would not remember her in the dedication or acknowledgments—HI!

Preface

A book of the "most wanted" requires certain choices—of both inclusion and exclusion. It was sometimes extremely difficult to restrict the list to only ten; occasionally, an honorable (or dishonorable) mention can help delineate the choices.

For the most part, these are personal choices, supported by argument and buttressed by fact. Attempting to define the overrated, underrated, or incompetent commanders is a task guaranteed to provide a lively discussion.

And that is largely the point of this book—it encourages frank and open discussion as to what the military has meant in a historical perspective, who has excelled, who has not.

The reader will note that there is a Western bias in the selections. This has been intentional, because the West has largely determined the shape of the world since 1500. For example, numerous Asian leaders could be named in many of China's wars over its 3,000-year history, but the impact beyond that nation's borders has been largely transitory. Similarly, the Huns and later the Mongols produced much history but little in permanent records. A tome of military leaders that would be totally unfamiliar to most readers would be a meaningless exercise.

It was particularly interesting to delve into the background of military leaders with an Ivy League education. Some schools were quite helpful (e.g., Brown, Dartmouth), while others (e.g., Harvard, University of Pennsylvania) thought that the mere question of military involvement demonstrated poor taste. As an alumnus of the University of Pennsylvania (class of 1970), I found it shameful that the university was reluctant to address any military matters—political correctness has run amok.

The movie selections have elicited more personal comments than any other section from pre-publication readers. The war movies are lists that elicit "fighting words"; everyone has his favorite movie. Some of them may have been mentioned here.

And for those of you who can't believe that I omitted your favorite commander or that famous general of the fifteenth century B.C. who drove the Hyksos out of Egypt, believe it (actually, it was Amosis)! Feel free to write or e-mail me (evan.brooks@pressroom.com) with your comments. In a future edition I might even concede that you were right.

Overall, this was a task that was more difficult than I initially anticipated. But it was also a task that reacquainted me with some periods of history that I had neglected and hope to pay more attention to in the future.

PERSONALITIES

The Great Captains of History

Eminent military historians (e.g., Liddell Hart, Dodge) as well as military leaders (e.g., Napoleon) have written detailed volumes on the Great Captains of History. As will be seen, victory does not always make a Great Captain (although it certainly helps!). Often, a Great Captain must endure the Chinese curse of "living in interesting times"; mediocre enemies do not contribute to Great Captains. The criteria I have used are based on the leader's accomplishments given the means available as well as an integration of technology and warfare. In choosing only ten, I have had to omit many worthy leaders; c'est la guerre (and writing). References to works by Liddell Hart, Dodge, and Napoleon are noted.

1. NAPOLEON BONAPARTE (August 15, 1769–May 5, 1821)

Beginning as a relatively impoverished junior officer, he rose to become Emperor of France by the age of 36. Promoted from captain to brigadier general for his conduct at the Siege of Toulon (September 4–December 19, 1793), he later saved the civilian government from the Parisian street radicals (with the "whiff of grapeshot") (October 5, 1794). As commander of the Army of Italy (1796), he showed how strategic planning coupled with tactical initiative could defeat a more numerous enemy. In the Egyptian Campaign

(1796–99), his military successes on land were not sufficient to counter the British successes at sea, but by 1800–01, he was the dominant leader in France, had secured a temporary peace with France's enemies, and had been elected consul for life (May 1802). When war began anew, he defeated his European opponents (Austria, Prussia, and Russia) and established domination over the continent, with only Great Britain remaining as an enemy. However, his failure to subdue Spain (1808) and his later invasion of Russia (1812) began his downfall. Other European generals learned his lessons of war, and at the Battle of Nations (Leipzig, October 16–19, 1813), the French were soundly defeated. Napoleon the general showed that his expertise had not waned; his retreat to Paris evidenced his old skill and he inflicted several defeats on the allies. The defense, while admirable, cannot win a war, and he was forced to abdicate on April 4, 1814, but returned for the Hundred Days' Campaign (1815), until finally defeated by a British-Prussian Alliance at Waterloo (June 18, 1815). His strategic insights were coupled with tactical initiative; his administrative skills in both military and civilian sectors were exemplary (the Code Napoléon remains the basis of the French legal system to this day). While one cannot point to any radical innovations he devised in the art of war, his synthesis of past lessons made him one of the greatest generals in history. (Dodge, *The Great Captains,* p. 178.)

2. **ALEXANDER THE GREAT**
(c. late July 356–June 10, 323 B.C.)

The son of Philip II of Macedonia (c. 383–336 B.C.), he showed early promise as a military leader when he successfully commanded the left flank at the Battle of Chaeronea (August 2, 338). Succeeding to the throne after his father's assassination (July 336), he subdued Greek unrest (336–335) and then began his conquest of the Persian Empire. His initial victory at the Battle of the Granicus (May 2, 334)

was followed by further successes at Issus (November 1, 333) and
Gaugamela (October 1, 331). He went on to conquer the Parthians
(330) and the Scythians (329) and began the conquest of India
(326), only to have his army declare that enough was enough.
Strategic insight coupled with tactical expertise, charisma, and a
willingness to place himself into the midst of the battle made him
a superb leader. Interestingly enough, his adroitness covered virtually every sphere of military activity—from guerrilla to siege to set-
piece battle to pursuit. (Napoleon in Chandler, *The Military Maxims
of Napoleon*, p. 245 and Dodge, *The Great Captains*, p. 1.)

3. JULIUS CAESAR (July 12/13, 100–March 15, 44 B.C.)

Caesar was a Roman politician whose military career became the
exemplar of Roman arms. His Gallic Wars (58–52), his invasion of
Britain (55), and his defeat of Pompey in the civil war (50–49) were
classic tactical feats. Unfortunately, he had the habit of being surprised by his enemies; then again, he also had the luck and battlefield initiative to overcome these early setbacks. Perhaps Napoleon
said it best when he declared that it was "better to be lucky than
good," and "Caesar's luck" was worth an army. His career established the basis of an empire, and his family name has come to
mean a ruler (the word "Caesar" has been adapted into other languages—for example "kaiser" and "tsar"). His oratory could inspire
his troops to accomplish things that were "impossible"; he knew
how to capitalize upon his enemy's errors. (Napoleon in Chandler,
The Military Maxims of Napoleon, p. 245 and Dodge, *The Great
Captains*, p. 73.)

4. GENGHIS KHAN (C. 1162–August 18, 1227)

An exiled claimant to a minor throne, he reclaimed his inheritance
before he was 30 and went on to become the ruler of Mongolia by
1204. He led his Mongol Empire in successful invasions of China

(1211), Central Asia (1218), Persia (1221), and Russia (1221–23). He was a strategic genius and an excellent civil-military administrator and may have been the most adept user of psychological warfare operations in history. He transformed the Mongol army from a light cavalry raiding party to a shock troop that could utilize both speed and force. (Liddell Hart, *The Great Captains Unveiled*, p. 1.)

5. HANNIBAL BARCA (c. 247–c. 183 B.C.)

He was a Carthaginian general whose family had sworn to avenge the Carthaginian defeat in the First Punic War (264–241 B.C.). After assuming command of the Carthaginian army in Spain, he invaded Gaul and crossed the Alps (218) to bring the devastation of war to the Roman heartland. For the next decade, he fought several pitched battles but was never strong enough to seize Rome itself. At the Battle of Cannae (August 2, 216), his double envelopment of the Roman army led to one of the worst defeats of Roman arms in history; the battle has continued to attract the attention of every general since who would seek to outdo the master. The Romans simply outlasted his army, since he could reinforce only with difficulty. Defeated by Scipio Africanus (c. 236–184 B.C.) at the Battle of Zama (202), he was pursued, harassed, and eventually driven to suicide by Rome ("Let us release the Romans from their long anxiety, since they think it too long to wait for the death of an old man" quoted in Lanning, *The Military 100*, p. 117). Strategic insight and tactical brilliance could not overcome the weight that Rome could bring to bear, but Hannibal did come close. (Napoleon in Chandler, *The Military Maxims of Napoleon*, p. 245 and Dodge, *The Great Captains*, p. 38.)

6. SALAH-AL DIN YUSUF IBN AYYUB (SALADIN)
(c. 1138–March 4, 1193)

A Kurd, he became vizier of Egypt (March 1169) and fought against Crusade expeditions. His genius lay in both political and military spheres, and he expanded the Egyptian navy and army and established control of Syria and Iraq (1174–86). Then, ready to confront the Christian Crusaders, he declared a *jihad* ("holy war") and seized most of Palestine (including Jerusalem in 1187). The Third Crusade was specifically tailored to reverse Saladin's gains, and when Richard I the Lionhearted (1157–99) defeated the Arabs at Arsuf (September 7, 1191), Saladin was astute enough to change his tactics and refused to meet the English ruler in an open-field battle. He was chivalrous (more so than most of his "Christian" opponents) and astute in recognizing goals and seeking the means to achieve them, but his military reputation has not been sufficiently recognized in his own Arab lands or in the West.

7. GUSTAVUS ADOLPHUS
(December 9, 1594–November 16, 1632)

King of Sweden, he spent most of his life on the battlefield. Beginning with wars against Denmark, Russia, and Poland, he displayed leadership in the Thirty Years' War (1618–48) that secured his place in history. At the Battle of Breitenfeld (September 17, 1631), he destroyed Tilly's Catholic mercenary army; he was later killed at the Battle of Leutzen. But he is known as the "Father of Modern Warfare" because of his innovations to integrate combined arms on the battlefield and develop a professional officer cadre. In addition, his logistical expertise allowed his army an unprecedented mobility, which he was able to use to maximize his opportunities. Willing to adapt his battlefield organization and tactics to changing times, he developed the first modern professional army. (Napoleon [who considered both Wallenstein {1583–1634} and Tilly {1559–1632} to be better generals; yet Gustavus's dynasty lasted longer than Napoleon's] in Chandler, *The Military Maxims of* Napoleon, p. 245; Dodge, *The Great Captains*, p. 107; Liddell Hart, *The Great Captains Unveiled*, p. 75.)

8. **FREDERICK THE GREAT**
(January 24, 1712–August 17, 1786)

King of Prussia, he was raised in a martial environment, although he seemed to have the soul of an artist. In the First Silesian War (1740–41), the War of the Austrian Succession (1740–48), the Seven Years' War (1756–63), and the War of the Bavarian Succession (1778–79), he exhibited a grasp of battlefield tactics coupled with an awareness of maneuver warfare. His *Instructions for His Generals* (1747) may still be read as one of the best theoretical treatises on warfare ever done. However, Frederick's reach always seemed to exceed his grasp; his concept of the offensive worked to a degree, but it decimated the economic underpinnings of his nation, especially since he often faced multiple enemies on more than one front. Napoleon regarded him as bolder than the French Emperor, but this boldness was eventually a negative factor. (Napoleon in Chandler, *The Military Maxims of Napoleon,* p. 245 and Dodge, *The Great Captains,* p. 140, whose proposed work on Frederick was never completed.)

9. **JOHN CHURCHILL, FIRST DUKE OF MARLBOROUGH**
(May 26, 1650–June 16, 1722)

During the Third Dutch War (1672–74), the War of the League of Augsburg (1688–97) and the War of the Spanish Succession (1701–14), he utilized the English army to achieve tactical dominance on the European battlefield. At the Battle of Blenheim (August 13, 1704), his oblique approach and judicious use of reinforcements to reinforce success destroyed the Franco-Bavarian army and restored the prestige of English troops to a level not attained since the Hundred Years' War. His strengths were in timing, morale, and maneuver; he was probably unequaled as a battlefield commander.

10. **ULYSSES S. GRANT** (April 27, 1822–July 23, 1885)

A Union general during the American Civil War (1861–65), he seized Forts Henry and Donelson (February 6 and 16, 1862), defeated the Confederate Army at the Battle of Shiloh (April 6–7, 1862), besieged and captured Vicksburg (November 1862–July 4, 1863), assumed command of the Army of the Potomac, and drove the Army of Northern Virginia back to Richmond in a series of battles (Wilderness, May 4–7, 1864; Spotsylvania, May 8–17, 1864; North Anna, May 23–26, 1864; Cold Harbor, June 3, 1864) before enveloping Richmond by the Siege of Petersburg (June 1864–March 1865). He finally compelled the main Confederate Army in the field to surrender at Appomattox Court House (April 9, 1865), thereby effectively forcing the conclusion of the war. Grant is the only leader of the Great Captains who earned his reputation in a civil war. However, his strengths were a perseverance in achieving his goals (which could occasionally go to an extreme, as at Cold Harbor), an ability to learn from his mistakes (e.g., the maneuvers of the Vicksburg Campaign), an ability to understand the strategic picture and handle large mass armies, and the ability to understand new technologies (e.g., use of the railroad and telegraph as force multipliers) and properly utilize them on the battlefield to achieve tactical and operational success.

The Great Admirals of History

While one may debate the Great Captain of History, there is no such dispute when it comes to the Great Admiral. He stands above the others in any rating. There are other admirals in history, but most are of relatively recent vintage. Why? Simply because the sea is an unforgiving environment, and much of naval warfare has had to do more with fighting the elements than with fighting an enemy. Ancient naval warfare was more akin to land warfare on an unstable platform; by the sixteenth century, naval warfare had begun to evolve into a separate and distinct form.

1. HORATIO NELSON
(September 29, 1758–October 21, 1805)

With his well-trained subordinates (the "Band of Brothers"), he defeated the French fleets or their allies at the Nile (August 1, 1798), Copenhagen (April 2, 1801), and Trafalgar (October 21, 1805). Nelson totally broke with the standard "Fighting Instructions" (British naval battle doctrine that had become ossified over the years into a rigid set of orders that prevented a decisive victory but also avoided the chance of catastrophic defeat) and allowed his fleets to engage the enemy at close quarters, knowing that their abilities were more than able to compensate for any enemy maneuvers. The "Nelson Touch" was a light one, but in an era of signal flags and obscuring smoke, it was enough. Although he was killed on his flagship at the moment of victory, this decisive engagement secured the supremacy of the seas for Great Britain and guaranteed that Napoleonic France would be unable to offer a viable challenge.

2. **THOMAS COCHRANE**
(December 14, 1775–October 30, 1860)

Cochrane was a visionary whose ability to understand new technologies was wasted on the British admiralty during the Napoleonic Wars. The real-life model for C.S. Forester's Horatio Hornblower, Cochrane was the best frigate captain in the British Navy. His missions were superbly planned and executed; the results were major successes with minimal casualties. His politics were radical (encouraging both parliamentary and naval reform), and this caused the Admiralty to consider him a liability. He became an admiral in the fleets of Chile, Peru, Brazil, and Greece before returning to Great Britain. His innovations in screw propellers and boilers presaged the changes accomplished by Admiral Fisher 50 years later.

3. **CHESTER WILLIAM NIMITZ**
(February 24, 1885–February 20, 1966)

During World War II, he was CINCPAC (Commander in Chief Pacific Fleet) and was primarily responsible for the Central Pacific "island-hopping" campaigns (i.e., the Gilbert Islands, November 20–23, 1943; the Marshall Islands, January 31–February 23, 1944; the Marianas, June 14–August 10, 1944; and Palau, September 15–November 25, 1944). Later, he joined with MacArthur in the liberation of the Philippines as well as the seizure of Iwo Jima (February 19–March 24,

1945) and Okinawa (April 1–June 21, 1945). A superb strategist, he was able to maximize the performance of his subordinates.

4. HEIHACHIRO TOGO (January 27, 1848–May 30, 1934)

Ably assisting in the modernization of the Japanese Fleet, he was the fleet commander at the Battle of Tsushima (May 27, 1905), where the Russian fleet was virtually annihilated by his superior firepower and maneuver. He was known as "The Nelson of the East."

5. MICHEL ADRIAANSZOON DE RUYTER (March 24, 1607–April 29, 1676)

The greatest Dutch admiral, he fought successfully against the Spanish (1641), the Barbary pirates (1642–50; 1654–59), Sweden (1659), and England (1652–53; 1664–67; 1672–76). He was renowned for his successful battles against larger fleets and literally captured the English flagship as a prize during a raid on the Thames River. His conduct as a fleet commander ensured the survival of the Dutch Republic during his lifetime.

6. ISOROKU YAMAMOTO (April 4, 1884–April 18, 1943)

As Japan's premier naval strategist, he was primarily responsible for the attack on Pearl Harbor (December 7, 1941) and the first six months of success. However, he had previously predicted that Japan could not hope to defeat the economically superior United States. Though he was responsible for an overly complex plan at Midway (June 4–6, 1942) that led to a major defeat, his strategic abilities were still recognized and feared by the Allies so much that they specifically targeted him for elimination and shot down his plane in one of the few direct terminations in World War II.

7. **DAVID GLASGOW FARRAGUT**
(July 5, 1801–August 14, 1870)

The first American naval officer promoted to the ranks of rear admiral, vice admiral, and admiral, he was the Union's best naval strategist during the Civil War (1861–65). His major victories included the capture of New Orleans (April 24, 1862) and Mobile Bay (August 5, 1864). During the latter battle, he cried out, "Damn the torpedoes [mines], full speed ahead," rallying the fleet to follow him through the minefields to victory.

8. **THEMISTOCLES** (c. 514–449 B.C.)

An Athenian leader, he fought at the Battle of Marathon (492 B.C.). He persuaded the Athenians to rely on their "wooden walls," according to a Delphic prophecy that he interpreted to mean a strong navy. Although the operational control of the Greek fleet was given to a Spartan, Themistocles was responsible for the strategic concept, which resulted in a naval victory over the Persians at the Battle of Salamis (480 B.C.).

9. **ANDREA DORIA**
(November 30, 1466–November 25, 1560)

He fought for Genoa against Barbary corsairs (1510) and for the French against Papal forces (1522–24). Later he commanded the Imperial-Genoese-Venetian combined fleets. For almost 40 years, he was the primary naval strategist of the Mediterranean—choosing his sides carefully in order to buttress his own reputation and fortune.

10. **DON JOHN DE AUSTRIA**
(February 24, 1547–October 1, 1578)

As commander of the Holy League (Spain, Venice, and the Papal States), he defeated the Turks at the Battle of Lepanto (October 7,

1571). This naval battle stopped Turkish expansion into the Mediterranean and was the high-water mark of Islamic growth into eastern Europe.

Honorable Mention

JOHN ARBUTHNOT FISHER (January 25, 1841–July 10, 1920)
What if they gave a war and no one came? What if one prepares for war, but it never comes (at least, not on your watch)? "Jackie" Fisher was a British admiral in a period of colonial wars and gunboat diplomacy but no fleet actions. Instead, he is recognized for bringing the Royal Navy into the twentieth century—scrapping sail and setting steam. In 1906, he was primarily responsible for the first modern battleship, HMS *Dreadnought*, which began a naval arms race that did not end before World War I—by which time he was retired. Called back for the national emergency, he could do little with Winston Churchill as First Lord of the Admiralty (only one prima donna in charge at a time, please).

WILLIAM FREDERICK HALSEY JR.
(October 30, 1882–August 16, 1959)
An American admiral during World War II in the Pacific campaigns against Japan, he was noted for his aggression, daring, and popularity among the fleet. Primarily responsible for the strategic victories at Santa Cruz (October 26–28, 1942) and the Solomons (June–October 1943), his initiative led him astray in the Leyte campaign (October 17–25, 1944) when he chased after the "carrier bait" of the Japanese fleet. Luckily, the transports in San Bernardino Strait were saved by a scratch task force (Taffy 3) of escort carriers and destroyers. As commander of the Third Fleet, he lost three destroyer escorts in a

typhoon and could have lost much more. Overall, he seems to have become the Jeb Stuart of the U.S. Navy in terms of strengths and weaknesses. The weaknesses have detracted from his rating, but in terms of combat effectiveness, he remains one of the best fighting admirals of all time.

The Distaff Side of Command: Female Combat Leaders

While history tells of many women who fought beside their spouses in the front lines (e.g., Molly Pitcher), there are surprisingly few examples of combat leadership.

1. JOAN OF ARC (January 6, 1412–May 30, 1431)

The "Maid of Orleans" remains the most significant female combat leader in history. Her "divine inspiration" catapulted her from a simple peasant girl into the leader of a French army in the Hundred Years' War. She resurrected the hopes of the French, and her martial victories permitted the coronation of Charles VII. Captured by the Burgundians, she was tried by the English and executed as a witch. Later rehabilitated by the Catholic Church, she was canonized on May 16, 1920 (interestingly, it took half a millennium for the Church to admit its mistake). Unlike many other female combat commanders, Joan did not succeed to her position by virtue of a parent or a spouse; she was a self-made woman.

2. BOUDICCA (?–A.D. 61)

Queen of a British tribe, she led a revolt against the Roman Empire when it attempted to seize her kingdom following her husband's death. Leading from the front, she was instrumental in the sacking

Joan of Arc, the Maid of Orleans, remains the most significant female combat leader in history. At the tender age of 17, this simple peasant girl was catapulted through "divine inspiration" to leadership of a French army in the Hundred Years' War.

of Colchester, London, and St. Albans before the Roman legions defeated her army. Rather than submit to Roman rule, she committed suicide.

3. **ZENOBIA** (A.D. 231?–273?)

Queen of Palmyra (A.D. 261–273), she rebelled against Roman suzerainty after the death of her husband. A capable field general, she was finally defeated by Aurelian and made part of his triumphal parade. She was allowed to retire in exile.

4. **DEBORAH** (C. 1100 B.C.?)

In the Bible, Deborah was a "prophetess, the wife of Lapidoth.... The children of Israel came up to her for judgment" (Judges 4:4–5). She developed a battle plan: "Go and draw toward Mount Tabor, and take with thee ten thousand men.... I will draw unto thee, to the river Kishon, Sisera the captain of Jabin's army, with his chariots and his multitude and I will deliver him into thine hand" (Judges 4: 6–7). In effect, Deborah planned a diversion that would lead the Canaanites into a fatal ambush. Her success was noted: "So God subdued on that day Jabin the King of Canaan before the Children of Israel" (Judges 4:23).

5. **RANI OF JHANSI** (C. 1825/1835–June 17, 1858)

Rani Lakshmi Bai was the queen *(Rani)* of Jhansi. When her husband died, the British forced her and her son to abdicate. With the beginning of the Indian Mutiny (1857), she led her bodyguard in a revolt against British rule. Defeated at Jhansi, she fled to join the main rebel army at Gwalior and died in combat. She is regarded as one of India's preindependence heroines.

6. **HATSHEPSUT** (C. 1500 B.C.)

The fifth ruler of the 18th Dynasty, Hatshepsut became regent upon the death of her husband Thutmose II (c. 1479 B.C.). Declaring herself

Pharaoh six years later, she presided over an Egyptian Golden Age. Donning male clothing and fake chin hair, she may well have led the armies of Egypt on a punitive expedition against a Numidian revolt ("I saw when HE overthrew the Nubian Bowman, and when their chiefs were brought to HIM as living captives. I saw when HE razed Nubia, I being in HIS majesty's following. . . ." As quoted in Dr. Leroy Vaughn, *Hatshepsut.* December 1, 2001. <*http://www.ccds. charlotte.nc.us/vaughn/Diversity/hatshepsut.htm*>.) She was overthrown by her son Thutmose III in 1458 B.C.

7. **THE TRUNG SISTERS** (August 1, A.D. 14–February 6, 43)

Twin Vietnamese sisters, Trung Trac and Trung Nhi were the daughters of a general. In A.D. 40, they openly revolted against the Chinese Han Dynasty, which had occupied Vietnam since 111 B.C. Their initial successes were countered three years later, when the Chinese committed major reinforcements and better field commanders. At the Battle of the Hat Giang River, the sisters and their forces were severely defeated; both women committed suicide rather than surrender to the Chinese. The first to launch a major revolt against China, they remain Vietnamese nationalist heroines.

8. **MARIA BOCHKAREVA** (July 1889–May 15, 1920?)

Peasant-born, she worked in a factory before enlisting in the Russian Army (1914). By 1917, she had been promoted to sergeant and wounded several times. With the February Revolution and the advent of the Kerensky Provisional Government, she offered to form the "Women's Battalion of Death." As a lieutenant and captain, she commanded this formation in one of the Provisional Government's final offensives against the German armies at the front (c. June 1917, where the unit suffered 80 percent casualties). In April 1918, she left Russia to seek assistance in the United States; she returned to Russia in October 1919. Captured by the Bolsheviks, she was sentenced to death by the Omsk Cheka (Soviet security police) on May 15, 1920. When or if the sentence was carried out is open to question, but Maria Bochkareva was never seen again.

9. LASKARINA BOUBOULINA (1771–1825)

Descended from a well-to-do fishing family, she purchased four ships and led them against the Turks in the Greek War of Independence (1821–32). She assisted in the blockade of Naupila and with a small land force, seized Tripoli. A partisan of armed resistance, she was killed in a family vendetta.

10. ANGELIQUE BRULON (1771–1859)

She fought in the French Revolutionary Wars (1792–99). As a sergeant, she commanded male troops at Calvi, who certified her courage in hand-to-hand combat. She was commissioned a lieutenant in 1822 and later received the Legion of Honor from Napoleon III.

Commanding Officers (Old)

Napoleon once stated that "a man has his day in war as in other things" (1805); obviously some men have days that last longer than others. Usually one finds that once a real war begins, the age of commanders will tend to decrease as the military gets rid of its peacetime commanders and replaces them with wartime leaders. But some men can retain command despite their advancing years. During World War II, anyone over the age of 25 in the U.S. Army Air Force was considered ancient. The commanders below truly constitute "old" by most definitions.

1. ENRICO DANDOLO (c. 1110/1120–June 1205) (c. 83/93?)

Elected doge of Venice on June 1, 1192, he became one of the leaders of the Fourth Crusade. Taking an active role in the assault of Constantinople, he was reportedly the first Venetian ashore in the attack (July 17, 1203).

2. AGESILAUS II (444–360 B.C.) (83)

A ruler of the Greek city-state of Sparta, he seems to have begun his military career at the age of 48, when he raided Phrygia (central Turkey). For the next three decades he spent most of his time in the field, fighting at the Battles of Corinth (394), Acarnania (389), and Thebes (382, 378, 377), and leading an invasion of Palestine (361) as a mercenary for the Egyptians.

3. JOSEF WENCESLAS RADETZKY
(November 2, 1766–January 5, 1858) (82)

An Austrian field marshal, he had a career that ran from the Russo-Turkish War (1787–92) through the revolutions of 1848. Although he had retired from military service, he was recalled to put down the nationalist revolutions in Italy (1848). He defeated the Italians at Custozza (July 24–25, 1848), captured Milan, and ended the rebellion (March 23, 1849). The classical *Radetzky March* by Johann Strauss was written in his honor.

4. NARSES (c. 478–c. 573) (76)

A Byzantine general, he operated against various barbaric tribes (e.g., Huns, Gepids, Lombards) to preserve the Byzantine Empire under Justinian. Aside from his advanced years, he was also blind. Justinian felt that Narses was politically trustworthy since he was a eunuch and would have no heirs to inherit his title.

5. GEBHARD LEBERECHT VON BLUCHER
(December 16, 1742–September 12, 1819) (73)

A Prussian field marshal, he was directly responsible for the defeat of Napoleon at Waterloo on June 18, 1815. Having bled the French Army during the Battle of Ligny (June 16, 1815) and despite being unhorsed and wounded on that battlefield, he insisted that the Prussian Army march to effect a juncture with the Duke of Wellington. The British Army was experiencing a "close-run thing"; it was the intervention of the Prussian Army that determined the ultimate victory.

6. CARL GUSTAV EMIL VON MANNERHEIM
(June 4, 1867–January 27, 1951) (72)

Appointed commander in chief of Finland's armed forces when the Soviet Union invaded (November 30, 1939), he led his troops to initial battlefield success. Eventually, Soviet numbers forced the Finns to compromise, but when the war resumed in 1941, von Mannerheim continued the war, eventually becoming an Allied power but always maintaining Finland's independence. On August 4, 1944, he was elected president of Finland.

7. PAUL LUDWIG HANS VON BENECKENDORFF UND VON HINDENBURG (October 2, 1847–August 2, 1934) (71)

Hindenburg had retired from the Imperial German Army in 1911; recalled for World War I, he and his chief of staff, Erich Ludendorff (1865–1937), proved a capable command team. Defeating the Russian Army at Tannenberg (August 25–31, 1914), he eventually became Chief of the General Staff (August 29, 1916) and was the senior officer in the German Army for the remainder of the war. He was later elected president of the Weimar Republic (April 26, 1925), and his inattention to detail materially assisted the rise of Adolf Hitler (1889–1945).

8. JEAN PARISOT DE LA VALETTE
(c. 1494–August 21, 1568) (71)

The 48th Grand Master of the Knights of St. John, he successfully commanded the defense at the Great Siege of Malta (May 18–September 7, 1565). The capital of Malta, Valletta, is named in his honor.

9. DOUGLAS MACARTHUR
(January 26, 1880–April 5, 1964) (70)

A serving general officer in three wars (World War I, World War II, Korea), he was made supreme commander of U.N. forces in Korea on July 8, 1950. His planning and execution of the amphibious landing at Inchon (September 15, 1950), led to the destruction of the North Korean Army, but his invasion of North Korea led to Chinese intervention. Eventually, he was relieved of command (April 11, 1951) after a dispute with President Harry S Truman.

10. **KARL RUDOLF GERD VON RUNSTEDT** (December 12, 1875–February 24, 1953) (70)

A German field marshal during World War II, he was primarily known for being the officer in charge of defending Western Europe from an Allied invasion and later as the overall commander of the Ardennes Offensive (December 16, 1944–January 18, 1945). His war record ran from the invasion of the Low Countries (1940) to the Russian Campaign (1941) to the defense of the Rhineland (1945).

Honorable Mention

WINFIELD SCOTT (June 13, 1786–May 29, 1866) (74)
A general officer in three wars (War of 1812, Mexican War, and Civil War), he was the senior officer of the U.S. Army when the Civil War began. As such, he developed the Anaconda Plan, which while derided as unrealistic, became the successful bedrock of the Union strategy to defeat the Confederacy. He retired in favor of George B. McClellan (November 1, 1861). He was not included in the top 10 list because he did not exercise a field command.

LEOPOLD I (July 3, 1676–April 7, 1747) (69)
Known as the "Old Dessauer," the prince of Anhalt-Dessau was a Prussian field marshal who was known for the invention of the iron ramrod and the marching step. He commanded the Prussian Army in its victory over Austria at the Battle of Kesselsdorf (September 30, 1745)—when he was only 69 years old.

Commanding Officers (Young)

Warfare is generally considered to be for the young. The average age of an American rifleman on Guadalcanal during World War II was under 19. It is difficult for one to achieve command at such an early age unless one is to subscribe to Mel Brooks's axiom "It is good to be the King" (or at least the son of a king). A number of the commanders listed herein did achieve their rank through heredity, but they succeeded on the basis of merit. The other method to youthful command is through civil war. As in a professional sports franchise that has expanded, there is a need for new commanders and ones who may be willing to experiment with new methods and technologies.

1. **ALEXANDER THE GREAT** (356–June 13, 323 B.C.) (16)

As the son of the king of Macedon (Philip II), he was appointed regent and defeated the Maedi during the Siege of Byzantium (340–339); he commanded the left wing of the Macedonian cavalry at the Battle of Chaeronea (August 2, 338). After his father's assassination, he became one of the Great Captains of History, defeating the Persian Empire and conquering much of the then-known civilized world.

2. GUSTAVUS ADOLPHUS
(December 9, 1594–November 16, 1632) (16)

Succeeding his father as King of Sweden (October 30, 1611), he immediately made his mark on military matters by leading his army during the War of Kalmar, during which he captured Oland and Christianopol (September–October 1611). During the Thirty Years' War (1618–48), he was one of the best field commanders and engaged in combat continuously until his death at the Battle of Leutzen (November 16, 1632). "The Lion of the North" is regarded as one of the Great Captains of History.

3. EDWARD THE BLACK PRINCE
(June 15, 1330–June 8, 1376) (16)

The eldest son of King Edward III of England, he was given command of the right flank at the Battle of Crécy (August 26, 1346), where he distinguished himself and was knighted. Thereafter, as part of the ongoing Hundred Years' War, he was given an independent command in France (1355), where he captured the French king at the Battle of Poitiers (September 19, 1356). He died of cholera before he could succeed his father to the throne; his nickname was derived from the distinctive armor that he wore in battle.

4. JOAN OF ARC (January 5, 1412–May 30, 1431) (17)

If you can't arrange to be the descendant of kings, then having God on your side is the next best thing. During the Hundred Years' War, she convinced the French Dauphin that she had been sent by God to assist the French in their struggle against the English. He appointed her commander of the relief force to lift the Siege of Orleans, which she successfully did (April 27–May 8, 1429).

5. **CHARLES XII** (June 17, 1682–November 30, 1718) (18)

The son of Charles XI of Sweden, he became king on April 5, 1697. He became active in the war against Russia, Poland, and Denmark (1700) as the field commander in chief of the Swedish Army. As a warrior-king, he spent the remainder of his life on the field of battle and was eventually killed during a siege.

6. **MARIE JOSEPH PAUL YVES ROCH GILBERT DU MOTIER, MARQUIS DE LAFAYETTE** (September 6, 1757–May 20, 1834) (19)

A French nobleman, he was a captain in the French Army. Volunteering to serve with the American colonies during the Revolutionary War, he was commissioned a major general by the Continental Congress (July 31, 1777). After his promotion, he distinguished himself at the Battle of Brandywine (September 11, 1777) and became one of George Washington's most trusted commanders.

7. **PUBLIUS CORNELIUS SCIPIO AFRICANUS MAJOR** (236/235–184/183 B.C.) (23)

Son of a Roman consul, he saved his father's life at the Battle of the Ticinus (November 218 B.C.). He was appointed to proconsular command of the Roman army in Spain. Scipio Africanus eventually defeated Hannibal at the Battle of Zama (202), thereby ending the threat to Rome during the Second Punic War.

8. **NAPOLEON BONAPARTE** (August 15, 1769–May 5, 1821) (24)

One of the Great Captains of History, Napoleon became Emperor of France at the age of 34 and embroiled Europe in a series of wars lasting from 1798 to 1815. During the Wars of the Republic (1792–98), he began as a junior regular officer and soon earned rapid promotion. At the Siege of Toulon, he distinguished himself and earned promotion to brigadier general (December 22, 1793).

9. GEORGE ARMSTRONG CUSTER
(December 5, 1839–June 25, 1876) (24)

Most famous for his "Last Stand" against the Sioux Nation, Custer had distinguished himself as an audacious Union cavalryman during the American Civil War. After the Battle of Chancellorsville (May 2–4, 1863), he was promoted to brigadier general of volunteers (June 1863), and thereafter did an excellent job in command of a Michigan cavalry brigade at the Battle of Gettysburg (July 1–3, 1863).

10. MIKHAIL NIKOLAEVICH TUKHACHEVSKY
(February 16, 1893–June 11, 1937) (25)

A junior officer in the Tsarist army during World War I, after the Bolshevik Revolution, he was placed in command of the First Red Army. Later succeeding to command of the Fifth and Eighth Red Armies in the Russian Civil War, he was promoted to supreme command in the west (April 1920), although his forces were defeated at Warsaw (August 16–25, 1920). One of the first marshals of the Soviet Union (November 21, 1935), he developed a "Deep Battle" theory of warfare with emphasis on combined arms and armor operations. However, he was executed at the beginning of Stalin's purges against his own military (posthumously rehabilitated February 15, 1963).

Disabled Commanders: The Sick, Lame, but Not Lazy

Combat is one of the most demanding physical activities. In the contemporary military, physical fitness is highly emphasized, and if one cannot pass a physical fitness training test, then involuntary separation from the military may result. The criterion for inclusion on this disabled list is more than a single amputation; thus, while there have been many soldiers who remained on active duty while suffering from blindness in one eye or a single limb amputation, the individuals on this list all suffered a more egregious form of disability.

1. DOUGLAS ROBERT STUART BADER
(February 21, 1910–September 4, 1982)

A combat pilot for the Royal Air Force, he lost both legs in a flying accident (December 1931). Refusing to accept his disability, he learned to fly anew and was allowed to reenter active duty (November 1939). As a squadron and group commander during the Battle of Britain, he was known for his leadership and aggressiveness. On August 9, 1941, he crashed in Belgium and spent the remainder of World War II in a POW camp. Interestingly enough, he tried to escape so many times that at one point the Germans took away his artificial legs.

2. JAN ZISKA (c. 1376–October 11, 1424)

A Bohemian Hussite general, he lost his eyesight in separate military engagements—the first eye between 1380 and 1419 and the second at the Siege of Rabi (1421). Despite total blindness, he retained command of the Taborite army and won two major victories (Nebovid Kuttenburg II on January 6, 1422, and Nemecky Brod on January 10, 1422). In the Hussite civil wars, he won several more important victories before dying of plague. He remains a national Czech hero.

3. JOSE MILLAN ASTRAY Y TERREROS
(July 5, 1879–January 1, 1954)

The founder of the Spanish Foreign Legion, he lost his left arm, right eye, and several fingers on his right hand during the Rif Rebellion (1920–27). Known as "El Glorioso Mutilado" ("The Glorious Mutilated One"), he instilled the "cult of death" in the Legion. During the Spanish Civil War (1936–39), he was named director general of the Corps of Mutilated Gentlemen (Wounded War Veterans).

4. HORATIO NELSON (September 29, 1758–October 21, 1805)

The admiral who established British supremacy of the seas during the Napoleonic Wars, he had lost his right eye during naval operations around Corsica (1794) and his right arm at Santa Cruz de Tenerife (July 24, 1797). At the Battle of Copenhagen (April 2, 1801), he used his disability to advantage: when ordered by signal flag to disengage, he put the telescope up to his blind eye and said that he saw no signal. He went on to secure a major victory.

5. HERMANN MAURICE, COMTE DE SAXE
(October 28, 1696–November 30, 1754)

A marshal-general of France, he secured his reputation through his leadership during the War of the Austrian Succession (1740–48) and victory at Fontenoy (May 11, 1745). However, he suffered from dropsy, a painful disease that causes fluid to accumulate in the body tissues; even in midbattle, he sometimes had to be carried by cart.

6. ENRICO DANDOLO (c. 1110/1120–June 1205)

A leader of the Fourth Crusade, he took an active role in the assault on Constantinople; he was reportedly the first Venetian ashore in the attack (July 17, 1203). His eyesight was notoriously poor, verging on legal blindness. The legend that he was blinded at Constantinople by Emperor Manuel Commenus is probably untrue.

Epileptics

The following leaders suffered from epilepsy. Was this disease more common in ancient times, was it caused by inbreeding, or was it simply a myriad of other diseases and symptoms lumped under a single name? There is no definitive answer, although the ancients often believed that an individual suffering an epileptic seizure was communicating with the gods. Thus, the disease may have contributed to a commander's charisma.

7. ALEXANDER THE GREAT
(c. late July 356–June 10, 323 B.C.)

He was the Macedonian ruler who conquered the Persian Empire and much of the known world.

8. JULIUS CAESAR (July 12/13 100–March 15, 44 B.C.)

He was the Roman politician and military leader who conquered Gaul and defeated Pompey (106–48) in the civil war (50–44).

9. HANNIBAL BARCA (c. 247–c. 183 B.C.)

He was the Carthaginian general who invaded Italy and devastated the mainland for 15 years during the Second Punic War (218–202).

10. **PETER THE GREAT** (June 9, 1672–February 8, 1725)

Possibly the greatest Russian tsar, he established the modern Russian Army and Navy. He led military expeditions to the White Sea (1694–95) and conquered Azov (1695–96). Attacking Sweden, he was defeated at the Battle of Narva (November 30, 1700). In turn, he defeated the Swedes decisively at the Battle of Poltava (July 8, 1709). Much of his remaining reign was spent at war on the peripheries of his empire.

Guerrillas

Guerrilla warfare is a relatively modern phenomenon. Until the Napoleonic Wars of the nineteenth century, the nation at arms was a little-known concept. Peasants may have enlisted or been conscripted, but the indigenous population rarely engaged in warfare other than to occasionally suffer the consequences of rape, pillage, looting, or wholesale destruction. But with the rise of the nation state, the population became more intimately involved with the consequences of warfare and the direct participation in such action. It is interesting to note that 5 of the 10 guerrilla commanders listed here were foreign nationals to their troops; they are marked by an asterisk (*).

1. PAUL EMIL VON LETTOW-VORBECK*
(March 20, 1870–March 9, 1964)

Who would ever think that a Prussian Junker would have been the most successful guerrilla in history? Lettow-Vorbeck was in charge of military forces in German East Africa at the beginning of World War I. By mobilizing black African troops *(askaris),* leavened with a few German noncommissioned officers (which together never amounted to more than 12,000 troops), he was able to tie down over 250,000 British and Commonwealth troops arrayed against him. Only the armistice compelled him to surrender.

2. **MAO TSE-TUNG** (November 19, 1893–September 9, 1976)

He literally wrote the book—the *Little Red Book*, a guidebook for Marxist revolutionaries everywhere. As the chairman of the Chinese Communist Party, he was able to successfully lead it from a splinter organization to dominance of the Chinese mainland by successfully battling warlords, Japanese invaders, and the Nationalist Government.

3. **THOMAS EDWARD LAWRENCE***
(August 15, 1888–May 13, 1935)

An academic, he became the exemplar for "going native": as a young British officer during World War I, he became the leader of the Arab Revolt in Palestine against the Ottoman Empire. Lawrence of Arabia, as he became known, was a celebrity and couldn't handle it. After the war, he attempted to start over in a number of anonymous positions before finally perishing in a motorcycle accident.

4. **JOHN SINGLETON MOSBY**
(December 6, 1833–May 30, 1916)

During the American Civil War, he conducted guerrilla operations in northern Virginia. "Mosby Country" ran from Loudoun and Fauquier Counties into Fairfax. During a daring raid into Fairfax itself, he kidnapped a Union general. Bold and resourceful, he led operations that were classics of their kind.

5. **ORDE CHARLES WINGATE***
(February 26, 1903–March 25, 1944)

A man seemingly out of his time, he was known for guerrilla operations in two environments: Palestine and Burma. As a British officer, he trained future military leaders of Israel (e.g., Dayan, Rabin) in offensive guerrilla tactics, and during World War II, he conducted irregular operations with his Chindits against the Japanese in the CBI (China-Burma-India) Theater. He was one of the most irregular British general officers in history, resembling an Old Testament prophet in his demeanor and actions.

6. **EMILIANO ZAPATA** (1877?–April 10, 1919)

An illiterate Mexican peasant, he led a guerrilla movement during the Mexican Revolution that was devoted to land reform. His military operations against the federal troops were instrumental in the overthrow of the regular government. Sadly, he and his followers were unable to sustain their movement.

7. **JOSIP BROZE TITO** (May 7, 1892–May 4, 1980)

During the Nazi occupation of Yugoslavia, his Communist forces were instrumental in tying down several German divisions. This was one of the few effective guerrilla movements against Nazi oppression.

8. **WENDELL W. FERTIG*** (December 16, 1900–March 24, 1975)

In 1941, he was a reserve lieutenant colonel in the U.S. Army in the Philippines; after Pearl Harbor (December 7, 1941), he promoted himself to brigadier general in order to secure legitimacy in the eyes of the indigenous personnel and led the Filipino resistance on Mindanao. Though he was initially discounted by the Regular Army establishment, his effective leadership during World War II resulted in a Philippine resistance army of 38,000.

9. **JAN CHRISTIAAN SMUTS**
(September 24, 1870–September 11, 1950)

Trained as an attorney, this self-taught military figure became one of the leaders of the Boer irregulars fighting the British Empire

(1900–04). Although he was extremely effective as a Boer commando, he was instrumental in the negotiation of a peace treaty with the British government. During World War I, he was not quite as effective in fighting guerrilla leader Paul Emil von Lettow-Vorbeck (see number 1), but he became a British field marshal in World War II and was instrumental in the founding of the United Nations.

10. JOHN NICHOLSON*
(December 11, 1822–September 23, 1857)

A British brigadier general, he was best known for his guerrilla activities along the Khyber Pass in what is now Pakistan. He established an irregular native police force to preserve order in the Punjab region. His reputation was such that a local religious cult was founded based upon Nicholson as a deity (the *Nikkalseynis*), although he considered such reverence sacrilegious. He was killed in action during the Indian Mutiny, and his indigenous acolytes soon disbanded. Sadly, he has been largely forgotten today in the areas of his service.

Mercenaries

One of the oldest occupations in history, the mercenary trade was a common occupation in ancient times. Soldiers hired themselves out to different city-states or kingdoms. However, the legions of imperial Rome eventually closed down the marketplace. After the fall of Rome, mercenary activity began an upswing, to reach its apogee in 13th- and 14th-century Italy. The *condottiere* (i.e., "for hire") became the principal military elements of the Italian city-states. Since the 1960s, mercenaries have staged a comeback, and there are even magazines for wannabes (e.g., *Soldier of Fortune*).

1. JOHN HAWKWOOD (c. 1321–March 16, 1394)

An English soldier of fortune, he fought at the Battle of Crécy (August 25, 1346) and was later knighted. During the interim peace, he joined the mercenary White Company (so named because of the polished armor of its troops). He became its commander (1363) and for the next three decades fought in the various city-state wars of Italy. He fought in Papal service (1372–77), for the anti-Papal alliance (1377), and as captain-general of Florence (1378–81), and he commanded the army of Padua (1387) and led the Florentine army (1390–92). Sir Arthur Conan Doyle (1859–1930), creator of

Sherlock Holmes, wrote a novel entitled *The White Company* (1891) about this group of mercenaries.

2. CLAIRE LEE CHENNAULT
(September 6, 1890–June 27, 1958)

A lieutenant colonel who retired from the U.S. Army Air Corps in 1937, he became the aeronautical adviser to the Chinese Nationalist Army in its struggle against Japan. In 1941, he formed the American Volunteer Group (AVG), better known as the "Flying Tigers." The U.S. government closed its eyes as a number of its military pilots joined this unit. Pilots received a monthly salary of $675 and a bonus of $500 for each Japanese plane shot down. Among the Flying Tigers was future ace Gregory "Pappy" Boyington. During World War II, Chennault was recalled to active duty in the U.S. military and achieved the rank of major general.

3. RODRIGO DIAZ DE VIVAR ("EL CID")
(c. 1043–July 10, 1099)

The national hero of Spain, he fought for the king of Castile. However, he was ordered into exile and became a mercenary leader for the Moorish kingdom of Saragossa (1081). The remainder of his career is clouded in generally successful campaigns designed to provide personal power and wealth rather than to advance any strong ideological cause.

4. MIKE ("MAD MIKE") HOARE (c. 1918–?)

In 1964, he led 5 Commando, a mercenary organization in the newly independent Republic of the Congo. While the United States supported the Belgian First ParaCommando in its air assault on Stanleyville, Colonel Hoare's 5 Commando was the ground support element and did a credible job. For the next two decades, he was

P-40s of Claire Chennault's American Volunteer Group (AVG), more popularly known as the "Flying Tigers," under guard at a Chinese airfield, circa 1942. It was comprised mostly of former military pilots, whom the Japanese considered little more than mercenaries for hire.

involved in numerous coups and countercoups in Africa. He became the embodiment of the modern mercenary.

5. **MONTREAL D'ALBARNO** (?–c. 1354)

Although not the first, he was the most famous of the commanders of the Grand Company in the Italian city-state wars of the 14th century. The company consisted of 7,000 cavalry and 1,500 elite infantry. Although Montreal established a discipline and organization that set the pattern for future mercenary companies, he was tried for public brigandage and murder and executed by city officials of Rome.

6. XENOPHON (c. 430–c. 355 B.C.)

He was an Athenian soldier who entered Persian service under Cyrus the Younger in his revolt against his brother Artaxerxes II. When Cyrus was killed at the Battle of Cunaxa (401), Xenophon became the commander of the Greek mercenary contingent ("The Ten Thousand") and led them on a legendary retreat to the sea. His personal account of this movement—*The Anabasis* (March Upcountry)—is one of the classic military narratives. Afterwards, he fought for Thrace and then Sparta.

7. JOHN PAUL JONES (July 6, 1747–July 18, 1792)

A hero of the American Revolution ("I have not yet begun to fight"), he was the only naval officer to receive a special Congressional gold medal (October 16, 1787). In 1788, he accepted an offer to serve as a rear admiral in the Russian Navy and defeated the Turks in the Battle of Liman (June 17–27, 1788). Shortly thereafter, he left Russian service and retired to Paris, France.

8. PATRICK SARSFIELD (?–August 21/22, 1693)

When William of Orange defeated James II, the latter's Irish troops were allowed to join their ruler in exile under the Treaty of Limerick (December 22, 1691). Although the English soon abrogated the treaty, Irish exiles for the next 150 years joined foreign armies as mercenaries and, just as often, to fight the English. Sarsfield was the founder of these "Wild Geese," who formed an Irish brigade in the French Army for the next century. As a lieutenant general in the French Army, he was mortally wounded at the Battle of Landen (August 19, 1693); his dying words were "Would it were for Ireland!"

9. **ANDREA DORIA**
(November 30, 1466–November 25, 1560)

A successful naval *condottiere,* he began in service to the pope and then branched out to other Italian princes. He fought for Genoa, the French, and Venice. For almost four decades, he was the primary naval strategist of the Mediterranean, choosing his sides carefully in order to buttress his own reputation and fortune.

10. **FRANCESCO SFORZA** (July 23, 1401–March 8, 1466)

Possibly the most successful *condottiere* in history, he assumed command of his father's army and later entered service for Milan. Over the next two decades, he fought for Milan and Venice, changing sides to suit his personal needs. He conquered the city of Milan (February 26, 1450) and became its duke. Cash and power were more important to him than ideology.

Honorable Mention

THE SWISS GUARD
Hired to provide papal security, these Swiss mercenaries have been on the job since the 16th century. Though no single individual stands out, as a mercenary unit, they have established a record for stability, professionalism, and longevity.

THE GURKHAS
Since the early 19th century, Nepalese hillmen have served in the British Army as mercenaries. Since 1913, when they first became eligible, 13 Gurkhas have been awarded the Victoria Cross.

Overrated Commanders

Some military leaders have reputations that may not be fully deserved. Popular opinion has exaggerated certain exploits and commanders beyond the acclaim to which they are entitled according to the historical record.

1. ERWIN JOHANNES EUGEN ROMMEL
(November 15, 1891–October 14, 1944)

The "Desert Fox" was probably the most famous German general officer of the Second World War. After his successful command of the 7th Panzer Division during the French Campaign (May–June 1940), he assumed command of the Afrika Korps on February 12, 1941, and for the next two years ran roughshod over British military forces in Africa; he was promoted to field marshal on June 22, 1942. Even Winston Churchill was impressed by his leadership and charisma: "We have a very daring and skillful opponent against us, and, may I say across the havoc of war, a great general." General Claude Auchinleck issued an edict to his British Eighth Army impressing upon everyone that Rommel was an ordinary German general and not a superman—troops were to talk not of Rommel but of the enemy or Axis Powers. After his defeat at the Battle of El Alamein

General Erwin Rommel with the 15th Panzer Division between Tobruk and Sidi Omar in North Africa, November 24, 1941. Though Rommel was a superb tactician, his concept of grand strategy was flawed, and he never proved he could command above the corps level.

(October 23–November 4, 1942), Rommel conducted a skillful withdrawal but was reassigned to Europe when it was obvious that the Axis had no chance of survival in the African Theater. In 1943, he was appointed to command Army Group B, and he bore some responsibility for the defenses of the French beachheads. Badly wounded shortly after D-Day, he was forced to commit suicide for having been privy to the plot to assassinate Hitler.

Having fought a clean war in Africa and participated in the assassination plot, he has become a legend. When the West German Navy launched one of its first destroyers, it was named in his honor. But the Desert Fox was in large part a creature of the German propaganda machine. It has been said that "he was not tainted by Nazism" (Barnett, *Hitler's Generals,* p. 314); he despised senior staff officers for their subservience to the Nazi Party (Young, *Rommel: The*

Desert Fox, p. 67), yet he was enthralled and subservient to the personal charisma of Hitler. In 1938, as a colonel, he commanded Hitler's personal security battalion and accompanied the Führer into the Sudetenland (October 1938) and Prague (March 1939). On August 23, 1939, he was promoted to major general and given primary responsibility for Hitler's safety; it was not until Germany began to lose the war that Rommel began to look askance at his leader.

He had a tendency to jump the chain of command, and while his from-the-front leadership could yield positive results, it often left his subordinates in the lurch. His concept of grand strategy was flawed and his operational use of logistics often exceeded his unit's capabilities. Overall, it may be said that he was a superb tactician and a gifted divisional/corps commander. As he was promoted, his actual accomplishments were diminishing. The Afrika Korps and Armeegruppe Afrika never became true army-sized commands, and Rommel never proved that he could command above the corps level.

2. THOMAS JONATHAN ("STONEWALL") JACKSON
(January 21, 1824–May 10, 1863)

Jackson was the poster boy of the Southern Cause, and his division and corps leadership is still studied around the world. But a closer look at his campaigns may well engender a different perspective. As a human being, Jackson may well be described as a dour, misanthropic, Bible-thumping, lemon-sucking prig whose treatment of his subordinate officers bordered on criminal cruelty; as a military leader, he rises above his station but not into the halls of martyrdom. An uninspiring mathematics professor at Virginia Military Institute, he was known as "Tom Fool"; as a divisional commander, he earned the sobriquet "Stonewall" for his inspiring stand at the Battle of First Manassas (July 21, 1861). The nickname may have come, however, from Confederate General Bernard Bee's (1824–61) reference to

Jackson's unwillingness to move and lend support to his unit (see Warner, *Generals in Gray,* and Freeman, *Lee's Lieutenants*).

Nevertheless, Bee did not survive the battle, and the positive publicity about Jackson made him into one of the Confederacy's first heroes. In November, he entered the Shenandoah Valley and for the next six months did an outstanding job by defeating multiple Union armies in a classic display of rapid maneuver and proper concentration. Note that his forte was operational and not tactical command; when he assumed tactical command during the Battle of Kernstown (March 23, 1862), he was soundly defeated. He unfairly blamed subordinate General Richard Garnett (1817–63) for his failure and relieved him from command (Garnett never recovered from the accusations against him and seemed to court death at the Battle of Gettysburg as a form of expiation).

When called back to support the main Confederate effort around Richmond during the Seven Days' Battles (June 26–July 2, 1862), Jackson offered a lackluster performance, arriving tardily and in the wrong place. He performed well at the battles of Second Manassas (August 29–30, 1862), Antietam (September 17, 1862), and Fredericksburg (December 13, 1862) and crowned his performance with his flanking maneuver of the Union Army at the Battle of Chancellorsville (May 2–4, 1863). Shot accidentally by his own men, Jackson died on May 10, 1863; Lee wrote that Jackson had "lost his left arm; but I have lost my right arm." Actually, Jackson's military reputation may have been guaranteed by his propitious death before he had to face the better Union generals. As an independent commander or one who was executing a plan that he devised, Jackson was outstanding; as a subordinate commander responsible for executing the commands of others, he was mediocre. Thus, his reputation as among the best and the brightest officers of the Confederacy is overblown.

3. **VO NGUYEN GIAP** (b. August 25, 1912)

Fighting successively against the Japanese (World War II), the French (Indo-Chinese War), and the Americans (Vietnam War), he was able to prevail strategically against all opponents. But his reputation has declined in recent years, and his is a time-sensitive rating: in 200 years, his campaigns will merit only a footnote. His strategic campaigns were studded with noteworthy failures. At the Red River (November 1950–February 1951), his set-piece offensives were decisively defeated by French forces; even his successful Siege of Dien Bien Phu (November 20, 1953–May 7, 1954) was significant for the number of casualties he incurred. When later confronting the Americans, he underestimated the impact of air mobility at the Battle of the Ia Drang Valley (October 19–November 26, 1965) and the durability and firepower of American units during the Tet Offensive (January 21–March 7, 1968). His ultimate victory did produce a united Vietnam, but the aggressive overspending of three generations of lives yielded a nation that will require another century to recover from the debilitating effects of its demographics.

4. **DOUGLAS MACARTHUR** (January 26, 1880–April 5, 1964)

A general officer serving in three separate conflicts (World War I, World War II, Korea), he probably did best in his first war when he commanded the 42nd Division. During the interwar years, he served on the court-martial of Billy Mitchell, served as Army Chief of Staff, and was responsible for ordering military forces to disperse the civilian Bonus Army in Washington, D.C. (summer 1932). When Japan attacked Pearl Harbor (December 7, 1941), his actions in the Philippines were ineffective, and eight hours later, Imperial Japanese airpower decimated his air assets, which were not dispersed and were vulnerable—an inexcusable error. As commander of the Southwest Pacific, he was responsible for a major portion of the island-hopping campaign. His campaigns were noted for their strategic efficacy as well as a low number of casualties. However, many of these low casualty rates were due to his declaring that particular campaign concluded and moving on, while U.S. and Allied military follow-on assets incurred additional casualties in truly pacifying the "secured" positions.

He treated Australian military assets and U.S. Marines under his command with an uncaring disdain. During the Korean War, his amphibious invasion of Inchon (September 15, 1950) was a masterpiece; however, he invaded North Korea and insisted that the Chinese would not intervene. They did so (November 25–26, 1950), and the war continued for an additional two years. He was relieved of command for insubordination to the president (April 11, 1951). Overall, his many successes were often overshadowed by egotistical blindness and actions that bordered on dereliction of duty.

5. **ROBERT EDWARD LEE**
(January 19. 1807–October 12, 1870)

Possibly the most revered and respected general in American history, he was the primary military leader of Confederate arms during the Civil War. Politically, he supported the Union, and socially he had no empathy for slavery; yet when he was offered command of the Union forces (April 18, 1861), he refused because he considered his primary loyalty to be to his home state of Virginia. Like Antaeus of Greek mythology (who became stronger each time he touched his mother earth), he had an attachment to his native soil that superseded all other obligations. He led the Army of Northern Virginia in its major battles—Seven Days' (June 26–July 2, 1862), Second Manassas (August 29–30, 1862), Antietam (September 17, 1862), Fredericksburg (December 13, 1862), Chancellorsville (May 2–4, 1863), Gettysburg (July 1–3, 1863), Wilderness (May 5–6, 1864),

Spotsylvania (May 8–12, 1864), Cold Harbor (June 3, 1864), Petersburg (June–October 1864), and Five Forks (March 29–31, 1865)—before finally surrendering at Appomattox (April 9, 1865).

Though he was masterful on the defensive, Lee's offensives were poorly planned and executed. In fact, there was little evidence of any planning whatsoever. Unlike most armies, the Army of Northern Virginia did not develop a full-fledged staff to do the routine work; instead, General Lee often remained awake in order to develop plans and orders that should have been within the purview of his subordinates. The only time the army did develop a plan was for the Antietam Campaign, and security was so lax that a copy of the battle plan fell into Union hands.

In addition to the lack of an effective and efficient staff, Lee's affinity for Virginia led him to misuse elements of his command, husbanding troops from Virginia while more freely expending North Carolinians or Texans. His gentlemanly demeanor was noted by everyone, but what this meant was that Lee was poor at removing incapable commanders and replacing them with more adept officers. Instead, he assumed many of their duties himself, thereby burdening himself with tasks clearly beyond the capabilities of any individual. Finally, Lee's strategic offensives were noteworthy for their lack of coherent and attainable goals. His tactical expertise on the defensive added years to a struggle that he could not win.

6. BERNARD LAW MONTGOMERY, FIRST VISCOUNT MONTGOMERY OF ALAMEIN
(November 17, 1887–March 25, 1976)

The most publicized British military commander since the Duke of Wellington, he established his reputation by defeating the Afrika Korps at the Battle of El Alamein (October 23–November 4, 1942). He had the advantage of reading the German radio traffic (via *Ultra* intercepts, the German signal codes had been broken), and his unsubtle frontal assault had a major force advantage—two to one in troops, artillery, armored vehicles, and aircraft. During the Sicilian Campaign (July 10–August 17, 1943), he was slow to exploit success. Denigrating American combat leadership, he forcefully complained to his political superiors that he should be placed in overall command of the Second Front and took it with ill-concealed grace when Eisenhower was named Overlord commander. His command of 21st Army Group at D-Day (June 6, 1944) was followed by multiple

General Montgomery watches his tanks move forward in North Africa, November 1942. Although many British historians still consider him the best Allied general of World War II, most Americans question his brilliance, citing his lack of aggression and dilatory pace when moving against the Germans.

unsuccessful attacks against Caen before the city finally fell on July 20, 1944. When the breakout from the beachhead occurred (Operation Cobra), Montgomery's dilatory advance prevented a decisive victory at the Falaise Gap.

But you can't keep a good whiner down; Montgomery developed a massive airborne assault in the Netherlands designed to jump across the German defenders. Operation Market-Garden (September 17–26, 1944) resulted in a British disaster; Montgomery's response was to demand a single thrust instead of a broad advance in the west (with his being the sole thrust). Relations became so strained that ultimately Montgomery was forced to apologize to General Eisenhower and assume a more humble posture—which still did not deter him from claiming credit for saving the American army during the Battle of the Ardennes (December 16 1944–January 15, 1945).

While many American military historians have questioned his brilliance, many British historians still regard him as the best general of the Allies during World War II. Montgomery was a skillful motivator and a self-aggrandizing commander. He knew that the British people would not be able to accept a large number of casualties as they had during the First World War, and he was able to accede to their implicit desires by simply not being as aggressive as he should have been. In terms of military competence, the British produced better combat leaders during the same period—Mountbatten, Slim, and O'Connor—but no one had his penchant for publicity in Great Britain. He and MacArthur would have been an interesting pair to observe together—public relations trumps results.

7. PAUL LUDWIG HANS VON BENECKENDORFF UND VON HINDENBURG (October 2, 1847–August 2, 1934)
ERICH LUDENDORFF (April 9, 1865–December 20, 1937)

The "undynamic duo" of imperial Germany during World War I, they achieved their initial reputation for the German victory at the Battle of Tannenberg (August 26–30, 1914). However, the operational

The "undynamic duo" of Imperial Germany, Hindenburg, *left,* and Ludendorff, *right,* brief Kaiser Wilhelm II at German headquarters in January 1917. Their tactical prowess was not supported by attainable strategic goals and this played a major role in the German defeat.

battle plan had been previously developed by staff officer Max Hoffman, and Hindenburg and Ludendorff simply accepted the plan in its entirety. The major success catapulted the pair to the forefront of the imperial German leadership, despite the fact that they had few original concepts to contribute. During the 1918 offensive, Hindenburg was so inert that he wrote his wife that Ludendorff was hard at work while he was going to read Faust "for there will be time on my hands" (Carver, *The War Lords,* p. 53). Ludendorff, on the other hand, was so busy that he worked himself into a nervous breakdown. His tactical victories were not buttressed by attainable strategic goals, and he ultimately bears major responsibility for the defeat of Germany.

8. **HORATIO HERBERT KITCHENER**
(June 24, 1850–June 5, 1916)

Possibly the best-known British general of the late Victorian Era, he had served in numerous imperial "little wars" with great success. His victory against the Dervishes at the Battle of Omdurman (April 7, 1898) cemented his reputation, although an examination of the conduct of the battle itself would reveal that General Hector Mac-Donald was primarily responsible for the victory. During the Boer War, Kitchener was defeated at the Battle of Paardeberg (February 18, 1900), although the Boers lacked the logistical wherewithal to continue the war. In the guerrilla campaigns, his inability to defeat the irregulars caused him to develop the concept of the concentration camp, an innovation used later by other nations. Appointed secretary for war during World War I, he refused to work with others and was unable to delegate authority. Thus his death by German mine while sailing to Russia may actually have been a propitious event.

9. **JOHN HUNT MORGAN** (June 1, 1825–September 4, 1864)

A Confederate cavalry general whose exploits rank with those of Jeb Stuart, he was regarded as a symbol of the Lost Cause. His cavalry raids into Tennessee, Kentucky, Indiana, and Ohio earned him thanks from the Confederate Congress. He penetrated as far north as the suburbs of Cincinnati, Ohio, before being captured. His escape electrified the South, although his later cavalry raids were characterized by unrestrained plunder and pillage. Though he was a regular officer in the Confederate military establishment, his actions were more akin to those of irregular William Quantrill (1837–1865), and his death in combat probably saved him from trial and execution for war crimes.

10. **ERICH VON MANSTEIN**
(November 24, 1885–June 10, 1973)

A German field marshal during World War II, he was often considered the "ablest of all the German generals" or the "most significant [German] personality" (Barnett, *Hitler's Generals*, p. 221). He personally developed the plan for the attack against France and later successfully assumed field commands in both France and Russia. While not a Nazi, he was, like Rommel, personally enthralled by Hitler's charisma. Adept as an army commander, he was one of the few senior commanders to preserve his units against Russian offensives, but he lacked any ability to foresee a strategic result that would yield success. He exercised no real strategic insight, no tactical innovations—he was an able commander but not a stellar leader of the first rank.

After the war, he was sentenced to imprisonment for war crimes committed by his troops (who were admittedly following his orders), although upon release, he was instrumental in the establishment of the West German Army (Bundeswehr)—which accounts for much of his reputation. In a Cold War era in which the United States and its allies might have to face Soviet arms, a German general who could testify as to the proper methods to defeat the Russians was a prized asset.

Underrated Commanders

Military immortality is dependent upon time, circumstance, and proper written or oral records. Certain leaders have been neglected because they were overshadowed by a peer or there were just not enough interested historians to commemorate their battlefield exploits. A classic example is Joshua L. Chamberlain; his battlefield reputation had faded from public memory until Michael Shaara revived his standing in his classic novel *The Killer Angels*. Perhaps the men in the list below will achieve a new and greater recognition.

1. RICHARD NUGENT O'CONNOR
(August 21, 1889–June 19, 1981)

The first and best commander of the British Western Desert Force during World War II in North Africa, he was responsible for some of the most lopsided victories in history (e.g., Sidi Barrani, December 9–12, 1940; Bardia, January 3–5, 1941; Beda Fromm, February 5–7, 1941). His troops, outnumbered four to one, ran roughshod over the Italian Army and were so successful that the British High Command decided they could better employ some of the combat divisions in Greece (which turned out to be a forlorn hope and a waste of men). He was captured while on a patrol shortly after Rommel had arrived in Africa. Imprisoned in an Italian POW camp until September 1943, he missed the opportunity to become Britain's premier combat leader of the Second World War. Instead, he became one of Montgomery's corps commanders in the Western Front, where he had to remain subservient to a leader who lacked his dash and brilliance.

2. **BELISARIUS** (c. 505–565)

A Byzantine general, he fought against the Persians, the Vandals, the Goths, and the Bulgars. Continuously outnumbered, he defeated his opponents by maneuver and flexibility. The Byzantine Emperor Justinian did not trust him because he feared that Belisarius's popularity might prove a threat to the imperial throne. But despite shoddy treatment by his emperor, Belisarius proved loyal throughout his career and steadfastly supported Justinian throughout his life.

3. **PYRRHUS** (319–272 B.C.)

He was one of the best commanders of the ancient period. King of Epirote (northwestern Greece), he had the poor timing to face both Rome and Carthage in their ascent. He defeated a number of Roman armies but was unable to consolidate his victories (thereby giving rise to the term "Pyrrhic victory"). Finally defeated by a Roman and Carthaginian alliance at the Battle of Beneventum (275), he died in a night skirmish, ending his dreams of Greek hegemony.

4. **WINFIELD SCOTT** (June 13, 1786–May 29, 1866)

The Douglas MacArthur of the 19th century, he also served as a general officer in three wars (War of 1812, Mexican War, Civil War). Both men were vain, arrogant, and pompous, but Scott was more consistently right. At the Battle of Chippewa (July 5, 1814) his troops defeated British regulars; at Veracruz (March 9, 1847) he conducted the most successful amphibious operation in American history; his march inland to Mexico City was a classic operation resulting in a series of victories (April 8–September 14, 1847). During the Civil War, his Anaconda Plan to blockade the South and seize the Mississippi River was initially derided by his critics, although it led to the preservation of the Union.

5. **RICHARD TAYLOR** (January 27, 1826–April 12, 1879)

The son of President Zachary Taylor (1784–1850), he was also Jefferson Davis's brother-in-law. Serving under Stonewall Jackson as a brigade commander, he performed exemplary service in the Valley Campaign. After the Seven Days' Battles (June 25–July 1, 1862), he was promoted and sent to Louisiana, where he bottled up Union forces in New Orleans. Again successful during the Red River Campaign (spring 1864), he was promoted to lieutenant general in command of the Department of East Louisiana, Mississippi, and Alabama. Whatever the assignment, whatever the location, he provided good results.

6. **JOHN MONASH** (June 27, 1865–October 8, 1931)

An Australian general officer during World War I, he served at Gallipoli (April 25, 1915–January 1916), the Sinai (January–September 1916), and the Western Front (1916–18). Becoming head of the Australian Army Corps, he led an assault at the Battle of Le Hamel (July 4, 1918) that included American troops. He was one of the few general officers of the First World War who would have been able to adapt to the changes and maneuvers of the Second.

7. **GEORGE HENRY THOMAS** (July 31, 1816–March 28, 1870)

During the Civil War, he was one of the best Union generals. Although he was a native Virginian, he remained loyal to the Union. His rearguard defense at the Battle of Chickamauga (September 19–20,

1863) earned him the nickname "The Rock of Chickamauga." Following up this defensive tour de force with a victory at the Battle of Chattanooga (November 24–25, 1864), he smashed the Confederate Army at the Battle of Nashville (December 15–16, 1864). His Southern birth led many to overlook his exploits—all too often, Southerners regarded him as a traitor and Northerners simply ignored him. But his tactical expertise demands a closer examination; he was one of the best generals that the United States has ever produced.

8. **WILLIAM JOSEPH SLIM**
(August 6, 1891–December 14, 1970)

During World War II, he commanded the 14th Army in the CBI (China-Burma-India) Theater of Operations. He stopped the Japanese at the Battles of Imphal-Kohima (March 6–July 15, 1944) and began the liberation of northern Burma and Mandalay. As commander in chief of Southeast Asian ground forces (August 16, 1945), he was responsible for the liberation of Malaysia and Indonesia. A superb troop leader and logistician, he provided some of the best leadership that Great Britain had during this period.

9. **CARL GUSTAV EMIL VON MANNERHEIM**
(June 4, 1867–January 27, 1951)

From the Russo-Japanese War through World War II, he served as a combat officer with inspiring results. Initially a Russian officer (since the Duchy of Finland was part of the Russian Empire), he became a corps commander during World War I. With Finnish independence, he supported the government against Communist invasion. Retiring in 1919, he returned to active duty and was the commander of Finland's armed forces during the Russo-Finnish War (1939–40). His leadership allowed the Finns to inflict a casualty rate of 10 Russians for every Finn, but it was not enough. Yet Mannerheim's political leadership allowed Finland to survive the armistice and its role during World War II when it became an Axis ally. Overall, he was responsible for the survival of the Finnish national state in the 20th century.

10. (Tie) The following three individuals are among the Great Captains of History. Whereas any historian knows their accomplishments, they remain generally unknown to the general public. The 17th century is generally regarded as a period of wigs and stockings; few people know how the art of warfare developed during this period. But these men were among the best practitioners of the art of warfare in any age.

EUGENE, PRINCE OF SAVOY-CARIGNAN
(October 18, 1663–April 21, 1736)

Although born a Frenchman, he served as an Austrian officer during much of the early 18th century. He served in the Austro-Turkish War (1682–99), War of the Grand Alliance (1688–97), War of the Spanish Succession (1701–14), Austro-Turkish War (1715–19), and War of the Polish Succession (1733–38). His joint operations with the Duke of Marlborough (1704–12) are among the best coalition warfare ever accomplished. He developed the use of cavalry as both reconnaissance elements and dismounted troops as well as establishing a meritocracy of officer promotion.

HENRI DE LA TOUR D'AUVERGNE, VISCOUNT OF TURENNE
(September 11, 1611–July 27, 1675)

A marshal of France, he fought in the Thirty Years' War (1618–48), the Franco-Spanish War (1635–59), the Fronde (1648–53), the War of Devolution (1666–68), and the Dutch War (1672–78). The Duke of Marlborough served under him, and Napoleon considered him one of the greatest military figures in history.

LOUIS II DE BOURBON, PRINCE OF CONDE
(September 8, 1621–December 11, 1686)

"The Great Conde" fought as a French officer in the Thirty Years' War (1618–48), the Franco-Spanish War (1635–59), the Fronde (1648–53), and the Dutch War (1672–78). He was an excellent strategist and tactician, although he was somewhat self-aggrandizing.

Incompetent Commanders

I n determining the incompetence of military leaders, one is faced with a dilemma—so many candidates, so few positions. Merely getting to the position of general officer should offer some hope of competency, but such is not always the case. Interestingly enough, most of the "winners" listed below did not receive their lofty ranks based on sheer inheritance. They were experienced officers, often highly decorated, who were simply placed in the wrong position at the wrong time. What they have in common is a tendency to dither—indecision is their forte, and it is damning. It is to better act decisively and be wrong than to be vague. In my military career, I have served under at least two commanding officers who could well join this confederacy of dunces, but luckily, they were given neither the time nor the opportunity to do so in a combat situation.

1. BRAXTON BRAGG
(March 22, 1817–September 27, 1876)

Possibly the greatest inadvertent American patriot, he may well have preserved the Union by his conduct in the Civil War. While no one ever questioned his personal bravery, the same could not be said of his popularity. It has been alleged that he was "fragged" as a young officer during the Mexican War—someone lit an artillery shell and rolled it into his tent (it was a dud). During the Civil War, he was a corps commander at the Battle of Shiloh (April 6–7, 1862) where he did credible service. However, soon afterwards, he assumed command of the Army of Mississippi, renamed it the Army of Kentucky, and moved across Kentucky toward Louisville. His indecisive approach allowed Union forces to seize that objective first, and he was defeated at the Battle of Perryville (October 8, 1862). Censured for his conduct, he advanced again, only to achieve a stalemate at the Battle of Murfreesboro (December 31, 1862–January 3, 1863). Outmaneuvered by Union forces, he fell back, only to attack and win a major victory at the Battle of Chickamauga (September 18–20, 1863). Once again, indecision allowed him to be decisively defeated at the Battle of Chattanooga (November 23–25, 1863). For some unknown reason, Confederate President Jefferson Davis regarded him highly and called him to Richmond as an adviser—to the detriment of the Southern cause. He argued with his subordinates, criticized his peers, and was always ready to turn a decisive victory into a middling stalemate. For sheer consistent incompetence, he ranks among those at the nadir.

2. **ACHILLE FRANCOIS BAZAINE**
(February 13, 1811–September 20, 1888)

At the beginning of the Franco-Prussian War, he was made commander of III Corps (August 1870). Appointed commander of the left wing (II, III, and IV Corps), he was in fact an army commander. He retreated from the border and fought the indecisive Battle of Mars-la-Tour (August 16, 1870). Thereafter, his indecision compelled him to withdraw to Metz instead of supporting VI Corps or attempting a breakout. Rather than communicate with his own government, he elected to surrender to the Prussians (October 28, 1870). Demanding a court of inquiry, he was censured; demanding a court-martial to overturn the censure, he was sentenced to death

(December 10, 1873). His sentence was commuted, but he fled France and spent the remainder of his life as an exile. His indecision and failure to capitalize upon success show consistent command incompetence.

3. DOUGLAS HAIG (June 19, 1861–January 29, 1926)

A British cavalry officer who served in the colonial campaigns rather successfully, Haig failed the test of adaptation when faced with the conditions of the First World War. The seeds of his failure may be traced to the Boer War, where he failed to contain the Boer commandos of Jan Smuts in an irregular war of movement. Maneuvering to become head of the British Expeditionary Force, he succeeded by bureaucratic intrigue (December 17, 1915). Thereafter, he was responsible for the virtual annihilation of a generation of British youth—the battles of the Somme (June 24–November 13, 1916) and Passchendaele (July 31–November 10, 1917). The German Army finally yielded (due in large part to the appearance of a new and fresh American army), and Haig's supporters and historians have spent the next three-quarters of a century justifying his decisions. Yet it is hard to sympathize with a "smart" officer who was keen on modern inventions but could not adapt them or a more modern set of tactics to the battlefield. He spent the remainder of his life working for the relief of ex-servicemen; if only he had done so when they were still on active duty.

4. ROBERT GEORGES NIVELLE
(October 15, 1856–March 23, 1924)

Nivelle and Haig were like Tweedledum and Tweedledee, but Nivelle's saving grace was that he did not have Haig's tenure in command. Beginning as a brigade commander in August 1914, he became the senior French Army officer on December 12, 1916—mainly through his self-confidence and belief in the offensive. The

Nivelle Offensive (April 16–May 5, 1917) accomplished little other than to bleed the French Army; the soldiers mutinied in 68 out of 112 divisions. His refusal to accept any blame and his inability to develop any new concepts reveal his lack of capacity for high command.

5. **WILLIAM GEORGE KEITH ELPHINSTONE**
(c. 1782–April 23, 1842)

Indecision is a decision in and of itself; the problem is that the choice indecision makes is generally the absence of any positive end state. Elphinstone was the commander of the British garrison in Kabul, Afghanistan. When he reached Kabul in April 1841, he found his cantonment area in an indefensible location, with the commissariat in a completely separate location. When the Afghans grew restive, Elphinstone was suffering from gout, rheumatism, and indecision. Only the latter was to prove fatal. The Afghans grew bolder and Elphinstone acceded to their demands and began an evacuation to Jalalabad (January 6, 1842). With 4,500 troops and 12,000 camp followers, the retreat soon turned into a rout—only one man (Dr. William Brydon) eventually reached Jalalabad. Elphinstone had relied on the Afghans' generosity and word of honor; he had refused to make a decision until his only decision was made for him. Everyone remarked that he was a gentleman and a nice person; it was not enough.

6. **HORATIO GATES** (c. April 1726/1728–April 10, 1806)

During the Revolutionary War, he did a superb job of organizing the Continental Army in Boston, Massachusetts. However, his sense of strategy and tactics was less than optimal. Although he was the commanding American general at the Battle of Saratoga (October 7, 1777), the officer most responsible for the victory was his second in command, Benedict Arnold. Gates clumsily attempted to use his newfound reputation to supplant George Washington, but with no success. He was transferred to South Carolina, and his leadership at the Battle of Camden (August 16, 1780) resulted in the worst American defeat of the Revolutionary War. If he had in fact replaced George Washington, we would be singing "God Save the Queen" at the present time.

7. LUIGI CADORNA
(September 4, 1850–December 23, 1928)

During World War I, this Italian Army commander showed the tenacity and lack of imagination of Haig coupled with Nivelle's care for his men. In 12 separate and distinct battles of the Isonzo (June 23–July 7, 1915; July 18–August 3, 1915; October 18–November 4, 1915; November 10–December 2, 1915; March 11–29, 1916; August 6–17, 1916; September 14–26, 1916; October 10–12, 1916; November 1–14, 1916; May 12–June 8, 1917; August 18–September 15, 1917; October 24–November 7, 1917), he showed a penchant for not learning from his mistakes. In fact, the 12th battle of the Isonzo (known as the Battle of Caporetto) resulted in the rout of the Italian Army. Cadorna had a habit of blaming his staff officers and subordinates and transferring them in disgrace to the rear, to prison, or to frontline units as a punishment; when he blamed the troops, he was quick to order executions and decimations of his own units. He achieved a standard of consistent incompetence tempered with a nasty personal streak.

8. ANTONIO LOPEZ DE SANTA ANNA
(February 21, 1794–June 21, 1876)

A Mexican general, he remains best known for his tactical success but strategic failure at the Siege of the Alamo (February 23–March 6, 1836). His costly victory paved the way for his defeat at the Battle of San Jacinto (April 21, 1836), which guaranteed the independence of Texas. He became dictator of Mexico in time for the Mexican

War (1846–48), where he achieved notable failures at the battles of Buena Vista (February 23, 1847), Cerro Gordo (April 18, 1847), and Chapuletpec-Mexico City (September 13–14, 1847). In each of these battles, he had larger armies and interior lines, and his troops were considered the best on the American continent. So much for leadership.

9. LEONIDAS POLK (April 10,1806–June 14, 1864)

Offering another valid argument for the separation of church and state, he was an ordained Episcopal minister and Bishop of the Southwest when he removed his priestly vestments to assume Confederate gray. A West Point graduate, he served credibly at the Battle of Shiloh (April 6–7, 1862), but the remainder of his service took a turn for the worse. Serving under Bragg, he commanded the Armies of Kentucky and Mississippi during their retreat into Tennessee. At the Battle of Chickamauga (September 19–20, 1863), he was censured by Braxton Bragg for his dilatory performance and relieved of command (September 30, 1863). A favorite of his troops and Jefferson Davis, he was respected even though his strategic and operational abilities seemed less than what would be expected of a field grade officer, much less a general officer.

10. ALEKSANDR VASILIEVICH SAMSONOV
(1859-August 30, 1914)
PAVEL KARLOVICH RENNENKAMPF (1854–1918)

During World War I, they were commanders of the Second and First Russian Armies, with orders to move into East Prussia in a coordinated assault. However, the men hated each other, the result of an argument going back to the Russo-Japanese War. Thus, instead of moving as a coordinated force, each moved separately, allowing the Germans to defeat them in detail at the Battle of Tannenberg (August 26–31, 1914) and the first Battle of the Masurian Lake

(September 9–14, 1914). Samsonov had the decency to kill himself; Rennenkampf was killed by the Bolsheviks in 1918. Both men had been promoted beyond their competency levels; they did not have the opportunity to maintain a consistent level of incompetence, but their actions merit censure in any event.

(Dis)Honorable Mention

CHARLES VERE FERRERS TOWNSHEND
(February 21, 1861–May 18, 1924)

During World War I, he commanded a British force in Mesopotamia, where he managed to surrender his 9,000-man element at the Siege of Kut (December 9, 1915–April 29, 1916). The problem was that while he was perfectly content to reside in a comfortable captivity, his troops were maltreated and he did nothing to stand up for them.

ARTHUR ERNEST PERCIVAL
(December 26, 1887–January 31, 1966)

During World War II, he was commander of the British garrison at Singapore, "The Gibraltar of the East." Despite outnumbering the Japanese attackers, he surrendered after a short siege (February 8–15, 1942) in what was the worst military defeat in the history of the British Empire. To add insult to injury, the Japanese were so short of ammunition that they would have had to withdraw unless he had agreed to surrender.

Commanders Blinded by Their Own Ego

A military commander is a leader. To successfully accomplish his mission, he must be self-confident and possess the ability to pass such confidence to his troops. A pessimistic general is one who is on his way to losing his next battle. However, some generals grow to believe in their own destiny no matter what the external situation. Eventually, such overconfidence may lead to defeat. You can't always believe your own press clippings, especially if you write them.

1. GEORGE BRINTON MCCLELLAN
(December 3, 1826–October 29, 1885)

During the American Civil War, he was promoted to command the Department (later Army) of the Potomac (July 1861) and was made general in chief of the army (November 1861); he began to believe his own press clippings. Disparaging the president, he treated Lincoln as an obstacle and not a superior. Relying on the Pinkerton Detective Agency as his primary intelligence source, he continuously overestimated the strength of the Army of Northern Virginia and refused to engage until he had sufficient numbers (in fact, he always outnumbered the Army of Northern Virginia). Outfought at the Seven Days' Battles (June 25–July 1, 1862), he was again outfought at the Battle of Antietam (September 17, 1862)—and this time, he had received a copy of the Confederate plan (his tactical victory should have been a strategic annihilation of the Army of Northern Virginia). A superb organizer and trainer of troops, he was reluctant to risk them in combat. Although he was always revered by his troops, he was a commander who could not command in time of war. Surrounded by an admiring press corps, he grew to believe that he was the "New Napoleon," while in reality he suffered from a severe case of what Lincoln charitably called "the slows." Running for president against Lincoln in 1864, he was shocked to learn that he had been decisively defeated.

2. **DOUGLAS MACARTHUR** (January 26, 1880–April 5, 1964)

An American general officer in command status in three wars (World War I, World War II, and Korea), he believed in his destiny. His mother had accompanied him to West Point to ensure that he performed superlatively, and he did. He became the commanding general of the 42nd Infantry Division during World War I, in what was probably his most successful experience in troop leading. After the war, he became Chief of Staff of the Army (November 1930–October 1935). Always publicity-hungry, he had continuously kept his name in the press; President Franklin D. Roosevelt regarded him as one of the two most dangerous men in the nation (the other being Louisiana Senator Huey P. Long). Retiring in 1936, he was called back to active service to defend the Philippines. Despite the Japanese attack on Pearl Harbor (December 7, 1941), his command was completely surprised when Japanese air elements hit Clark and Iba airfields several hours later (December 8, 1941). He partially compensated for this inexcusable performance by conducting a successful withdrawal to Bataan (December 23, 1941–January 1, 1942).

After leaving the Philippines (while declaring "I shall return"), he was made commander of Allied forces in the Southwest Pacific Area (April 1942). During the Pacific Campaigns, he performed superbly,

In a characteristic (posed) photograph, General MacArthur, pipe clenched between his teeth, surveys the Leyte beachhead at the moment in October 1944 when he made good his 1942 promise that "I shall return."

although his large press corps contingent made it sound like he was fighting the war on his own. He disparaged or ignored the U.S. Marines fighting under his command as well as his Australian and New Zealand allies. Following the conclusion of World War II, he became the de facto ruler of reconstruction Japan (1945–50). During the Korean War, his brilliant amphibious invasion at Inchon (September 15, 1950) was offset by his insistence that the Chinese would not intervene. Oops—on November 25–26, 1950, they did.

MacArthur insisted that they could be defeated by the use of nuclear weapons, and when his disagreements with President Harry S Truman grew public, he was relieved of command. He was a superb orator, but his concept of leadership in a democratic society was flawed by his arrogance and ego.

3. **BERNARD LAW MONTGOMERY**
(November 17, 1887–March 25, 1976)

A British general during World War II, he achieved international renown for his defeat of Rommel's Afrika Korps at the Battle of El Alamein (October 23–November 4, 1942). By this time, British logistics had so outstripped the German supplies that Montgomery had an overwhelming superiority in men, aircraft, and armored vehicles, and he was informed of Axis plans through Ultra intercepts (this decryption of the German codes was not made public until 1975!).

Montgomery developed a press coterie that made him into the next Duke of Wellington. During the invasion and capture of Sicily (July 9–August 17, 1943), his careful and methodical approach showed poorly against George Patton's rapid advance. For the invasion of France, he was made commander in chief of ground forces, where his hesitancy and slowness led to stalemate in multiple battles around Caen (June 6–August 7, 1944). His insistence that all Allied efforts be diverted to his army, his defeat during the large airborne Operation Market-Garden (September 17–26, 1944), and his criticism of things American did little to endear him to his superiors. At the Battle of the Ardennes (December 16, 1944–January 18, 1945), he single-handedly took credit for rescuing the Americans from the German attack. After Britain's demographic bloodletting during World War I, the nation could not tolerate similar losses again; Montgomery's careful planning minimized casualties but at the price of combat success. His denigration of others did little to enhance his reputation.

4. **MARK WAYNE CLARK**
(May 1, 1896–April 17, 1984)

An American general during World War II, he was chief of staff of Army Ground Forces (May 1942). In preparation for the Allied landings in North Africa (Operation Torch), he infiltrated Vichy-held territory by submarine to ascertain how the French would most likely respond. He later commanded Allied forces in North Africa under Eisenhower (November 1942). In 1943–44, he was commander of Fifth Army in Italy and was responsible for the Italian Campaign. Instead of seeking to fix and destroy the enemy opposition, he opted to liberate Rome for the history books. This respite allowed the German defenders to firm up their defensive lines and present a much more formidable defense. Clark's Italian offensives were more successful in print than in reality and were hard-fought, miserable actions against an entrenched enemy in difficult terrain.

5. **MAXWELL DAVENPORT TAYLOR**
(August 26, 1901–April 19, 1987)

As commander of the 101st Airborne Division, he dropped into Normandy (June 5–6, 1944) during the invasion of France. He participated in Operation Market-Garden (September 17–25, 1944) and successfully led his division through to the end of World War II. So far, so good; but after he retired from the Army (July 1959), he began to support the doctrine of "flexible response" as opposed to "massive retaliation." Popular with the new Kennedy Administration, he was recalled to active duty as Chairman of the Joint Chiefs of Staff (October 1, 1962). His counsel was effective in the Cuban Missile Crisis (October 22–November 2, 1962) but ineffective on Vietnam. He dissembled between the president of the United States and the Joint Chiefs of Staff (H. R. McMaster, *Dereliction of Duty*), and in the interest of promoting his own agenda and historical record, he ensured that the Joint Chiefs would not be able to freely advise the president.

Through 1959, he was an excellent military officer; thereafter, he became a political officer more interested in the verdict of history.

6. GEORGE ARMSTRONG CUSTER
(December 5, 1839–June 25, 1876)

One of the most successful Union cavalrymen during the American Civil War, he fought at the battles of Antietam (September 17, 1862), Fredericksburg (December 13, 1862), Chancellorsville (May 2–4, 1863), Gettysburg (July 1–3, 1863), Yellow Tavern (May 11, 1864), and Five Forks (April 1, 1865). Breveted as a brigadier general of regulars, he reverted to the permanent rank of captain when the war ended. Promoted to lieutenant colonel with the Seventh Cavalry, he fought successfully against the Sioux in the West. Custer's demise in battle with the Sioux at the Little Big Horn (June 25, 1876) was engendered by his desire to gain favorable press notices. He was hoping to secure the Republican nomination for president of the United States and wanted a major victory to seal his fate. "Custer's Last Stand" instead secured immortality within the military annals of the United States.

7. GEORGE SMITH PATTON
(November 11, 1885–December 21, 1945)

Patton was probably the best armor officer that the United States ever produced, but his actions seemed to guarantee his self-destruction. After successfully commanding the Western Task Force landings as part of Operation Torch (November 8, 1942), he was relieved after arguing with the British (March 15, 1943). Directing the Seventh Army during the Sicilian Campaign (July 10–August 17, 1943), he was again relieved after slapping two shell-shocked soldiers (August 16, 1943). A believer in his own destiny, he found it hard to accept that such a minor incident would result in his removal from command.

In January 1944, he assumed command of the First Army, a phantom unit used to deceive the Germans concerning the invasion of France. After D-Day (June 6, 1944), he was given command of the Third Army and led the breakout from the Normandy beachhead (August 1, 1944) and the subsequent exploitation across France and into Germany. During the Battle of the Bulge (December 16, 1944–January 18, 1945), he successfully shifted his army 90 degrees in order to relieve the German pressure to his north. But as the war was ending, his outspoken comments once again caused him grief: he stated for the record that the Russians were now the enemy and that the United States should ease up on its deNazification process because it would need Nazi personnel to reconstitute Germany. Again, he was relieved of command.

8. NAPOLEON BONAPARTE
(August 15, 1769–May 5, 1821)

His star rose quickly as he went from unknown artillery captain to emperor of France in 13 years. However, he began to believe in his own destiny. He liberally distributed crowns of Europe to his family (Jerome, King of Westphalia; Joseph, King of Naples, King of Spain; Louis, King of Holland). During the Waterloo Campaign, he discounted the Duke of Wellington: "Because you have been beaten by Wellington, you think him a great general. I tell you, Wellington is a bad general, the English are bad troops, and this affair is nothing more than a picnic" (Howarth, *Waterloo: Day of Battle,* p. 57). Well, the English ants definitely spoiled his lunch, and the French were decisively defeated by the "bad general" at Waterloo (June 18, 1815). In effect, Napoleon was defeated by his prior successes; his opponents learned lessons of war from him, while he could not be everywhere. During his exile on St. Helena (1815–21), he spent much of his time dictating his memoirs, which justified his actions and decisions in a self-serving manuscript.

9. **EPAMINONDAS** (C. 418–362 B.C.)

A Theban general, he decisively defeated the Spartans at the Battle of Leuctra (371). He attempted to destroy any potential Spartan offensive threat by invading the Peloponnesus and liberating those city-states previously in thrall to Sparta. Yet his belief that he was right led him to ignore the Theban constitution and retain control of the army for a second invasion of Sparta (in 368, leading to a formal charge of treason), and the city-states that he had "liberated" rose up in rebellion within 10 years against their very liberator. He was killed fighting the Spartans yet again at the Battle of Mantinea (362).

10. **CHARLES ANDRE JOSEPH MARIE DE GAULLE** (November 22, 1890–November 9, 1970)

A junior brigadier general at the time of France's defeat in World War II, he fled to England and called for resistance to the Nazis (June 18, 1940). He organized the Free French Forces, which eventually became the Provisional Government of the French Republic. His defense of French interests as well as the interests of de Gaulle became quite exasperating to the Allies (although the statement is attributed to Winston Churchill, it was actually liaison officer Edward Spears [1886–1974] who said that "the hardest cross I have to bear is the Cross of Lorraine" quoted at the Winston S. Churchill Home Page. December 1, 2001 <*http://www.winstonchurchill.org/bonmots2.htm*>). Following the war, he became the last president of the Fourth Republic (June 1, 1958) and first president of the Fifth Republic (September 28, 1958). But he often seemed to think that the interests of France and de Gaulle were synonymous.

Military Nicknames

Military leaders have had nicknames dating back to the beginnings of history. However, some of those names echo with martial pride while others leave a little to be desired. "Nicholas the Nice" or "Peter the Pious" may be what history remembers, but would they really strike fear into their opponents?

1. ABU-AL-ABBAS (THE BLOODSHEDDER) (c. 721–54)

A great-great grandson of Muhammad's uncle, he declared himself the precursor of the *mahdi* and assumed the caliphate in 750, having defeated his Umayyad predecessors and later defeated the Chinese in Central Asia. His nickname referred to the cleansing of the unholy rather than to the wholesale slaughter of enemies.

2. CHARLES MARIE EMMANUEL MANGIN (THE EATER OF MEN) (1866–1925)

Mangin was a senior French Army officer during World War I (1914–18) whose aggressive leadership gave him his nickname not because of what he did to the enemy, but rather because of what he did to his own men. As 6th Army commander during the Nivelle Offensive, he failed, but was later given command of the 10th Army during the final Ludendorff Offensive (July 1918).

3. **BASIL II BULGAROCTONOS (BULGAR SLAYER)**
(958–December 15, 1025)

A Byzantine emperor, he won a decisive victory over the Bulgars at Balathista (July 29, 1014). He blinded 99 out of every 100 prisoners, and sent them back in groups being led by the 100th prisoner, who had only had one eye removed.

4. **FELIX MARIA CALLEJA DEL REY (THE BUTCHER)**
(1759–1828)

During the struggle for Mexican independence (1811–23), he established a reputation for malice and cruelty. He defeated numerous insurgents but in 1816 returned to Spain, where he was appointed governor of Cadiz. Three years later, his men mutinied and imprisoned him for his harsh administration.

5. **MATTHIAS GALLAS, COUNT OF COMPO (DESTROYER OF ARMIES)** (September 16, 1584–April 25, 1647)

An Austrian field marshal during the Thirty Years' War (1618–48), he was successful under both Generals Tilly (1559–1632) and Wallenstein (1583–1634), although he was instrumental in the latter's assassination.

6. **BANASTRE TARLETON (BLOODY BAN)**
(August 21, 1754–January 25, 1833)

Possibly the best unconventional warfare leader of the British Army during the Revolutionary War, he often fought against Francis Marion (1732–95) in South Carolina. He was hated by the Americans for his conduct at Waxhaws (May 29, 1780), where he refused quarter, and he was later defeated by Daniel Morgan (1736–1802) at the Battle of Cowpens (January 17, 1781).

7. **ABD-EL-KRIM (THE WOLF OF THE RIF)**
(1881–February 6, 1963)

A Moroccan Berber leader, he led the Rif Rebellion against the colonial powers of Spain and France (1920–26). Facing both the Spanish and French Foreign Legions, he established a reputation of competence but was eventually overwhelmed and forced into exile by the French forces. For two interesting though different perspectives, compare Porch's *The French Foreign Legion* and Alvarez's *The Betrothed of Death* (the latter covering the Spanish Foreign Legion's role in the Rif Rebellion).

8. **GUSTAVUS ADOLPHUS (THE LION OF THE NORTH)**
(December 9, 1594–November 16, 1632)

King of Sweden during the Thirty Years' War (1618–48), he was one of the Great Captains of History. As a commanding general, he was both a strategist and a tactician as well as an administrator. His major failing was a tendency to lead from the front, which resulted in his death at the Battle of Leutzen.

9. **ALBERT I (THE BEAR)** (c. 1100–November 13, 1170)

The margrave of Brandenburg, he fought against the Wends (c. 1136–40). He was one of the leaders of the German drive into eastern Europe during the Guelf conflicts (1135–82).

10. **TOMOYUKI YAMASHITA (THE TIGER OF MALAYA)**
(1888–February 23, 1946)

In December 1941, he led the Japanese 25th Army in its conquest of the British colony. On February 15, 1942, he forced the Crown Colony of Singapore to surrender, despite his being outnumbered by two to one. By 1944, he was commanding the 14th Area Army responsible for the defense of the Philippines. He was tried and executed for war crimes committed by his troops in Manila. The fairness of his war crimes trial has been questioned, since he was clearly not in control of his garrison in Manila when the atrocities occurred. But Douglas MacArthur seems to have insisted on his condemnation.

Honorable Mention

CONSTANTINE V COPRONYMUS (THE ILL-ODORED)
(718–September 14, 775)

A Byzantine emperor, he fought the Arabs (741), his own in-laws (742–43), the Arabs once again (746), and the Bulgars (756–63). His nickname derived not from his military exploits but rather from his baptism: as a newborn being baptized, he defecated in the baptismal font. Talk about history being unforgiving!

Don't Ask, We'll Tell: Commanders of Dubious Sexual Proclivities

Heterosexual commanders have been the norm throughout history, but there are always exceptions. The following officers and leaders have, at the very least, been alleged to skirt normal morality. In most cases, it should have been immaterial; in one case, a sexual serial killer would never have been accepted in any society.

1. GAIUS JULIUS CAESAR
(July 12/13, 100–March 15, 44 B.C.)

Early in his public career, he had an extended stay as the guest of the king of Bithyia (80). Allegations were made that in fact Caesar had become the king's "boy toy," a story that Caesar always vehemently denied. Nevertheless, his troops later referred to their commander as "every woman's husband, every man's wife."

2. GORGIDAS AND THE SACRED BAND (375–338 B.C.)

Gorgidas founded the Sacred Band of Thebes, a picked troop of 150 pairs of Boetian male lovers. "If a state or an army could be formed only of lovers and their beloved, how could any company hope for greater things than these . . ." (Plato, *Symposium*, quoted in

Ben Bison. December 1, 2001. <*http://www.fortunecity.com/rivendell/rhydin/111thebes.htm*>). This brotherhood of war was an elite shock troop formation until annihilated by Alexander the Great and his father at the Battle of Chaeronea.

3. GILLES DE RAIS
(c. September/October 1404–October 26, 1440)

During the Hundred Years' War, he was a close companion of Joan of Arc as well as a marshal of France. He was also a sadistic serial killer who delighted in torturing and murdering young children of either sex. He was accused of murdering over 100 children between the ages of 6 and 18.

4. ALEXANDER THE GREAT
(c. late July 356–June 10, 323 B.C.)

While he was busy conquering the world, he also had time to devote to both sexes. There is strong evidence that he was bisexual, a somewhat standard sexual more of the period.

5. ALCIBIADES (c. 450–404 B.C.)

One of the greatest and most ambitious generals of the Greek city-states, he was also reputed to be a homosexual—not that there was anything wrong with that at the time.

6. CHARLES D'EON DE BEAUMONT (CHEVALIER D'EON)
(October 5, 1728–May 22, 1810)

A captain of dragoons, the chevalier was very fond of cross-dressing—so much so that polite society could not determine what sex he actually was. Large sums were gambled on this question, but the answer had to wait until his death, when it was conclusively proved that he was in fact a male.

7. **THOMAS EDWARD LAWRENCE**
(August 15, 1888–May 13, 1935)

Lawrence of Arabia was known to have masochistic and homosexual affairs. Driven by his self-perceived "failings," his guilty feelings over his sexual orientation may have contributed to his early demise.

8. **CHARLES GEORGE "CHINESE" GORDON**
(January 28, 1833–January 26, 1885)

A British major-general, he was the commanding officer of the Ever Victorious Army during the Taiping Rebellion in China and died at the Siege of Khartoum in the Sudan. Although he had a somewhat obsessive interest in young newsboys and other prepubescent males, there is no direct evidence that he ever engaged in any sort of sexual activity—homosexual or heterosexual. Like many Victorian officers, he may have repressed his sexual inclinations for the honor of the Queen.

9. **HORATIO HERBERT KITCHENER**
(June 24, 1850–June 5, 1916)

Lord Kitchener, most famous for his recruiting poster ("Britons Want You") and as commander at the Battle of Omdurman (September 2, 1898), was a Victorian general with few or no sexual inclinations. There were rumors of homosexuality and a newspaper reported gossip that he had "the failing acquired by most of the Egyptian officers, a taste for buggery" (quoted in L1 News. December 1, 2001. <*http://www.lineone.net/express/99/09/28/features/fcolcomment1-d. html*>).

10. **HECTOR MACDONALD** (April 13, 1853–March 22, 1903)

One of the few men to ever begin as a private in the British Army and achieve flag rank, Major General MacDonald was responsible for Kitchener's victory at the Battle of Omdurman (September 2, 1898). He was later accused of taking indecent liberties with young children; such charges were never proved. Despondent at the accusations, he committed suicide.

Amateur Commanders

To be a successful commander, one does not have to be a product of a military school or a scion of a military family—but it helps! Yet certain talented amateurs have hearkened to the call of the trumpet and successfully performed a leading role in the martial arts.

1. **JOAN OF ARC** (January 5, 1412–May 30, 1431)

Joan is one of the true anomalies in history. Her prior training seemed to suit her well for being a simple peasant. Yet, either through divine inspiration, delusions, or madness, she was allowed to lead the armies of France against the English during the Hundred Years' War.

2. **JULIUS CAESAR** (July 12/13, 100–March 15, 44 B.C.)

A wealthy playboy politician, he originally intended to use the military as a stepping-stone to increase his political influence. Yet Caesar became one of the Great Captains of History. His Gallic Wars, his invasion of Britain, and his war against Pompey the Great all gave credence to an expertise that seemed to be inherent rather than learned. Perhaps this was true: Caesar's legions often referred to "Caesar's luck" as a major basis for success, and even Napoleon stated that it was better to be lucky than good.

3. **OLIVER CROMWELL** (April 25, 1599–September 3, 1658)

A rural gentleman planter, he did not begin a military career until after he turned 40. Yet he displayed a talent for military operations, and in the English Civil Wars (1641–51), he became the leader of the Parliamentarians and eventually Lord Protector of England (December 16, 1653).

4. **ROBERT BLAKE** (c. August 1599–August 7, 1657)

Like his contemporary and ally Oliver Cromwell, he did not have any military experience until after he turned 40. Previously a wealthy mercantilist, he distinguished himself as a general officer for the Parliamentarian forces; when he was almost 50, he turned to the navy and became a British admiral. He defeated Dutch forces at the Battle of Kentish Knock (October 8, 1652) and materially assisted in the British victory at Gabbard Bank (June 12, 1653). He was probably Britain's finest admiral until Horatio Nelson (1758–1805) and is considered one of the founders of the Royal Navy.

5. **JAN CHRISTIAAN SMUTS**
(September 24, 1870–September 11, 1950)

Trained as an attorney, he became the state attorney general in the Transvaal Republic. With the advent of the Second Boer War (1899–1902), he showed a talent for military operations and became a Boer general fighting the British. With the conclusion of that war, he returned to politics and became Colonial Secretary of Transvaal Colony. When World War I began, he became a British general and was invited to join the Imperial War Cabinet (1917). During the Second World War, he was made a British field marshal (1941) and afterwards was instrumental in the establishment of the United Nations (1945).

6. JOHN MONASH
(June 27, 1865–October 8, 1931)

After Joan of Arc, he probably had the most surprising civilian background for a military officer. An Australian Jew, he had degrees in liberal arts, law, and engineering. A polymath, he served as a citizen-soldier in the forces of Australia. With the advent of World War I (1914–18), he became a brigade commander at Gallipoli (April 1915), a division commander in Australia (July 1916), and commander of the Australian army corps on the Western Front (May 1917). British Prime Minister David Lloyd George was so impressed with Monash that he said the Australian might have become commander in chief if the war had not ended (bloody unlikely given that he was both a colonial and Jewish). After the war, he became chairman of the Victoria State Electricity Commission and an educator. Monash University in Australia is named in his honor.

7. FREDERICK FUNSTON
(November 9, 1865–February 19, 1917)

Until the age of 30, he had difficulty holding down a job and became a federal employee with the U.S. Department of Agriculture. In 1896, he volunteered to serve with the Cubans during the Cuban Insurrection (1895–98), during which he showed a natural military flair and achieved the rank of lieutenant colonel with the rebels. In the Spanish-American War, he was made a colonel of volunteers, but the war ended before he saw action. In the Philippine Insurrection, he won the Medal of Honor (1899) and was promoted to brigadier general of volunteers. His request for a regular commission was denied; meanwhile, he captured the Philippine rebel leader, Emilio Aguinaldo (1869–1964), and was rewarded with a commission as a brigadier general in the Regular Army.

8. **RICHARD TAYLOR** (January 27, 1826–April 12, 1879)

A wealthy Southern planter, he had no military training, but his father was Zachary Taylor (1784–1850) and his brother-in-law was Jefferson Davis (1808–89). As a Confederate general during the Civil War (1861–65), he fought under Stonewall Jackson during the Valley Campaign, under Robert E. Lee at the Seven Days' Battles and on his own at the Red River Campaign. He became a lieutenant general and was one of the more successful Confederate officers in the war. He was an excellent field commander as well as a successful administrator.

9. **GEORGE WASHINGTON**
(February 22, 1732–December 14, 1799)

A Virginia surveyor and planter, he first gained military experience in the state militia during the French and Indian War (1754–63). Instead of remaining in the military, he became justice of the peace for Fairfax County, Virginia (1760–64) and a gentleman farmer. During the Revolutionary War, he became the general commanding the colonial forces and eventually defeated the British through judicious use of guerrilla warfare, attrition, and carefully selecting his battles. While he could never have completely defeated the British in direct engagements, his strategy forced the British to eventually abandon the attempt to regain the rebellious colonies.

10. **DAVID BELL BIRNEY** (May 29, 1825–October 18, 1864)

Born in Alabama, he became a successful businessman in Philadelphia, Pennsylvania. During the Civil War (1861–65), he was commissioned as a Union brigadier general of volunteers and fought successfully at the Seven Days' Battles (June 25–July 1, 1862), Antietam (September 17, 1862), and Chancellorsville (May 1–6, 1863). Promoted to major general, he fought with distinction at Gettysburg (July 1–3, 1863), the Wilderness (May 5–6, 1864), Spotsylvania

(May 8–18, 1864), Cold Harbor (June 3–12, 1864), and Petersburg (June 15–18, 1864). When he died, he was commander of X Corps in the Army of the Potomac.

Honorable Mention: The Theory of the Leisure Class

With apologies to Thorstein Veblen (1857–1929), there does seem to be a dangerous correlation between the gainfully unemployed and leaders of revolution. The following persons generally lacked employment until the revolution awakened their talents.

SIMON BOLIVAR (July 24, 1783–December 17, 1830)
Born in Caracas, he was a moderately wealthy dilettante who lived in Spain and traveled widely in Europe. By 1810, the Spanish Americas had degenerated into political chaos, and he began his career as a revolutionary leader. He liberated what are now Colombia, Ecuador, Venezuela, and Bolivia over a 15-year period and is considered the George Washington of Latin America.

ERNESTO "CHE" GUEVARA (May 14, 1928–October 9, 1967)
Trained as a medical doctor, this upper-middle-class Argentine became a revolutionary and assisted Fidel Castro in the overthrow of the Batista government in Cuba (1959). However, he believed in his own publicity and eventually left to achieve revolution throughout South America. In Bolivia, political theory came face to face with reality, and his appeal to the peasants was generally ignored. Captured by the Bolivian Army with CIA assistance, he was executed. He made a better dead martyr than a living guerrilla leader and still exercises a romantic appeal for the New Left.

Ivy League
Graduates

The Ivy League has prided itself on producing America's leaders. But when one thinks of the military, the Ivies seldom come to mind. These eight northeastern universities (Brown, Columbia, Cornell, Dartmouth, Harvard, Princeton, the University of Pennsylvania, and Yale) have established a reputation for liberalism and perhaps even political correctness. But there have been illustrious military figures who received an Ivy degree.

1. SYLVANUS THAYER (DARTMOUTH COLLEGE, CLASS OF 1807) (June 9, 1785–September 7, 1872)

Superintendent of West Point (1817–33), he is commonly credited with being the "Father of the Military Academy." Upon his arrival, he immediately upgraded academic standards, instilled military discipline, and emphasized the honor code, which emphasized that "a cadet will not lie, cheat or steal, and will not tolerate those who do." Instead of offering a loose curriculum with a nondegree status, the United States Military Academy (USMA) became the chief institution in the United States for producing civil engineers. With the rapid territorial expansion of the United States (1800–50), the Academy's graduates were responsible for the roads, bridges, harbors, and railway lines.

Thayer later founded the engineering school at Dartmouth, which is named in his honor.

2. WILLIAM JOSEPH "WILD BILL" DONOVAN (COLUMBIA UNIVERSITY, CLASS OF 1905, BACHELOR'S DEGREE/LAW DEGREE) (January 1, 1883–February 8, 1959)

A battalion commander and later acting regimental commander of the 69th Regiment, during World War I, he earned the Medal of Honor. During World War II, he founded and ran the Office of Strategic Services (OSS), which after the war became the Central Intelligence Agency. Because of Donovan's extensive use of Ivy alumni as OSS operatives, the organization was often referred to as "Oh So Social."

3. RICHARD TAYLOR (YALE UNIVERSITY, CLASS OF 1845) (January 27, 1826–April 12, 1879)

The son of President Zachary Taylor (1784–1850) and the brother-in-law of Confederate President Jefferson Davis (1808–89); he served as a Confederate general officer during the Valley Campaign (May 1862) and the Seven Days' Battles (June 25–July 1, 1862), where he did an excellent job. He was promoted to command the District of Western Louisiana, where his Red River Campaign defeated the Union forces (spring 1864). He was later promoted to lieutenant general in charge of East Louisiana, Mississippi, and Alabama, and his command was the last major force to surrender east of the Mississippi River (May 4, 1865).

4. THEODORE ROOSEVELT JR. (HARVARD UNIVERSITY, CLASS OF 1908) (September 13, 1887–June 12, 1944)

The son of President Theodore Roosevelt (1858–1919), he participated in both World Wars I and II. During the latter, he was the assistant division commander of the Fourth Infantry Division. On

D-Day (June 6, 1944), he landed with the first wave on Utah Beach and led his troops inland. For his actions, he was recommended for the Distinguished Service Cross, but when he had a heart attack and died on June 12, 1944, the War Department upgraded his decoration to the Medal of Honor. Interestingly enough, his father was awarded the Medal of Honor for his actions during the Spanish-American War (1898) posthumously on January 16, 2001. The Roosevelts were one of two sets of fathers and sons to win the Medal (the other set being Arthur MacArthur and his son, Douglas MacArthur).

5. HENRY "LIGHT HORSE HARRY" LEE (PRINCETON UNIVERSITY, CLASS OF 1773)
(January 29, 1756–March 25, 1818)

A Revolutionary War hero, he commanded an independent combined arms strike force (Lee's Legion), consisting of dragoons and light infantry in the South Carolina Theater of Operations. Afterwards, he commanded the troops involved in suppressing the Whiskey Rebellion (1794). But he is best known for his eulogy of George Washington ("first in war, first in peace, and first in the hearts of his countrymen," 1799) and as the father of Robert E. Lee (1807–70).

6. MATT LOUIS URBAN (CORNELL UNIVERSITY, CLASS OF 1941) (August 25, 1919–March 4, 1995)

Assigned to the 60th Infantry Regiment, 9th Infantry Division, he rose to become battalion commander and served in six campaigns during World War II. He was known as the Ghost to the Germans because of the way he kept coming back to combat after being wounded. He was awarded the Medal of Honor for his heroism.

7. STEPHEN VAN RENSSELAER (HARVARD UNIVERSITY, CLASS OF 1782) (November 1, 1764–January 26, 1839)

A wealthy landowner and politician, he was promoted to major general after participating in the state militia (1801). During the War of 1812, he was ordered to defend the northern boundary of New York State and invaded Canada in October 1812. His force was soundly defeated (proving once again that you can always tell a Harvard man, you just can't tell him much), and he resigned his military commission to return to political activities. He later founded Rensselaer Polytechnic Institute (1826).

8. WILLIAM CURTIS CHASE (BROWN UNIVERSITY, CLASS OF 1916) (March 9, 1895–August 21, 1986)

A major general and commander of the 38th Infantry Division during World War II, he was responsible for the liberation of Manila. His troops recovered the American flag that had flown over General MacArthur's headquarters in the Manila Hotel and had been captured by the Imperial Japanese Army in 1941–42. The flag was presented to Brown University, where it currently is located in the basement of the John Hay Library on campus.

9. PERSIFOR FRAZER SMITH (PRINCETON UNIVERSITY, CLASS OF 1815) (November 16, 1798–May 17, 1858)

He fought in the Second Seminole War (1836–38) and served with distinction under General Zachary Taylor and as a brevet brigadier general under Winfield Scott. He was later brevetted as a major general and commanded the Division of the Pacific (1849–50).

10. TENCH TILGHMAN (UNIVERSITY OF PENNSYLVANIA, CLASS OF 1761) (December 25, 1744–April 18, 1786)

During the American Revolution, he was commissioned as a captain in the Pennsylvania Battalion of the Flying Camp. In August 1776, he became an aide-de-camp and secretary to George Washington (1732–99). After the British surrender at Yorktown, he carried the Articles of Capitulation to the Continental Congress in Philadelphia, where he was awarded a sword and a horse by Act of Congress.

Educators

"**O**ld soldiers never die, they just fade away"—Douglas MacArthur (1880–1964). Actually, some become teachers and educators. This transition is a relatively modern phenomenon because it requires a culture with a great degree of literacy. Thus, it has occurred only within the last 200 years. It is an increasing trend as longer life expectancies allow for military veterans to return to academia and pass on their knowledge and the fruits of their experience.

1. JOSHUA LAWRENCE CHAMBERLAIN
(September 8, 1828–February 24, 1914)

During the American Civil War, he was a Union general. The hero of Little Round Top at the Battle of Gettysburg (July 2, 1863), he ended the war as a major general of volunteers and was chosen to accept the surrender of the Army of Northern Virginia. A former college professor, he returned to Bowdoin University, where he was elected president (1876); by the time he retired, he had taught every subject in the curriculum except mathematics. He is the major protagonist in Michael Shaara's classic novel *The Killer Angels*.

2. **ROBERT EDWARD LEE**
(January 19, 1807–October 12, 1870)

The foremost Confederate general of the American Civil War (1861–65), he commanded the Army of Northern Virginia in some of the classic battles of the war—the Seven Days' (June 26–July 2, 1862), Second Bull Run (August 29–30, 1862), Antietam (September 17, 1862), Fredericksburg (December 13, 1862), Chancellorsville (May 2–4, 1863), Gettysburg (July 1–3, 1863), and the Wilderness (May 5–6, 1864). Named general in chief of the Confederate armies, he surrendered his army at Appomattox Court House on April 9, 1865. After the end of the war, he became president of Washington College in Lexington, Virginia, and remained there until his death. The college was renamed Washington & Lee University in his honor.

3. **OLIVER OTIS HOWARD**
(November 8, 1830–October 26, 1909)

Although a general in the American Civil War (1861–65), he was best known for his campaigns during the Indian Wars, especially his negotiations with Cochise and the Chiricahua Apaches (1872) and the campaign against Chief Joseph and the Nez Perce (1877). After his retirement from the military, he founded Lincoln Memorial University, Tennessee (1895).

4. **DANIEL HARVEY HILL** (July 12, 1821–September 24, 1889)

A Confederate general during the American Civil War (1861–65), he fought in the Army of Northern Virginia as a divisional commander. Promoted to corps command, he fought under Braxton Bragg (1817–76) at the Battle of Chickamauga (September 19–20, 1863). After the war, he was president of the University of Arkansas (1877–84) and president of the Middle Georgia Military and Agricultural College (1885–89; now known as Georgia Military College).

5. ERNEST NASON HARMON
(February 26, 1894–November 13, 1979)

A veteran of both World Wars I and II, he served as a division com-
mander in the invasion of North Africa (November 1942), Salerno
(September 9–18, 1943), Anzio (January 22–May 23, 1944), the
Siegfried Line (October 1944), and the Ardennes (December 16,
1944–January 18, 1945), ending the war as a corps commander.
After the war, he became president of Norwich University (1950–65).

6. DWIGHT DAVID EISENHOWER
(October 14, 1890–March 28, 1969)

An American general officer during World War II, he commanded
the invasion of North Africa (November 1942), Sicily (July 9–August
17, 1943), and Italy (September 3–October 8, 1943). Appointed
Supreme Commander, Allied Expeditionary Force, he was responsible for the D-Day invasion (June 6, 1944) and the subsequent Anglo-
American operations across France, Belgium, and Germany that
resulted in the surrender of Nazi Germany (May 7–8, 1945). After
the war, he became president of Columbia University (February
1948–December 1950) before becoming president of the United
States (1952–60).

7. TROY H. MIDDLETON
(October 12, 1889–October 9, 1976)

An American general during World War II, he was appointed commander of the 45th Infantry Division. After the Battle of Salerno
(September 10–14, 1943), he was made commander of VIII Corps
in Normandy, France (June 12, 1944). As part of Patton's Third Army,
he was responsible for clearing out Brittany; during the Battle of the
Ardennes (December 16, 1944–January 18, 1945), his corps took the
brunt of the German attack. After the war, he became comptroller
(1945–50) and president (1951–62) of Louisiana State University.

8. **MARK WAYNE CLARK** (May 1, 1896–April 17, 1984)

An American general during World War II, he was commander of Allied forces in North Africa under Eisenhower (November 1942). In 1943–44, he was commander of the Fifth Army in Italy and was responsible for the Italian Campaign. In December 1944, he was made commander of the 15th Army Group. During the Korean War, he succeeded Matthew B. Ridgway (1895–1993) as commander of UN Forces. After retiring from the army, he was president of the Citadel (1954–60).

9. **WILLIAM RIDDELL BIRDWOOD**
(September 13, 1865–May 17, 1951)

During World War I, he was commander of the Australian-New Zealand Army Corps (ANZAC) in the landings at Gallipoli (April 25, 1915). The exploitation of the landings failed miserably, but he performed credibly during the evacuation (December 1915–January 1916). After the war, he was master of Peterhouse, Cambridge University (1931–38).

10. **NATHAN GEORGE "SHANK" EVANS**
(February 6, 1824–November 30, 1868)

A Confederate officer during the Civil War, he was promoted to brigadier general at the Battle of Balls Bluff (October 21, 1861). Later battles included Second Bull Run (August 28–30, 1862), South Mountain (September 14, 1862), and Antietam (September 17, 1862). His battlefield service ended in 1863 when he was court-martialed for intoxication, but he was returned to duty in 1864 (although not in a command position). After the war, he became a high school principal in Midway, Alabama.

General Officers
for Both Sides

I t is difficult to achieve flag rank in any military organization and even more unusual to achieve actual command rank in the military organizations of more than one nation. European monarchs were often granted senior ranks in other national armies (e.g., Kaiser Wilhelm of Germany was a field marshal in the British Amy). But to serve as a general officer for one nation and then serve in a similar capacity for another nation is relatively rare in modern history. It may be achieved by merit, longevity, or treason.

1. BENEDICT ARNOLD (January 14, 1741–June 14, 1801)

Promoted as a brigadier general in the Continental Army (January 1776), he was promoted to major general following his exploits on Lake Champlain and Danbury (1777). As second in command, he was primarily responsible for the American victory at the Battle of Freeman's Farm (September 19, 1777). Following his defection to the British (September 25, 1780), he was commissioned a brigadier general and was instrumental in British raids on Virginia, including the seizure and burning of Richmond (January 5–6, 1781).

2. **JOSEPH WHEELER**
(September 10, 1836–January 25, 1906)

As a Confederate officer, he distinguished himself at the Battle of Shiloh (April 6–7, 1862) and was promoted to brigadier general of cavalry in October 1862, major general in January 1863, and lieutenant general in February 1865. During the Spanish-American War, he was commissioned a major general of volunteers and commanded the cavalry division in V Corps. An apocryphal story states that during the Battle of San Juan Hill (July 1, 1898), he said "Let's go, boys! We've got the damn Yankees on the run again!" He held only two ranks in the U.S. Army during his career—second lieutenant and brigadier general.

3. **FITZHUGH LEE** (November 19, 1835–April 28, 1905)

A nephew of Robert E. Lee (1807–70), he served as a cavalry commander in the Confederate Army of Northern Virginia. He was promoted to brigadier general (July 24, 1862) and major general (August 3, 1863). After the Civil War, he became governor of Virginia and later the American consul-general in Havana (1896); during the Spanish-American War, he was made a major general of volunteers, although he did not see combat. After the war, he was made the military governor of Havana. He was buried in his U.S. military uniform, prompting someone to say, "What'll Stonewall think when Fitz turns up in Heaven wearing that!"

4. **JAN CHRISTIAAN SMUTS**
(September 24, 1870–September 11, 1950)

Trained as an attorney, this self-taught military figure became one of the leaders of the Boer irregulars fighting the British Empire (1900–04). He became a Boer general in mid-1900 and fought against the British until the Treaty of Vereeniging (May 31, 1902). During World War I, he became a British general officer and entered the Imperial War Cabinet (1917); he was made a British field marshal in 1941.

5. ANTOINE HENRI JOMINI (March 6, 1779–March 22, 1869)

A Swiss national, during the Napoleonic Wars he was invited by French Marshal Michel Ney to join his staff. Jomini fought at the battles of Ulm (October 1805), Austerlitz (December 2, 1805), Jena (October 14, 1806), Eylau (February 7–8, 1807), and others. As a brigade general, he had incurred the enmity of Marshal Louis Berthier (1753–1815), who had him arrested in lieu of promotion to division general. He deserted to the Allies (August 1, 1813), and was made a lieutenant general in the Russian army.

6. MARIE JOSEPH PAUL YVES ROCH GILBERT DU MOTIER, MARQUIS DE LAFAYETTE
(September 6, 1757–May 20, 1834)

A French nobleman who volunteered to serve with the colonies during the Revolutionary War, he was commissioned a major general by the Continental Congress (July 31, 1777). He was made a major general (December 1781) and lieutenant general (1791) in the French army.

7. THOMAS COCHRANE
(December 14, 1775–October 30, 1860)

Possibly the best frigate commander during the French Revolutionary and Napoleonic Wars (1792–1815), he was (improperly) charged with stock fraud and imprisoned. Leaving England, he accepted positions as admiral in the naval fleets of Chile, Peru, Brazil, and Greece (1817–28). Upon his return to Britain, he reentered the Royal

Navy (1832) and became an admiral in 1851. It is likely that he served as a role model for the fictional Hornblower or Aubrey.

8. ANDREI ALEKSEEVICH BRUSILOV
(August 19, 1853–March 17, 1926)

A tsarist general during the First World War, he led the Brusilov Offensive (June 4–September 20, 1916), which was one of the most successful Russian military initiatives and captured 375,000 Austrian prisoners. During the Civil War, he joined the Bolsheviks out of loyalty to the motherland. He was appointed commander of all Bolshevik armed forces (May 2, 1920) and subsequently served as inspector general of cavalry (1921–24).

9. GIDEON JOHNSON PILLOW
(June 8, 1806–October 8, 1876)

Appointed by President Polk as a brigadier general of volunteers (July 1846) during the Mexican War, he spent much of his time fighting with his commander, General Winfield Scott (1786–1866). He became a Confederate brigadier general during the Civil War (July 1861) where he did not distinguish himself by his flight from Fort Donelson (February 1862).

10. MIKHAIL DMITRIEVICH BONCH-BRUEVICH (1870–1956)

A staff officer and general in the Tsarist army, he was one of the first imperial senior officers to switch his allegiance to the Bolsheviks. It probably did not hurt that his brother, Vladimir, was an Old Bolshevik and a close personal friend of Lenin. Between November 1917 and August 1918, he was one of the senior commanders of the Bolshevik army, eventually becoming the Stavka chief of staff. He retired shortly after the Civil War and became a scientist. Interestingly enough, he is one of the few senior commanders of the

Red Army to have survived the military purges of the 1930s. His personal memoirs were titled *From Tsarist General to Red Army Commander.*

Honorable Mention

JEAN BAPTISTE JULES BERNADOTTE
(January 26, 1763–March 8, 1844)

A sergeant in the Royalist Army, he became a brigadier general in the Army of the Republic (late 1793) and a marshal under Napoleon (May 14, 1804). His military expertise may have been questionable, but his political instincts were first-rate. When Sweden's dynastic line died out, he was elected crown prince and regent of Sweden (August 21, 1810) with the concurrence of Napoleon. He led the Swedish Army against his former commander at the Battle of Leipzig (October 16–18, 1813) and was later crowned king of Sweden (February 5, 1818). His dynastic line rules to this day.

Traitors

One man's traitor is another man's patriot. The men listed below have the dubious distinction of having been commissioned officers in the army of their nation and having been convicted either of espionage or of taking up arms against that nation.

1. **BENEDICT ARNOLD** (January 14, 1741–June 14, 1801)

His very name has entered the lexicon as a synonym for treason. A major general in the Continental Army during the Revolutionary War, he was probably most responsible for the victory at the Battle of Saratoga, thereby engendering French recognition for the fledgling United States. On September 25, 1780, he fled to the British after his attempt to betray the fort at West Point, New York, became known. He ended the war as a brigadier general for Great Britain. He was probably the most adept American general officer on a tactical level, but his ambition and arrogance led to his treason.

2. **ALFRED REDL** (March 14, 1864–May 25, 1913)

A colonel in the Austro-Hungarian Army, he had been chief of counterintelligence and later chief of staff for the Eighth Corps. But

Engraving of Benedict Arnold by H. B. Hall published in 1879. Arnold was one of the most adept American generals of the Revolutionary War, proving his mettle at Saratoga. If not for his betrayal of West Point to the British, he might have gone down in American history as one of its greatest heroes rather than as its greatest traitor.

the Russians had discovered that he was both a pedophile and a man who needed money. With his security clearances threatened, he betrayed the Austro-Hungarian war plans to Imperial Russia. When caught, he committed suicide.

3. FERDINAND WALSIN-ESTERHAZY
(December 26, 1847–May 21, 1923)

A major in the French Army, he was the officer who actually committed espionage on behalf of Germany in the Dreyfus Affair (see the chapter on courts-martial). He was never convicted because he fled France and lived in Great Britain for the remainder of his life. Although he admitted his actions late in life, there are still some people who believe to this day both that Dreyfus was guilty and that Esterhazy was innocent—despite the vast preponderance of evidence clearly pointing to the opposite conclusion.

4. JEAN BAPTISTE JULES BERNADOTTE
(January 26, 1763–March 8, 1844)

Who says treason never pays? A Napoleonic marshal, he did well at Austerlitz (December 2, 1805), but his conduct at the Battles of Jena-Auerstadt (October 14, 1806) was so bad that it is hard to accept it as mere incompetence. At Wagram (July 5–6, 1809), he continued his losing ways only to assume the regency of Sweden on August 21, 1810. From 1812 onward, he fought with the Allies against his mother country, especially at the Battle of Leipzig (October 16–18, 1813). While technically he had been released from his allegiance to France, his conduct was morally questionable. He was crowned king of Sweden (February 5, 1818), his dynastic line rules to this day—which is more than can be said for Napoleon.

5. ALCIBIADES (c. 450–404 B.C.)

An Athenian general and admiral during the Peloponnesian Wars, he defected to Sparta (415), defected back to Athens (411), and defected to the Persians (404) before he was assassinated. His strongest allegiance was to himself.

6. ANDREI VLASOV (September 1, 1900–August 1, 1946)

During World War II, he was a lieutenant general in the Red Army. Captured by the Germans, he agreed to fight against Stalin and the Communists. His army of Russian ex-prisoners of war fought as German allies on the Eastern Front. With the end of the war, he was tried for treason and hanged.

7. LOUIS AUGUST VICTOR DE BOURMONT
(September 2, 1773–October 27, 1846)

In another example of the price of treason, on the eve of Waterloo, General de Bourmont defected to the Allies with four of his principal staff officers (June 15, 1815). When the Bourbons were restored, he eventually became a marshal of France (1830).

8. CHARLES FRANCOIS DU PERRIER DOMOURIEZ
(January 25, 1739–March 14, 1823)

During the French Revolutionary Wars, he was chief general of the Army of the North. On April 5, 1793, he defected to the Allies and the French royalists in exile.

9. OLEG VLADIMIROVICH PENKOVSKIY
(April 23, 1919–May 16, 1963)

Penkovskiy was a colonel in the Soviet GRU (Military Intelligence) whose career hit a dead end when the KGB (Soviet state security) discovered that his father had been a White officer during the Russian Civil War (1918–21). In retaliation for his treatment, Penkovskiy became a prime espionage asset for British and American intelligence agencies until he was executed by the Soviets.

10. **MEIR TOUBIANSKI** (192?–June 30, 1948)

A captain in the Hagannah (Israeli Army), he was tried for espionage, convicted, and executed the same day. Supposedly, he had intentionally given information to Great Britain. On July 1, 1949, Prime Minister David Ben-Gurion apologized to his widow. There is still debate in Israel as to his guilt, with some hard-liners contending that his posthumous pardon was political in nature. During Israel's existence, he was one of two men to be executed by the state, the other being Adolf Eichmann (1906–62), a prime architect of the Holocaust in the Third Reich.

(Dis)Honorable Mention

ARTHUR WALKER (b. October 25, 1934)
A special "salute" of disgrace is due to Lieutenant Commander Walker (Retired). Whereas all the other officers were apprehended while on active duty, this man's activity was not discovered until after his retirement. Agreeing to commit espionage under the tutelage of his brother, Chief Warrant Officer John Anthony Walker Jr. (b. 1938), he assisted his brother and nephew, Yeoman Third Class Michael Lance Walker (b. 1962), in the theft and transmittal of classified data regarding cryptology and nuclear submarine technology—a family of spies, a family of disgrace.

Collaborators

Collaboration is a dirty word. However, prior reputation, political considerations, or just plain luck can save one from the
repercussions of a poor choice. During World War II, the radio pro-
pagandists were convicted of collaboration (e.g., Lord Haw-Haw, Axis
Sally, Tokyo Rose). Generally, those in the arts and letters survived
unimpeded.

1. FLAVIUS JOSEPHUS (C. 37–C. 100/101)

Josephus was a Jewish military commander and historian who managed to survive a suicide pact. At the conclusion of a rebellion in
Judea, he and his men were surrounded by the Romans and determined to take their own lives. Lots were drawn, and each individual
killed his predecessor. Somehow Josephus was the last man standing, at which time he surrendered to the Romans. He became a vas-
sal of the Emperor Vespasian and retired as a wealthy Roman citizen.

2. VIDKUN QUISLING (July 18, 1887–October 24, 1945)

A Norwegian politician, he formed a government under the Nazi
Occupation during World War II. When the legitimate government
returned at the war's end, Quisling was executed. His name has
entered many languages as a synonym for traitor.

3. **PIERRE LAVAL** (June 28, 1883–October 15, 1945)

A French politician, he was the quisling of France and suffered the same fate. The titular head of state, Marshal Henri Philippe Petain (1856–1951), was also convicted of treason but had his sentence commuted to life imprisonment due to his laudable record during World War I.

4. **MAURICE AUGUSTE CHEVALIER**
(September 12, 1888–January 1, 1972)

We may "thank Heaven for little girls," but the French Al Jolson could thank his public for their short-term memories. Not only did he collaborate with the Germans in the Second World War, but he preceded his collaboration with suspected similar activity during the First. He claimed that he had actually been working for the Maquis; it is more likely that he was working for both sides. As an entertainer, he may have been first-rate; as a moral exemplar, he was lucky to have escaped death by summary execution.

5. **EZRA POUND** (October 30, 1885–November 1, 1972)

An American expatriate poet living in Italy during the Second World War, he was not content to maintain a discreet silence. His anti-Semitic and fascist broadcasts forced even the United States to place him on trial for treason. He was determined to be mentally incompetent and committed to St. Elizabeth's Hospital in Washington, D.C. In 1958, he was released and returned to Italy. But for his literary talent, he would likely have been hanged.

6. **JANE FONDA** (b. December 21, 1937)

It was easy to be against the war in Vietnam. To be against a war is one thing; to give aid and comfort to the enemy is another. Actress Jane Fonda made a visit to Hanoi during the Vietnam War, made propaganda broadcasts from Hanoi, and posed for pictures sitting at an antiaircraft weapon. "Hanoi Jane" deserved the censure of even the New Left, but instead, she has made a career of tracking every new craze and megacapitalizing upon it—from exercise to Ted Turner to Christianity.

7. **JEAN-PAUL SARTRE** (June 21, 1905–April 15, 1980)

The philosopher of existentialism was a well-known collaborator in Paris during the Second World War. Only his academic reputation kept him from judicial trial.

8. **GRAND MUFTI OF JERUSALEM (HAJ AMIN AL-HUSSEINI)** (c. 1893–July 5, 1974)

An Arab leader, he declared a *fatwah* (decree of death) against Great Britain in 1941 and spent part of World War II in Berlin, where he made radio broadcasts actively supporting the Axis Powers. After the war, he returned to Jerusalem, where he was one of the major Arab leaders in the struggle to destroy the State of Israel. His family includes Yasser Arafat.

9. **PAUL DE MAN** (December 6, 1919–December 2, 1983)

De Man was a philosopher best known for the school of deconstructionism—an intellectual theory of moral relativism. He had been an anti-Semitic fascist in his native Belgium during World War II and decided that being known as a fascist was not a healthy occupation in the postwar period. Therefore, he fled to the United States and began his career as an academic. If man and God were indeed at Yale, the latter was not looking too closely into the moral fiber of the professorial staff. De Man's theories of moral relativism masked his moral bankruptcy until his death, after which his reputation suffered a downward spiral.

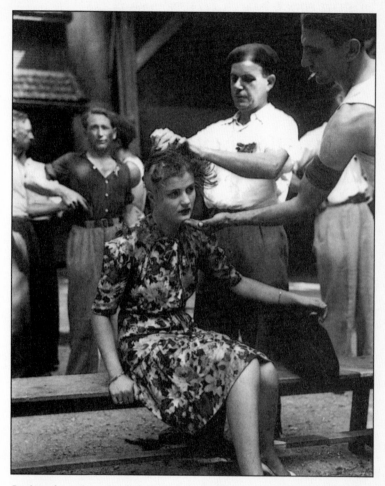

Paying the price of collaboration in France after the Allied liberation in August 1944. French women, like the one pictured here, who had "personal relations" with the German occupiers, had their heads shaved as a public mark of shame.

10. **RENE FONCK** (March 27, 1894–June 18, 1953)

The Allied "Ace of Aces" during World War I with 75 downed enemy planes to his credit, he was known as being arrogant, vainglorious, and difficult. His glory during World War I was severely tarnished by his active collaboration with the Germans during World War II as part of the Vichy government.

Honorable Mention

WILLIAM FRANKLIN (c. 1729/1731–November 17, 1813)

The illegitimate son of Founding Father Benjamin Franklin, he was the last royal governor of New Jersey. But then again, he did not collaborate with the Crown; he was once and always a British citizen. He merely retained his loyalty, unlike his father and the other Founding Fathers.

Wretched Refuse: Generals in Exile

The United States of America has offered a refuge to a number of exiled flag officers. Such personages often had to leave their countries on short notice and would have found a return inimical to their health. And sometimes, they just came without any threats at all.

1. **JEROME BONAPARTE** (November 15, 1784–June 24, 1860)

Napoleon's youngest brother, he was supposed to be a naval officer but proved a failure. Napoleon made him commander of the Bavarian division (1806) and corps (1807). Although he was made king of Westphalia in 1807, his regime was not overly successful. In 1809, he was made commander of X Corps; at the Battle of Waterloo (June 18, 1815), he was a division commander in Reille's Second Corps. His leadership made the Hougomont intended diversion into a major escalation of the battle. But in 1802–04, he had lived in Baltimore, Maryland, where he married Elizabeth Patterson; his brother the emperor would later have the marriage annulled, although Betsy was to become an aggravation to the Bonaparte family for the next half century.

2. JOSEPH BONAPARTE (January 7, 1768–July 28, 1844)

Napoleon's oldest brother, he was named king of Naples and later king of Spain. However, in 1806, he had been named commander of the Army of Naples and in 1814, he was made commander of the Paris National Guard. Between 1815 and 1832 and 1837 and 1839, he lived in Bordentown, New Jersey.

3. NGUYEN CAO KY (b. September 8, 1930)

He was premier (1965–67) and vice president (1967–71) of South Vietnam but was best known for his prior service in the South Vietnamese Air Force. As an air force general, he was known for his flamboyant attitude and his white silk scarf (which he continued to use as his trademark, even when forced into exile). After the fall of Vietnam, he fled to the United States and currently lives in California.

4. ANTON IVANOVICH DENIKIN
(December 16, 1872–August 8, 1947)

Commander in chief of the White Army during the peak of the Russian Civil War (1918–21), he fled to Paris after the Bolshevik victory. In 1946, he moved to Ann Arbor, Michigan, where he assumed a teaching position at the University of Michigan.

5. GIUSEPPI GARIBALDI (July 4, 1807–June 2, 1882)

The "liberator of Italy," he had a long and hazardous path to achieve his destiny. After fleeing Italy for the first time, he served in the military forces of Brazil and Uruguay. Returning to fight in Italy, he was again forced to flee, and entered into exile in the United States (1849–54) until returning to Italy once again. While it would be nice to say that the third time was the charm, in fact, his military successes waxed and waned over the next 15 years.

6. **EMMANUEL GROUCHY** (October 23, 1766–June 7, 1847)

The last man to receive his marshal's baton from Napoleon (April 15, 1815), he was given command of the right wing of the Army of the North during the Waterloo Campaign (June 16–18, 1815). Failing to fix the Prussians in place, he allowed them to join the British at Waterloo and decisively defeat Napoleon. He followed his orders, and did not "march to the sound of the guns." With the fall of Napoleon (1815), Grouchy spent the next years in exile in the United States until he returned to France in 1831.

7. **JOSE MIGUEL DE CARRERA**
(October 15, 1785–September 4, 1821)

A Chilean general during the Wars of Independence (1810–25), he made himself dictator in 1811 but had to flee two years later. In 1815, he went to the United States, but he returned to Argentina in 1816, where his continuing intervention in local politics resulted in his execution in 1821.

8. **NGUYEN NGOC LOAN** (c. 1930/1931–July 16, 1998)

A brigadier general and commander of the police in South Vietnam, he was best known for the photograph taken of him executing a Viet Cong guerrilla on February 1, 1968. This became one of the most famous pictures taken during the Vietnam Conflict. After the fall of South Vietnam, he fled to the United States, where he ran a pizza parlor in Dale City, Virginia (a suburb of Washington, D.C.).

9. **FULGENCIO BATISTA** (January 16, 1901–August 6, 1973)

Former chief of the general staff of Cuba, he became president of Cuba until his retirement in 1944. He then lived in Florida until returning to assume the presidency of Cuba once again, only to be overthrown in February 1959 by then-young revolutionary Fidel Castro.

10. **VICTORIANO HUERTA** (March 23, 1854–January 14, 1916)

In the midst of the Mexican Revolution, he overthrew President Francisco Madero and declared himself president (1913–14). Forced to resign by continuous revolts, he spent some of his time in exile in the United States before returning to Mexico, where he was then imprisoned.

Murder (and Death) Most Foul

Generals do not always die peacefully in bed. The objective of war often is to inflict bodily harm on the opposing force and this can lead to unacceptable insurance risks. But the fact remains that certain individuals have fallen to horrific fates or caused such fates to befall others.

1. MARCUS LICINIUS CRASSUS (c. 115–53 B.C.)

Descended from a wealthy family, he became the richest man in Rome (deriving much of his wealth from what is now regarded as fire insurance fraud). He defeated the slave revolt of Spartacus (71–70) and became a member of the First Triumvirate (consisting of Caesar, Pompey, and himself). To enhance his military reputation, he invaded Parthia, only to have his legions annihilated at Carrhae (53) by the mounted enemy. Tradition says that he was captured and executed by being made to swallow molten gold as a "reward" for his avarice.

2. DANIEL EDWARD SICKLES (October 20, 1819–May 3, 1914)

A Union corps commander and political general at the Battle of Gettysburg (July 1–3, 1863), he was best known for disobedience of orders. He directed his III Corps forward into the Peach Orchard, where it was virtually annihilated (and lost his leg, which is still on display in the Walter Reed Army Medical Museum in Washington, D.C.).

Although Meade removed him from command, Sickles was awarded the Medal of Honor for his actions. Politically astute, he spent the remainder of his life dodging accusations of corruption (which were probably all true). However, before the Civil War, he showed true indications of his character. In Lafayette Park (across from the White House), he gunned down Philip Barton Key (son of "Star-Spangled Banner" composer Francis Scott Key) in cold blood (February 27, 1859) in front of numerous eyewitnesses. The cause for the shooting was that Key had been having an affair with Sickles's wife. But that would not be a sufficient reason for an acquittal. Instead, his defense attorney, Edwin M. Stanton, successfully gained his client's acquittal on the grounds of temporary insanity—the first successful use of such a defense in the United States. To top it off, Sickles then forgave his wife for her adultery.

3-4. JEFFERSON COLUMBUS DAVIS
(March 2, 1828–November 30, 1879)
WILLIAM NELSON
(September 27, 1827–September 29, 1862)

Davis was a Union general officer during the Civil War (1861–65). Beginning the war as a lieutenant at Fort Sumter (where his name on the plaque has been the source of much confusion to tourists), he became a brigadier general of volunteers by May 1862. On the other hand, Nelson was a professional sailor who left the navy as a lieutenant commander in order to accept a commission as a brigadier general of volunteers (September 1861). Promoted to major general of volunteers (July 1862), he had an argument with his subordinate, Davis, who took the matter in a professional manner and simply shot the unarmed Nelson to death in a hotel.

Because of political influence, Davis was never court-martialed, although his promotion to major general was canceled because of the incident.

5. WILLIAM WALLACE (c. 1270–August 23, 1305)

A Scots partisan and leader who fought against English rule (and subject of the Mel Gibson 1995 film *Braveheart*), he was captured on August 5, 1305. Tried for treason, he asserted the defense that he was not a subject of the English Crown; found guilty, he was sentenced to death. His public execution involved being dragged alive through the streets, hanged at the gallows and cut down before death, and finally drawn (having his intestines pulled from his body and burned) and quartered (having his arms, legs, and head cut off—the last of which finally resulted in death).

6. LOUIS FRANCIS ALBERT VICTOR NICHOLAS MOUNTBATTEN (June 25, 1900–August 27, 1979)

A great-grandson of Queen Victoria, he was the British royal liaison between the 19th and 20th centuries. A veteran of World Wars I and II, he became Supreme Allied Commander for Southeast Asia (1944), last Viceroy of India (1945–47) and First Sea Lord (1956–59). He and his grandson Nicholas were killed by an Irish Republican Army terrorist bomb that had been placed on his yacht. If ever there was a call for massive retaliation . . .

7. ALEXANDER THE GREAT
(c. late July 356–June 10, 323 B.C.)

The Macedonian conqueror could be a mean drunk. Egged on by his mistress, Thais, he burned down the city of Persepolis (330). Later, he discovered that one of his subordinates had not come forward with evidence of a plot and had both the man (Philotas) and the accused's father (Parmenion) executed (December 330). Parmenion had been one of his most reliable and loyal generals; his execution may have avoided a potential blood-feud, but it was definitely cold-blooded.

8. JOAN OF ARC (January 6, 1412–May 30, 1431)

The great French war leader of the Hundred Years' War was captured by the Burgundians and turned over to the English. Sentenced to "perpetual imprisonment," she initially confessed (under torture) but recanted, at which time she was tried as a "relapsed heretic." Upon being found guilty, she was burned alive at the stake.

9. EARL VAN DORN (September 17, 1820–May 8, 1863)

A Confederate general during the Civil War (1861–65), he was commander of the Trans-Mississippi Department (January 1862). Defeated at the Battle of Pea Ridge (March 7–8, 1862), he still retained control of Confederate forces in Mississippi. However, it seems he had time for some activities other than combat. On May 8, 1863, an aggrieved husband walked into his headquarters and shot the general through the back of the head for alienation of affections.

10. ERWIN JOHANNES EUGEN ROMMEL
(November 15, 1891–October 14, 1944)

The Desert Fox of World War II fame and a German field marshal, he had been implicated in the plot against Hitler (July 20, 1944). Although he was the most popular German officer in the Third Reich, he was given the choice of standing trial (and almost certainly having his family suffer retaliation) or taking poison. He made the logical choice and committed suicide. Hitler gave him a state funeral and a large funeral wreath to honor his warrior general who had "succumbed to combat injuries."

Honorable Mention (Irony Division)

JOHN SEDGWICK (September 13, 1813–May 9, 1864)

A Union general during the Civil War (1861–65), he had been offered command of the Army of the Potomac (which he declined) but retained control of his VI Corps. Probably the most loved general officer in the Union Army, he was called "Uncle John" by his men. At the Battle of Spotsylvania Courthouse (May 9, 1864), he was inspecting the Rebel positions from his own entrenchment—a distance of 800 yards. He told his troops to stop flinching at the enemy's fire and said, "They couldn't hit an elephant at this distance"—at which time a Confederate sniper placed a fatal bullet below the general's left eye.

Friendly Fire Casualties and Collateral Damage

In an era of stand-off weapons, the likelihood of friendly fire casualties and simply hitting the wrong target has increased substantially. To sum it up, smart weapons aren't. It is still up to the soldier using the weapon system to properly identify, engage, and destroy the enemy. Poor training, confusion, the fog of combat, simple chaos theory—all contribute to the likelihood of an incorrect decision. If this is not historically new, it is still a problem that requires avoidance. And this does not address the problem of the "fragging" or the inadvertent error. During my tenure in Kuwait City, I was personally familiar with such a problem. A lieutenant colonel assigned to the 352nd Civil Affairs Command was warned by the Kuwaitis to stay out of a certain area. He returned to that area and was shot and seriously wounded by a Kuwaiti soldier. While there were allegations of looting, nothing was ever proved; the rumors were that the colonel received a Purple Heart.

1. THOMAS JONATHAN "STONEWALL" JACKSON
(January 21, 1824–May 10, 1863)

The "right arm" of the Army of Northern Virginia, Jackson was one of Robert E. Lee's corps commanders during the Civil War. Best known for his Valley Campaign (1862), he was primarily responsible for the Confederate victory at the Battle of Chancellorsville (May 2–4, 1863), but while on reconnaissance, he was accidentally shot by his own troops. He died six days later from complications after his arm was amputated.

2. **LESLIE JAMES MCNAIR** (May 25, 1883–July 25, 1944)

Chief of Army Ground Forces (AGF), he directed the expansion and training of the U.S. Army (1941–44). While visiting the Normandy beachhead, he was killed during the breakout (Operation Cobra) when U.S. Army Air Force bombers dropped their loads short of their intended target. A lieutenant general, he was the highest-ranking American officer killed during the Second World War.

3. **DAVID DANIEL "MICKEY" MARCUS**
(February 22, 1901–June 10, 1948)

A graduate of West Point, Colonel Mickey Marcus volunteered to fight in the Israeli War of Independence. He became the first general of a Jewish army since biblical times; however, shortly before a truce was declared, he was shot and killed by one of his own sentries. He did not speak Hebrew, and the sentry assumed that anyone speaking English would be an Arab (since that was the language of Jordan's Arab Legion).

4. **JAMES LONGSTREET** (January 8, 1821–January 2, 1904)

Another of Lee's corps commanders during the Civil War, he was shot by his own men during the Battle of the Wilderness (May 6, 1864). Like Jackson, he was shot in the arm; unlike Jackson, he survived.

5. ANTON VON WEBERN
(December 3, 1883–September 15, 1945)

An Austrian composer best known for his contributions to classical 12-tone music, he was shot and killed in Vienna by an American soldier for violating curfew.

6. *GUARDFISH* (SS-217)
(January 23, 1945)

This American attack submarine was on its 10th war patrol when it identified a target in the South China Sea as an enemy submarine and destroyed it by torpedo fire. Unfortunately, it was the U.S. naval salvage vessel *Extractor*. This was the only time in history that an American warship sank an American vessel.

7. THE DESTRUCTION OF THE GENOESE BOWMEN
(August 26, 1346)

The Battle of Crécy was a major defeat for the knights of France, who were incapable of learning that the English longbow had changed the face of warfare. At the beginning of the battle, Philip VI sent out his Genoese bowmen to engage the English. They were ineffective, and rather than allow them time to retire behind friendly lines, he told his knights to "kill me those scoundrels, for they stop up our road without any reason"—one of the worst examples in history of caring for one's troops.

8. THE DESTRUCTION OF AUGEREAU'S CORPS
(February 8, 1807)

At the Battle of Eylau, French Marshal Charles-Pierre-Francois Augereau (1757–1816) led his VIIth Corps in an assault in the midst of a blinding snowstorm. Visibility was zero, and the French marched into a dead zone where they were virtually annihilated by both the enemy Russian artillery and their own French batteries.

9. **THE COMMANDER OF THE 15TH FOOT** (August 13, 1704)

The major commanding the 15th Foot was not a popular officer. Shortly before the Battle of Blenheim began, he told his troops that he requested to be killed by the enemy; the soldiers replied that there was a battle to be fought. As the victory was achieved, he doffed his hat, turned to his troops in celebration, only to be shot through the head.

10. **PORK CHOP HILL** (April 16–18, 1953)

The subject of a book by S. L. A. Marshall and also a movie starring Gregory Peck, this was an American assault on a Korean hill held by the Chinese. The 31st Infantry Regiment was assigned to take the hill—and it did. The problem was that when Company K seized the hill, Company L did not realize this, and only stopped firing after it ran out of ammunition.

Military Commanders as Specific Targets

The history of warfare is defined by the killing of the enemy. While objectives may be territorial or otherwise limited, the destruction of the enemy's military forces has always been one of the main objectives. Thus, it is interesting to note that the deliberate targeting of an enemy commander is relatively rare. One may see the enemy commander on the battlefield and attempt to kill him, but that seems to be qualitatively different from specifically arranging a situation so that the commander will be the tactical target and end state of the mission.

1. **ISOROKU YAMAMOTO** (April 4, 1884–April 18, 1943)

The best admiral of the Imperial Japanese Navy during World War II, he was responsible for planning the assault on Pearl Harbor, Hawaii. He recommended against attacking the United States, but when the decision was made, he dutifully obeyed. He was sufficiently feared by the Americans that when they learned he would be inspecting a forward area, it was decided to send a special mission to shoot down his plane. This decision was made at the highest levels (i.e., the White House); its success was apparent when the Japanese Navy was unable to replace him.

2. **REINHARD HEYDRICH** (March 7, 1904–June 4, 1942)

During World War II, he was one of Hitler's favorites. As a major figure in the SS, he had been primarily responsible for the implementation of the Final Solution. Appointed Deputy Reich Protector of Bohemia and Moravia, he was assassinated in Prague by a Czech team from the British Special Operations Executive (SOE).

3. **COUNT FOLKE BERNADOTTE AF WISBORG** (January 2, 1895–September 17, 1948)

A Swedish army officer (and descendant of Napoleonic Marshal Jean-Baptiste Bernadotte), he was appointed by the United Nations to mediate between the Arabs and the Jews during the 1948 Israeli War of Independence. Believing that he was partial to the Arabs, the LEHI (known as the Stern gang after its founder) planned and carried out his assassination.

4. **EMILIANO ZAPATA** (August 8, 1879–April 10, 1919)

A Mexican revolutionary, he was assassinated when an enemy cavalry officer offered to defect to him. As a token of good faith, Zapata demanded that the officer execute 50 renegades, and when he did so, Zapata accepted his bona fides and walked into a fatal trap.

5. **PANCHO VILLA** (c. 1878–July 20, 1923)

A Mexican revolutionary, he was assassinated by "parties unknown." He had been in semiretirement, but his enemies obviously had long memories.

6. **E. R. S. (EDWARD RICHARD SPRIGG) CANBY** (November 9, 1817–April 11, 1873)

An American general, he met with the Modoc tribal leader Captain Jack for a truce conference in order to end the Modoc Indian War

(1872–73). At the conference, Captain Jack and his men assassinated General Canby and three of his subordinates.

7. **FRANZ FERDINAND** (December 18, 1863–June 28, 1914)

As the inspector-general of the Austro-Hungarian Army (and third in line to the dual throne), he was attending military maneuvers in Bosnia when he made a side trip to Sarajevo. He was assassinated by Gavrilo Prinzip (1894–1918), a student revolutionary. This assassination was the match that ignited World War I.

8. **DWIGHT DAVID EISENHOWER** (October 14, 1890–March 28, 1969)

During the Battle of the Ardennes (December 16, 1944–January 18, 1945), German troops who spoke American slang infiltrated the American lines with multiple missions—to confuse the Americans, misdirect traffic, and assassinate General Eisenhower. Under the command of German commando Otto Skorzeny (1908–75), Operation Greif became a mission that caused a security scare but was ultimately a failure.

9. **ERWIN JOHANNES EUGEN ROMMEL** (November 15, 1891–October 14, 1944)

The Desert Fox was such a threat to British forces in North Africa that the Long Range Desert Group (precursor to the Special Air Services, SAS, developed a mission to kidnap or assassinate the German general; they were unsuccessful.

10. **LOUIS FRANCIS ALBERT VICTOR NICHOLAS MOUNTBATTEN** (June 25, 1900–August 27, 1979)

Although retired from active service, this former Commander for Southeast Asia (1944), last Viceroy of India (1945–47), and First Sea Lord (1956–59) was assassinated by the Irish Republican Army.

Honorable Mention

PHOENIX PROGRAM

During the Vietnam War, both the North Vietnamese and the United States attempted to assassinate senior military and governmental officials. The Phoenix Program was the institutional entity established by the United States to accomplish such missions.

Biblical Commanders

While almost everybody says they read the best-selling book of all time and most people indeed have a copy in their home, how many have read and understood the military history enunciated in the multigenerational conquest of the Holy Land? Whether one accepts it as the immutable word of God or simply as a historical tale entwined with moral and ethical considerations, the text relies heavily on military implications. But who were the true military leaders?

1. **JOAB** (C. 1000 B.C.)

Israel achieved the dominance of western Asia during the reign of King David, and Joab was his commander of the regular army. During the civil war between the houses of Saul and David (1051–1049 B.C.), Joab faithfully led David's military forces. When David granted an armistice to Abner, his most dangerous military opponent, Joab assumed responsibility for his elimination. As David assimilated the tribes of Israel and conquered his capital of Jerusalem, it was Joab who stood as his military bulwark. In a separate campaign, Joab defeated the Edomites in the Salt Valley (1 Kings 11:14–15). When David's son, Absalom, revolted against his father, it was the loyal

Joab who restored the throne to David. Throughout his military career, Joab remained true to David, despite being slighted many times. With David's demise, Joab was executed by Solomon's adherents—a shameful reward for a lifetime of faithful service.

2. JOSHUA (C. 1300 B.C.)

Responsible for the strategic plan for the conquest of Canaan, he began with the Siege of Jericho. The city's capture gave the Israelites their first foothold west of the Jordan River. Thereafter, in order to minimize the effect of the Canaanite war chariots, he formed an alliance with the Gibeonites (see Joshua chapter 9), and set up a barrier defense in the mountains. His operational campaign led to the conquest of Ai and further inroads of territorial expansion (although his exploits may in fact be an amalgam of several generations of various leaders).

3. DAVID (C. 1040–968 B.C.)

He established the Kingdom of Israel and formed the beginnings of the Jewish people as a cohesive national group. Beginning as a humble shepherd, he engaged Goliath in single combat and became the hero of Israel (1 Samuel 17:11–13). A combination of Davy Crockett ("killed him a lion and a bear"), Robin Hood (robbing from the rich to give to the poor), Robert the Bruce (winning against overwhelming odds), and Damon (in his friendship with Jonathan), he became the greatest statesman in the history of Israel. His conquest of Jerusalem and defeat of the Philistines established a reputation that has become embedded within the gestalt of the Jewish people.

4. DEBORAH AND BARAK (C. 1200–1100 B.C.)

Together, they defeated the Canaanites. Deborah planned a three-phased campaign to minimize the effects of the enemy chariots by

(1) concentrating her forces, (2) drawing the enemy toward marshland where wheeled vehicles would lose mobility, and (3) executing an assault with a secondary force attacking the rear of the enemy. Although the Bible refers to this period as the rule of the judges, it was actually a military leadership that was responsible for the governing of the polity. These two individuals achieved a coordination rarely seen in history.

5. **SAUL** (C. 1050–1006 B.C.)

A warrior-king condemned by his own martial prowess, he waged wars against the Philistines that were characterized by oft-repeated tactics—quick night marches, division of force into multiple columns, and simultaneous assault from separate avenues of approach. Such tactics can often be successful, but they require a coordination often lacking without a reliable means of communication and can lead to defeat in detail (e.g., Custer at the Little Big Horn). Saul's success in the Michmash Campaign (1 Samuel 14:4) led to his fatal confrontation at Mount Gilboa, when the Philistine war chariots were able to meet his forces on favorable terrain.

6. **JONATHAN** (C. 1030–1006 B.C.)

The son of Saul, he was raised as a warrior and lived his entire life in battle. During the Michmash Campaign, he was responsible for his father's victory by utilizing psychological operations. He and a single sword bearer maneuvered into the rear of the Philistine garrison and stampeded the enemy blocking force into the main force. Saul then took advantage of the confusion and launched a decisive frontal assault, thereby winning the battle (see 1 Samuel 14:11–13). He was killed with his father at the Battle of Mount Gilboa (see 2 Samuel 1:17–27).

7. **GIDEON** (C. 1100 B.C.)

Gideon was renowned for his successful night attack against the Midianites. Without a reliable means of communication, night attacks were difficult endeavors, subject to confusion and often failure. But during the Harod Campaign, he selected a picked group of 300 warriors (Judges 7:4–7). After a personal reconnaissance (Judges 7:10–14), he ordered his elite troops to attack shortly after a new changing of the enemy guard. The night assault was successful, although the pursuit of the defeated enemy could have been more forceful.

8. **AHAB** (C. 870 B.C.)

To prevent the southern Kingdom of Israel from becoming a regional power, the Damascene ruler Ben-Hadad II engaged in a preemptive war (1 Kings 20:1). Ahab's forces were besieged in Samaria but again engaged in a deception operation. A small force of 232 troops acted as a decoy while the remainder surprised and defeated the enemy (1 Kings 20:19–22). Thereafter, Ahab seized the Golan Heights, presumably by flanking operations.

9. **UZZIAH** (C. 750 B.C.)

The son of Amaziah, he totally defeated the Philistines (2 Chronicles 26:6–8). In addition, he completed his father's work with reference to the total defeat of the Edomites (2 Kings 14:22). His strategic victories gave his kingdom a moderately secure and defensive base.

10. **AMAZIAH** (C. 785 B.C.)

This king of Judah planned and executed a strategic plan to reconquer the Edomites (2 Kings 14:7; 2 Chronicles 25). His victory at the

Vale of Salt was decisive and began the subjugation of Edom to the kingdom of Judah.

Honorable Mention

JUDAH MACCABEUS (C. 197–160 B.C.)

After Alexander the Great's conquest of the Middle East, his various generals inherited the separate kingdoms and satrapies. Seleucus inherited the region of Palestine and Syria. His descendant, Antiochus IV, determined to forge his kingdom into a coherent whole by a compulsory common Greek culture. However, many of the Jews had no interest in becoming Hellenized. Judah, his father, and his siblings began a guerrilla campaign against the Greek forces. Outnumbered in his first battle by odds exceeding four to one, Judah attacked the enemy on the march and not in a set-piece battle. At Nahal el-Haramiah, he annihilated the Greek forces in a classic ambush. Thereafter, he defeated another Seleucid army at the Battle of Beth-horon. At Emmaus and Beth-zur, he continued to defeat the mercenary Greek armies.

In 164 B.C., he rededicated the temple in Jerusalem, with a single day's supply of oil lasting for a miraculous eight days (this has become the still-celebrated Festival of Hanukkah). But Judah's success was the root cause of his defeat. As his reputation increased, the Seleucid Empire had to take him more seriously and bring more capable troops to bear. When Judah signed an alliance with Rome, the Seleucids were determined to defeat the rebellion. At Elasa, Judah faced odds of over 20 to 1 (800–20,000). Believing that a noble defeat would serve as an inspiration to his people, he died on the battlefield (see 1 Maccabees 9:11–16). The rebellion continued for a further period but eventually subsided. Interestingly enough, while contemporary Jews celebrate the miracle of Hanukkah, few know of the eventual Maccabean fate. So why isn't Judah a biblical commander? Simply because the story of the Maccabees is not in the standard Jewish or Protestant Bible; it is in the Apocrypha (additional books included in the Roman Catholic version).

OMRI (C. 875 B.C.)

Ruler of the northern Kingdom of Israel, he was called the "David of the North." Establishing his capital at Samaria, he defeated the Moabites. Although he was a biblical king, his lack of piety and/or lack of a decent chronicler resulted in his virtual omission from the Bible. Most of our knowledge of his reign has been derived from the Moabite Stone of the ninth century.

Native American Commanders

"M" anifest Destiny," "westward expansion," or "extermination of the indigenous population" (depending on one's degree of political correctness) has portrayed the Indian wars as a clash of cavalry and Indians on the plains (Sioux) or in the desert (Apache). However, the Indian wars were actually concluded by 1815; there would be threats and serious reverses, but there was little likelihood that the Native American population would be able to destroy the transplanted European population. It is the early leaders who had the best opportunity to do so, and the degree of their success has been obscured by the writers of history.

1. KING PHILIP (METACOM) (c. 1639–August 1676)

When the Pilgrims needed assistance to survive their first winter, it was Massasoit who stepped forward. Ironically, his son King Philip led the first and most successful Indian war in American history, one that remains little known at the present time. It was ostensibly a dispute over land rights, but the deeper cause was simply a struggle between two cultures. The Wampanoag Indians rose to destroy the Massachusetts Bay and Plymouth Bay Colonies and came close to succeeding. King Philip's War lasted for two years (1675–76), and ended only with Metacom's death. The colonists' losses approximated those the English had endured in centuries of Viking raids (almost one-third of the population), but the victory destroyed tribal power in New England forever.

2. **PONTIAC** (c. 1720–69)

Chief of the Ottawa, he fought with the French during the French and Indian War (1754–63). Thereafter, he formed one of the largest Indian coalitions ever seen on the North American continent and attempted to destroy all British forts in the trans-Appalachian territory. Pontiac's War (1763–64) destroyed 12 of 16 forts, but ultimately British troops were able to defeat him.

3. **TECUMSEH** (March 8, 1768–October 5, 1813)

Chief of the Shawnee, he fought against white settlers during the latter part of the Revolutionary War and continued the struggle in the Northwest Indian War (September 1790–August 1795). Refusing to compromise with American colonists, he was defeated at the Battle of Fallen Timbers (August 20, 1794). He continued to resist and was commissioned a brigadier general in the British army during the War of 1812. He was killed at the Battle of the Thames (October 5, 1813).

4. **CRAZY HORSE** (c. 1842–September 5, 1877)

Chief of the Oglala Sioux, he fought with Red Cloud. Afterwards, he was responsible for forming the coalition of the Plains tribes with Sitting Bull (who was more of a medicine man than a warrior leader), which resulted in the defeat of George A. Custer at the Battle of the Little Big Horn (June 25, 1876).

5. **BLACK HAWK** (c. 1767–October 3, 1838)

Chief of the Fox and Sauk, he fought with Tecumseh during the War of 1812. Afterwards, he ran afoul of American territorial interests and declared war in 1832. After a few minor successes, he was decisively defeated at the Battle of the Bad Axe River (August 2, 1832).

6. RED CLOUD (c. 1822–December 10, 1909)

He was the first of the great Sioux chiefs who fought against the Americans. His war (1866–68) was ended by the Treaty of Fort Laramie (April 1868). The North Platte territory was returned to Indian control, and having achieved his limited goals, he never took up arms again.

7. CHIEF JOSEPH (c. 1840–September 21, 1904)

Chief of the Nez Perce, he led his entire tribe in a 1,300-mile retrograde operation across Oregon, Idaho, Wyoming, and Montana seeking sanctuary in Canada. Stopped by the army when he was only 30 miles from the border, he stated that "From where the sun now stands, I will fight no more forever."

8. MANGUS COLORADO (c. 1797–January 17, 1863)

The greatest war chief of the Chiricahua Apache, he fought the Mexicans and Americans for almost 30 years. He was captured through treachery and executed "while trying to escape."

9. COCHISE (c. 1812–June 8, 1874)

Chief of the Chiricahua Apache, he was the son-in-law of Mangus Colorado. He led his tribe against the Mexicans and the Americans for a decade in northern Mexico and Arizona.

10. GERONIMO (c. 1829–February 17, 1909)

Another Chiricahua chief, he is probably the Native American best known to the general population. Though he was a talented guerrilla leader, his band was quite small (his 35 warriors kept 5,000 U.S. troops pursuing him through New Mexico and Arizona for five months in 1886).

Senior Flag Officers
of the United States

	Army/Air Force/Marine Corps	Navy
1-Star	Brigadier General	Rear Admiral (Lower Half)
2-Star	Major General	Rear Admiral (Upper Half)
3-Star	Lieutenant General	Vice Admiral
4-Star	General	Admiral

The reason the major general is ranked lower than the lieutenant general is that the initial two-star rank derived from the sergeant-major general. Also, it has been difficult for the other services to differentiate between the one- and two-star naval officer. But there have been special senior ranks above and beyond the ones listed.

General of the Armies
of the United States

1. **GEORGE WASHINGTON**
(February 22, 1732–December 14, 1799): July 4, 1976 (posthumous)

2. **JOHN J. PERSHING**
(September 13, 1860–July 15, 1948): September 3, 1919

General of the Army of the United States

1. ULYSSES S. GRANT
(April 27, 1822–July 23, 1885): July 25, 1866

2. WILLIAM T. SHERMAN
(February 8, 1820–February 14, 1891): March 4, 1869

3. PHILIP H. SHERIDAN
(March 6, 1831–August 5, 1888): June 1, 1888

General of the Army

The five-star rank was created during World War II so that American general officers would have rank structure equivalent to that of British field marshals. Supposedly, President Franklin Delano Roosevelt asked George C. Marshall about the title, and the latter replied that under no circumstances did he want to be known as Marshal Marshall.

1. GEORGE C. MARSHALL
(December 31, 1880–October 16, 1959): December 16, 1944

2. DOUGLAS MACARTHUR
(January 26, 1880–April 5, 1964): December 18, 1944

3. DWIGHT D. EISENHOWER
(October 14, 1890–March 28, 1969): December 20, 1944

4. HENRY "HAP" ARNOLD
(June 25, 1886–January 15, 1950): December 21, 1944
(changed to General of the Air Force, May 7, 1949)

5. **OMAR N. BRADLEY**
(February 12, 1893–April 8, 1981): September 22, 1950

Fleet Admiral (the Naval Equivalent to the General of the Army)

1. **WILLIAM D. LEAHY**
(May 6, 1875–July 20, 1959): December 15, 1944

2. **EARNEST J. KING**
(November 23, 1878–June 25, 1956): December 17, 1944

3. **CHESTER W. NIMITZ**
(February 24, 1885–February 20, 1966): December 19, 1944

4. **WILLIAM F. HALSEY**
(October 30, 1882–August 16, 1959): December 4, 1945

Marshal-Generals of France

The highest rank in the French Army is not marshal of France but rather Marshal-General of France. The rank has been awarded on only four occasions. Although it was supposedly offered to Charles de Gaulle (1890–1970), he turned it down; after being de Gaulle, anything else would have been a demotion.

1. HENRI DE LA TOUR D'AUVERGNE, VISCOUNT OF TURENNE (September 11, 1611–July 27, 1675)

According to Napoleon, Turenne was the greatest general that France ever produced. During much of the 17th century, he was noted for his grasp of strategy and tactics as well as his popularity among his troops. He was created Marshal-General on April 4, 1660, to give him command authority over other French marshals. His principal wars include the Thirty Years' War (1618–48), the Franco-Spanish War (1635–59), the Fronde (1648–53), the War of Devolution (1666–68), and the Dutch War (1672–78). He was killed by enemy artillery fire while conducting a personal reconnaissance.

2. **HERMAN MAURICE, COMTE DE SAXE**
(October 28, 1696–November 30, 1750)

Though the German-born Saxe began his military service in the Saxon army, he transferred to the command of a German regiment in French service (1719) and spent the remainder of his life in the French military. He particularly distinguished himself during the War of the Austrian Succession (1740–48). Promoted to Marshal-General in 1747, he was probably the best soldier of the mid-18th century. His writings on strategy and tactics later influenced Napoleon and others.

3. **DUKE CLAUDE LOUIS HECTOR VILLARS**
(May 8, 1653–June 17, 1734)

Having distinguished himself during the War of the League of Augsburg (1688–97), he became one of France's leading generals with the War of the Spanish Succession (1701–14). Villars was made Marshal-General of France on October 18, 1733.

4. **NICHOLAS JEAN DE DIEU SOULT, DUKE OF DALMATIA**
(March 29, 1769–November 26, 1851)

Although he enlisted in the Bourbon army as a private (1785), the French Revolution recognized his talents and he achieved promotion to general officer. Under Napoleon, he became a Marshal of the Empire (May 19, 1804). Defeated by the Duke of Wellington (1769–1852) in Spain, he nevertheless fought several additional campaigns with distinction. During the Waterloo Campaign (June 1815), he served as Napoleon's chief of staff. After Napoleon's downfall, Soult went into exile but was recalled to France, where he eventually served as Minister of War (1830–34/1840–45) and in several other government posts. On September 15, 1847, he was made marshal-general of France.

Addendum

Two additional officers may have held a similar title (Maréchal Général des Camps et Armées du Roi), but they were more akin to royal aides (e.g., minister of the royal bedpans) than exemplars of military leadership:

ARMAND DE GONTAUT-BIRON (1524–92)

FRANÇOIS DE BONNE, DUC DE LESDIGUIÈRES (1543–1626)

Air Aces

The top air aces of history are all German pilots from the Second World War. This is due to two major factors: (1) number of combat operations and (2) target-rich environments. The Allies had the luxury of rotating their pilots into staff commands or training assignments, so their aces had less opportunity to rack up kills; most of the German pilots had to fly until the end of the war. The Japanese aces had been flying longer than the Germans (because they had been fighting China since 1937), but their air environment did not offer the number of targets that the Germans faced.

1. ERICH HARTMANN (352 KILLS)
(April 19, 1922–September 19, 1993)

"Bubi" Hartmann initially wanted to go to medical school; the war changed his occupation. He began combat operations on the Eastern Front in August 1942 and became known as the "Black Devil of the Ukraine" (from the nose coloration of his aircraft). He flew over 1,400 missions, of which 800 involved enemy contact. He emphasized closing with the enemy over marksmanship and was proudest of the fact that he never lost a wingman during his combat career.

2. GERHARD BARKHORN (301 KILLS)
(May 20, 1919–August 1, 1983)

Known as a dependable pilot, not a flashy one, he was shot down nine times. After the war, he became a general officer in the West German Air Force. Barkhorn and his wife were killed in a car crash.

3. GUNTHER RALL (275 KILLS) (b. March 10, 1918)

A superb marksman, he was one of the best deflection shots in the Luftwaffe. After the war, he became the commanding officer of the West German Air Force.

4. OTTO KITTEL (267 KILLS)
(February 21, 1917–February 14, 1945)

Initially an enlisted pilot, he received a battlefield commission in April 1944. He was killed by flak on the Eastern Front.

5. WALTER NOVOTNY (258 KILLS)
(December 7, 1920–August 11, 1944)

A natural leader, "Nowi" became a wing commander by the time he was 24. He was killed flying an ME-262 jet.

6. WILHELM BATZ (237 KILLS) (May 12, 1916–1987/1988)

Batz entered the Luftwaffe in 1935 and established a reputation as an outstanding flight instructor. Though his flight skills were excellent, his marksmanship developed slowly, and it took 18 months of combat before he became an outstanding fighter pilot. After the war, he joined the West German Air Force.

7. ERICH RUDORFFER (222 KILLS) (b. November 11, 1917)

Known as one of the best marksmen in the Luftwaffe, he once shot down 13 Russian planes in 17 minutes (November 6, 1943).

8. **HEINRICH BAER(220 KILLS)**
(May 25, 1913–April 28, 1957)

A member of the Luftwaffe before the war, he had wanted to be a civilian pilot for Lufthansa. He was shot down 18 times during the war, only to be killed in a sports aircraft after the war.

9. **HERMANN GRAFF (212 KILLS)** (b. 1912)

An enlisted pilot, he rose from flight sergeant to major in three years. A darling of the Nazi propaganda machine, he was ostracized after the war because of his pro-Soviet attitudes. Most Luftwaffe pilots imprisoned by the Russians after the war remained anti-Communist; Graff did not and the other pilots never forgave him.

10. **HEINRICH EHRLER (209 KILLS)**
(September 14, 1917–April 4, 1945)

His combat record was scarred by a court-martial in which he was deemed responsible for the loss of the battleship *Tirpitz*. He was sentenced to death for dereliction of duty (an unjust verdict), but the sentence was suspended and he died in an ME-262 jet fighter near the war's end.

Submarine Aces

The top submarine aces of history are all from the Second World War. During the First World War, the submarine was still an experimental weapon and lacked the lethality and endurance it would later develop. Most of the aces are German. As with the air war, this is due to two major factors: (1) number of combat operations and (2) target-rich environments. The Allies had the luxury of rotating their personnel into staff commands or training assignments; many of the German submarine commanders were kept doing combat missions until their deaths. Also, the German targets (i.e., Allied shipping) were much larger and more numerous than the Japanese merchant marine, which was the target of the American submarines.

1. OTTO KRETSCHMER (238,327 TONS/42 ½ SHIPS)
(May 1, 1912–August 5, 1998)

In a period of less than 18 months, the captain of the U-99 established the tonnage record for any submarine commander in history. His boat was sunk by the British on March 17, 1941, and he spent the remainder of the war in a prisoner-of-war camp.

2. **WOLFGANG LUTH (229,000 TONS/47 SHIPS)**
(October 15, 1913–May 12, 1945)

Many of his kills were accomplished on the East Coast of the United States during the "happy times" (that period in which the U-boats had the advantage over the Allies in technology and tactics). He was killed ashore by a German sentry when he gave the wrong password near the war's end.

3. **RICHARD H. O'KANE (227,800 TONS/31 SHIPS)**
(February 11, 1911–February 16, 1994)

The top American submarine commander in terms of tonnage, he was sunk by his own defective torpedo. He was later promoted to flag rank.

4. **GUNTHER PRIEN (211,843 TONS/32 SHIPS)**
(January 16, 1908–March 18, 1941)

The most famous U-boat commander (the U-47 *Snorting Bull*), he was best known for infiltrating the British naval base at Scapa Flow and sinking the battleship *Royal Oak*. His death in combat was a severe blow to the Kriegsmarine.

5. **VIKTOR SCHUTZE (187,279 TONS/36 SHIPS)**
(February 16, 1906–September 23, 1950)

He was the skipper of the U-25.

6. **ERICH TOPP (185,434 TONS/34 SHIPS)** (b. July 12, 1914)

In the U-57 *(The Red Devil Boat),* he established a reputation for competency and coolness under fire.

7. HERBERT SCHULTZE (183,432 TONS/28 SHIPS)
(July 24, 1909–June 3, 1987)

Skipper of the U-48, he sank eight ships in two patrols (52,000 tons).

8. HEINRICH LIEBE (171,003 TONS/31½ SHIPS)
(January 29, 1908–July 27, 1997)

He was the skipper of the U-38.

9. HEINRICH LEHMANN-WILLENBROCK (170,163 TONS/ 27 SHIPS) (December 11, 1911–April 18, 1986)

Commander of the U-96, he was the basis for the submarine officer in Lothar-Gunther Buchheim's novel (and later movie) *Das Boot*.

10. HEINRICH BLEICHRODT (162,491 TONS/28 SHIPS)
(October 21, 1909–January 9, 1977)

He was a later commander of the U-48.

Military Chaplains

It has been said that there are no atheists in foxholes. Military chaplains do occupy foxholes and offer spiritual relief to military personnel regardless of creed. According to the Geneva Convention, a chaplain is a noncombatant, and his special status should be recognized by all parties to a conflict. This has not always been observed.

1.–4. (Tie) **FATHER JOHN P. WASHINGTON** (Catholic) (July 18, 1908–February 3, 1943);

REVEREND CLARK V. POLING (Dutch Reformed) (August 7, 1910–February 3, 1943);

RABBI ALEXANDER D. GOODE (Jewish) (May 10, 1911–February 3, 1943);

REVEREND GEORGE L. FOX (Methodist) (March 15, 1900–February 3, 1943)

The four chaplains were immortalized for their conduct on board the *Dorchester*, a U.S. Army troopship. On February 3, 1943, the German submarine U-233 torpedoed the ship. Over 900 men were on the ship, and the four chaplains gave their life jackets to those who did not have any; almost 700 men died, making this the third largest loss of life that the United States suffered during World War II in transporting troops. As the ship was sinking, the four chaplains were observed standing arm in arm on the deck, each praying in his own way for the troops. In 1948, the United States issued a commemorative stamp honoring the four chaplains—a rare exception to philatelic policies, which normally require a 10-year period to have occurred between death and issuance of a stamp (except for U.S. presidents).

The U.S. Postal Service issued this stamp on May 28, 1948, to honor the memory and heroism of the chaplains (*left to right,* George L. Fox, Clark V. Poling, John P. Washington, and Alexander D. Goode), who had sacrificed their lives in order to save others when a German submarine sank the troop transport *Dorchester* on February 3, 1943.

5. FATHER FRANCIS L. SAMPSON
(February 29, 1912–January 28, 1996)

Known as the "Parachuting Padre," he served with airborne forces in both World War II and Korea. Interestingly enough, his wartime experiences have been portrayed in two separate war movies. In *The Longest Day,* he was the chaplain diving into the water looking for his Mass kit; in *Saving Private Ryan,* he was the Tom Hanks role which transformed him into a hard-bitten infantry captain. Chaplain Sampson had to secure Fritz Niland's return from the front lines since Niland's three brothers had recently been killed or missing in action. Later, Sampson became a major general and the chief of chaplains and afterwards the head of the USO.

6. MONSIGNOR JAMES H. O'NEILL (?–?)

On December 8, 1944, the Third Army chaplain received a call from the Army Commander, George S. Patton, who requested a prayer for good weather. The weather had been rainy, which forced air support missions to be canceled. Colonel O'Neill could not find an appropriate prayer for the occasion and wondered whether praying for good weather to assist in the killing of human beings was morally acceptable. But he felt that a quick victory would lessen the suffering and number of deaths. Therefore, he composed the following prayer, which was read throughout Patton's army: "Almighty and most merciful Father, we humbly beseech Thee, of Thy great goodness, to restrain these immoderate rains with which we have had to contend. Grant us fair weather for battle. Graciously hearken to us as soldiers who call upon Thee that, armed with Thy power, we may advance from victory to victory, and crush the oppression and wickedness of our enemies and establish Thy justice among men and nations."

7. FATHER FRANCIS P. DUFFY (May 2, 1871–June 26, 1932)

The chaplain of the 69th Infantry Regiment, a New York unit, Duffy was renowned for his willingness to help "his boys" in the trenches. During a German offensive July 15–17, 1918, he worked continuously in the front lines, offering aid and solace to the troops as well as assisting in carrying wounded to the battalion aid station. In 1940, a movie was made about the regiment and the chaplain *(The Fighting 69th)*.

8. **FATHER WILLIAM CORBY**
(October 2, 1833–December 28, 1897)

Corby achieved his fame by being the chaplain of the Iron Brigade during the American Civil War. At the Battle of Gettysburg, he addressed the brigade on July 2, 1863. Afterwards, he placed his right hand in the air and began giving absolution. The brigade went to its knees and the entire Second Corps of the Union army fell silent. Afterwards, the brigade went on to its destiny in a pitched battle that became a Union victory. A statue of the chaplain at this famous moment was placed on the Notre Dame campus, where it may be seen today; however, in a testimonial to college priorities, the statue is popularly referred to as "Fair Catch Corby."

9. **FATHER VINCENT ROBERT CAPADONNO**
(February 13, 1929–September 4, 1967)

A Navy chaplain, he was assigned to the Marine's Third Battalion of the Fifth Regiment in Vietnam. On September 4, 1967, he was ministering to his men in a firefight. He had been wounded several times while assisting the wounded and giving Last Rites; a mortar round nearly blew off his right arm. He gave his gas mask to a Marine and had to endure tear gas being dropped in an effort to keep the enemy from overrunning the Marine positions. He noticed a wounded Marine in the enemy line of fire and placed himself between the man and the enemy; he was hit by 27 rounds and killed instantly. For his actions, he was awarded the Medal of Honor. A naval warship was named in his honor (DD-1093)—the first U.S. naval vessel to receive a papal blessing.

10. **FATHER EMIL KAPAUN** (April 20, 1916–May 23, 1951)

Although he served in the CBI (China-Burma-India) Theater of Operations during World War II, he is remembered primarily for his service in Korea. When the Chinese entered Korea, Captain Kapaun stayed behind with the wounded of the Third Battalion, Eighth Cavalry Regiment, First Cavalry Division (November 1950). In a Chinese prisoner-of-war camp, he ministered to all faiths. The Chinese responded by denying him medical help and letting him starve to death. In 1993, the Vatican declared Kapaun a "Servant of God," the first step toward possible sainthood.

Camp Followers and Mistresses

Most people assume that history is filled with camp followers and mistresses of military personnel. That may be true, but the surprising fact is that most of these personnel remain unknown to history. Even for those who are known, there is generally little additional information available. There are more details available on the horses that the generals rode.

1. EIGHT UNNAMED ACTRESSES

Hermann Maurice, Comte de Saxe (October 28, 1696–November 30, 1754), was a marshal-general of France. His leadership during the War of the Austrian Succession (1740–48) and victory at Fontenoy (May 11, 1745) established his reputation. The name(s) of his mistresses are unknown, but he and they deserved a prominent position in this pantheon of prurience. He died after "interviewing" eight young actresses; the cause of death is listed in the death certificate as "une surfeit des femmes."

2. LADY EMMA LYON HAMILTON (c. 1765–January 15, 1815)

The mistress of Charles Greville, she was "sold" by him to his uncle, Sir William Hamilton (British ambassador to Naples), for the consolidation and settlement of his debts. Hamilton married her in 1791, and she became a favorite at the Neapolitan court. She met British naval hero Horatio Nelson (1758–1805) in Naples about 1793 and became his mistress about 1798. After the Battle of the Nile (August 1, 1798), she and her husband joined Nelson, and the three lived together until Sir William's death in 1803. Although both her husband and Nelson had left her separate fortunes, she exhausted her assets by extravagant living and died a pauper.

3. THAIS (?–?)

An Athenian *hetaira* (courtesan), she was reputedly one of the mistresses of Alexander the Great (356–323 B.C.). After he captured the Persian capital at Persepolis, she suggested that the city be burned to avenge the prior Persian sack of Athens; it was destroyed in a drunken bacchanalia. After Alexander's death, she married one of his generals, Ptolemy I Soter (367–283 B.C.).

4. ELIZABETH LORING (?–?)

Wife of a British commissary officer, she was also the New York mistress of British General William Howe (1729–1814). Because Howe was so entranced with his paramour, he was dilatory in his pursuit of George Washington. American Tories circulated a ditty: "Awake, arouse, Sir Billy, / There's forage on the plain. / Ah, leave your little filly, / And open the campaign."

5. ISABEL ROSARIO COOPER (1914–June 29, 1960)

A Scotch-Filipino, "Dimples" was brought to the United States by General Douglas MacArthur in 1930 when he assumed the duty of chief of staff of the army. Ensconced in a Washington, D.C. hotel, she had limited but apparent duties; at the time, she was 16 years old! She committed suicide in 1960.

Napoleon's Mistresses

"Not tonight, Josephine" may have been the emperor's watchword simply because he was literally sleeping all over Europe. The emperor of France may well be able to also claim the title of "Father of Europe"—if all his illegitimate descendants are counted.

6. **MARIE WALESKA** (1789–1817)

A Polish countess, she had an affair with Napoleon that may have been one of his longest.

7. **PAULINE BELLISLE FORES** (March 15, 1778–1869)

The wife of a French cavalry officer, she also served as Napoleon's mistress during the Egyptian Campaign, earning the sobriquet "Napoleon's Cleopatra."

8. **MARGUERITE-JOSEPHINE WEYMER** (1787–1867)

An actress with a stage name of Mme. George, she was Napoleon's mistress about 1803.

9. **JOSEPHINE GRASSINI** (April 8, 1773–January 3, 1860)

In addition to being a mistress of Napoleon, she was a well-known operatic diva.

10. **ALBINE DE MONTHOLON**

The wife of one of Napoleon's general officers, she accompanied him to exile on St. Helena. Her husband, Charles Tristan de Montholon (1783–1853), has been accused of being the man who poisoned Napoleon during his final exile.

Honorable Mention

KAY SUMMERSBY (c. 1918–January 1975)

As a British soldier, she was assigned to be General Dwight Eisenhower's driver during World War II. He had her commissioned as an officer in the American Army. Although there were rumors and innuendoes throughout the war as to the nature of their relationship, no hard evidence has yet been adduced that would prove an illicit affair.

Hollywood Actors

Entertaining the home front and the troops on USO tours is one thing; risking your life in combat is another. There are actors and entertainers who have gone in harm's way either before or after their military service.

1. **AUDIE MURPHY** (June 20, 1924–May 28, 1971)

The most decorated American soldier of World War II (with over 28 combat medals), he became an actor because of his military experience. His most noteworthy films were *Red Badge of Courage* and *To Hell and Back* (his own wartime autobiography).

2. **STIRLING HAYDEN** (March 26, 1916–May 23, 1986)

In late November 1941, he joined the COI (Coordinator of Information, later to become the OSS, Office of Strategic Services). After airborne training (1942), he broke his ankle and enlisted in the Marine Corps (October 1942). Commissioned as a second lieutenant (April 21, 1943), he transferred to the OSS and became commander of a Yugoslav partisan band. He was awarded the Silver Star.

3. **SABU DASTAGIR** (January 27, 1924–December 2, 1963)

Known by his first name, he starred in *Elephant Boy* (1937) and *The Thief of Baghdad* (1940). An Indian national, he had become an American citizen and enlisted in the Army Air Force (September 1943). He flew 42 combat missions in the Pacific as a ball turret gunner (one of the most dangerous and uncomfortable assignments) on B-24 Liberators. He was awarded the Distinguished Flying Cross and the Air Medal with four Oak Leaf Clusters.

4. **JIMMY STEWART** (May 20, 1908–July 2, 1997)

Joining the Army Air Force in March 1941, he took flying lessons on his own time and was commissioned in January 1942. By January 1944, he had deployed to Europe; after flying over 20 combat missions in B-17s, he became a colonel and chief of staff of the Second Combat Wing, Eighth Air Force. He was awarded the Distinguished Flying Cross and the French Croix de Guerre. Remaining in the reserves, he was promoted to brigadier general (May 31, 1968), the highest rank ever achieved by a movie star.

5. **CHARLES DURNING** (b. February 28, 1923)

Drafted into the army in 1943, he was in the first wave on Omaha Beach on D-Day (June 6, 1944). Later wounded by bayonet (eight times in the right shoulder, arm, and back), he recuperated in time for the Ardennes Offensive. Captured by the Germans, he escaped and thus narrowly avoided execution at the Malmedy Massacre; he helped identify the victims after American forces recaptured the forest. His military service ended when he was shot in the chest. He was awarded the Silver Star and three Purple Hearts.

6. EDDIE ALBERT (b. April 22, 1908)

Enlisting in the Navy on September 9, 1942, he was commissioned as a lieutenant (jg) (February 1, 1943). On November 21, 1943, he took command of several landing craft and rescued 13 wounded marines at Tarawa. He was cited for outstanding bravery under fire.

7. CLARK GABLE (February 1, 1901–November 16, 1960)

Enlisting in the Army Air Force, he graduated officer candidate school on October 28, 1942. Reichmarschall Herman Goering offered a reward to any German pilot who shot Gable down. He flew five combat missions and was awarded the Distinguished Flying Cross and the Air Medal before being discharged as a major in June 1944.

8. DOUGLAS FAIRBANKS JR.
(December 9, 1909–May 7, 2000)

Commissioned in the navy in April 1941, he participated in escort duty with the PQ-17 (a Murmansk-bound convoy that took egregious casualties from U-boat attacks, July 2–4, 1942). Later, he was trained in commando operations and participated in the invasions of Sicily and Salerno. In the August 1944 invasion of southern France (Operation Dragoon), he commanded a squadron of PT boats. He was awarded the Silver Star, the French Croix de Guerre, and the British Distinguished Service Cross.

9. WAYNE MORRIS (February 17, 1914–September 14, 1959)

His most famous movie role was a champion boxer in *Kid Galahad* (1937). As a navy pilot, he became an ace, shooting down five Japanese aircraft. He flew 57 combat missions and earned three Distinguished Flying Crosses and two Air Medals. He is the only Hollywood actor to achieve ace status.

10. **DAVID NIVEN** (March 1, 1910–July 29, 1983)

The son of a British captain who died at Gallipoli (1915), he was a graduate of Sandhurst (the British equivalent of West Point). Rejoining the British army during World War II, he rose to become a lieutenant colonel in the commandos and was at Normandy on June 6, 1944. He was awarded the Legion of Merit by the United States. Interestingly enough, as a senior British officer, he was entitled to a batman (valet). His was a young private who had acting aspirations of his own, Peter Ustinov (b. April 16, 1921).

Military Theorists

Military theory has been studied, ignored, and studied again. Liberal academics often decry the attempt to synthesize the principles of war, but history has given certain guidelines that can maximize a nation's martial success. The following individuals are those whose writings have stood the test of time or are the current doctrinal sources of military thought.

1. KARL MARIA VON CLAUSEWITZ (June 1, 1780–November 16, 1831)

A veteran of the Napoleonic Wars, he served as chief of staff to the Prussian III Corps at the battles of Ligny (June 16, 1815) and Wavre (June 18, 1815). An ardent nationalist, he wrote *On War* (1819), an attempt to synthesize strategy and the conduct of war within the state. He was still editing and rewriting when he died, and he left instructions that the treatise be destroyed. Instead, his wife published it, and it has become the standard reference for military theory. The problem is that as an unfinished work, much of it is contradictory, and one must be careful in arriving at a conclusion.

2. SUN TZU (C. 500 B.C.)

Reputedly a general for the King of Ch'i, he wrote *The Art of War*, the earliest known book on military strategy and one that can still be read in a contemporary environment. He emphasized surprise, mobility, flexibility, and deception—all of which are basic maneuver concepts in the U.S. Army today. Mao Tse-tung's *Little Red Book* of guerrilla tactics derives largely from Sun Tzu.

3. NICCOLO MACHIAVELLI (May 3, 1469–June 21, 1527)

A Florentine politician, he commanded the Florentine militia against Pisa (1509) and accompanied the papal army in its campaign against Rome (1526–27). His major writings include *The Prince* (1513) and *The Art of War* (1520)—both of which emphasize moral factors in warfare and attempt to define a coherent system of strategy, although the former work with its emphasis on statecraft has had a larger impact.

4. ALFRED THAYER MAHAN
(September 27, 1840–December 1, 1914)

The sine qua non of naval theorists, this American admiral's *Influence of Sea Power upon History, 1660–1783* (1890) became the standard naval treatise on theory immediately upon its publication. His theory mandated control of the seas as a prerequisite to national security and integrated sea power into the context of national policy. Mahan later became the president of the Naval War College (1892–93).

5. JOHN FREDERICK CHARLES (J. F. C.) FULLER
(September 1, 1878–February 10, 1966)

A British general officer and military theorist, he developed in his writings the basic concepts of combined arms operations that were synthesized by Germany during World War II into the blitzkrieg ("lightning war"). In addition to his early writings, he wrote *A Military History of the Western World* (three volumes; 1954–56). It is a valuable study until it reaches 1865, when the author's personal prejudices begin to jaundice the remainder of the work. Basil Liddell Hart

(1895–1970) also wrote in a similar vein, although there is some question today over the originality of his work (much of which seems derived from Fuller).

6. ANTOINE HENRI JOMINI (March 6, 1779–March 22, 1869)

A general officer during the Napoleonic Wars (for both Napoleon and the tsar), he attempted in his *Art of War* (1838) to elucidate the theory of war into certain set-piece immutable principles—particularly mass and decisive point of attack. While his writings were more influential than those of Clausewitz in the 19th century, his rigor and lack of flexibility have led to a lessening of influence in contemporary combat doctrine.

7. JULIAN STAFFORD CORBETT
(November 12, 1854–September 21, 1922)

A British naval historian, he was an attorney and a lecturer at the Naval War College. His primary writings include works on British naval history and *Principles of Maritime Strategy* (1911), which attempted to develop a synthesis of maritime operations.

8. GIULIO DOUHET (May 30, 1869–February 15, 1930)

The first well-known air theorist, he argued in his *Command of the Air* (1921) that airpower was a quantum change in the history of warfare. Postulating a form of "total war" against the enemy's infrastructure, he saw no real defense against airpower.

9. BILLY MITCHELL (December 29, 1879–February 17, 1936)

An army brigadier general, he was court-martialed for insubordination as a result of his outspoken defense of airpower in the 1920s. Many of his writings were in the military professional journals, but his *Winged Defense* (1925) is indicative of his theories. He believed that an independent air force was necessary and that basically the bombers would be able to penetrate enemy air defenses. Though much of his analysis was later proven wrong, in 1924, he predicted that the start of a Pacific war would begin with a Japanese air and sea attack upon Pearl Harbor accompanied by an air attack in the Philippines ("Attack will be launched as follows: Bombardment, attack to be made on Ford Island [Hawaii] at 7:30 A.M.... attack to be made on Clark Field [Philippines] at 10:40 A.M."); on December 7, 1941, the Japanese attacked Pearl Harbor at 7:55 A.M. and the Philippines at 12:35 P.M.

10. JOHN A. WARDEN III (b. December 21, 1943)

His *Air Campaign: Planning for Combat* (1988) served as the basis for the air campaign in Desert Storm (February 1991). Later, his "Five-Ring Theory" postulated a parallel strike at the enemy's war-fighting capabilities (leadership, key production, infrastructure, population, and fielded military forces). Warden had a tendency to overemphasize the capabilities of airpower and assume an environment of air supremacy. Like his predecessor Billy Mitchell, he was isolated within his own military by his abrasive support of his theories, and he retired from active duty as a colonel.

Honorable Mention

WAYNE P. HUGHES (b. 1930)

A captain in the post–World War II U.S. Navy, he wrote *Fleet Tactics: Theory and Practice,* the standard reference for contemporary naval operations. His book emphasizes history, tactical analysis, and fleet operations.

The Greatest Command Staff in History

I s there a rock-and-roll heaven? If so, there must surely be a Valhalla. Suppose you had the ability to recruit an army without restrictions, to let your mind roam throughout history and choose the proper commanders and staff. Who would you choose and why? Positions should be filled with personnel who excel at that particular level of command.

THEATER ARMY COMMANDER: SALAH-AL DIN YUSUF IBN AYYUB (SALADIN) (c. 1138–March 4, 1193)

This Arab political leader and general conquered most of the Holy Land. He was a commander who understood the proper dynamic between political objectives and military means.

CHIEF OF STAFF: HELMUTH KARL BERNHARD VON MOLTKE (October 26, 1800–April 24, 1891)

A Prussian general who was chief of staff during the domination of Prussia in Europe in the mid to late 19th century, he developed a decentralized command structure that allowed him to train his sub-ordinates and let them maximize the results. Simultaneously, he understood the use of technology and was able to effectively use it to military advantage.

G1 (ADMINISTRATION): WILLIAM JOSEPH SLIM
(August 6,1891–December 14, 1970)

A British general who commanded the 14th Army in World War II (China-Burma-India Theater), he was responsible for the liberation of Mandalay and Burma (1944–45). His careful planning and care for his troops in a geographically hostile environment showed him to be a leader who would get the most from his troops by ensuring that they were properly supplied.

G2 (INTELLIGENCE): MAX HOFFMAN
(January 25, 1869–July 8, 1927)

At the beginning of World War I, he was deputy chief of operations for the Eighth Army in East Prussia. Noticing the gap between the two Russian armies, he devised a plan that was utilized to decisively defeat the enemy in detail at the Battle of Tannenberg (August 26–31, 1914). He was a fine staff officer who could maximize the opportunity to strike a decisive blow by adequately interpreting the battlefield.

G3/5 (OPERATIONS/CIVIL-MILITARY): ALEXANDER THE GREAT (c. late July 356–June 10, 323 B.C.)

The Macedonian leader who conquered most of the known world, he was adept at all types of warfare—set-piece battle, siege, defense, pursuit—and he excelled at civil-military operations. By adopting some of the customs of lands that he conquered, he forced an amalgam between Greek and Persian culture. Overall, his operational excellence and ability to "read" the battlefield mandates his selection.

G4 (LOGISTICS): LAZARE NICOLAS MARGUERITE CARNOT (May 13, 1753–August 2, 1823)

A French general, "the Organizer of Victory" was able to reconstitute an entire army force structure during the French Revolutionary Wars (1792–99) and have it withstand the combined armies of Europe.

ARMY COMMANDER:

SUBOTAI (c. 1172–c. 1245)

The principal general of Genghis Khan (c. 1162–1227), he conquered much of China, Russia, Poland, and Hungary while maintaining a steadfast loyalty to his commander.

BELISARIUS (c. 505–565)

Justinian's best general, he defended Rome against the Goths and other barbarians. Despite his emperor's doubts and misgivings, Belisarius maintained his loyalty even though he was given the opportunity to secure a throne for himself.

CORPS COMMANDER:

LOUIS NICOLAS DAVOUT (May 10, 1770–June 1, 1823)

Napoleon's best marshal, he was one of the few French commanders capable of handling an independent command without supervision. A stern taskmaster, "the Iron Marshal" inspired respect and obedience rather than affection.

GEORGE THOMAS (July 31, 1816–March 28, 1870)

A Union general during the American Civil War (1861–65), he showed that his handling of corps and even larger elements was as good on defense (Battle of Chickamauga, September 19–20, 1863) as on offense (Battle of Nashville, December 15–16, 1864).

He was solicitous of his troops, an overachiever in results, and a good subordinate.

JAMES LONGSTREET (January 8, 1821–January 2, 1904)
"Lee's Old War Horse," he was a corps commander in the Army of Northern Virginia during the American Civil War (1861–65). Often blamed for the defeat at the Battle of Gettysburg (July 1–3, 1863), he was correct in wishing to assume the tactical defensive in a strategic offensive posture. He recognized the impact of new technology and was able to adapt such innovations to the battlefield at Petersburg and elsewhere.

GEORGE SMITH PATTON
(November 11, 1885–December 21, 1945)
Patton was the best armor officer that the United States has ever produced, and his Third Army operations during World War II were models of flexibility and success.

DIVISIONAL COMMANDER:

ERWIN JOHANNES EUGEN ROMMEL
(November 15, 1891–October 14, 1944)
The African Campaign of the Desert Fox during World War II was a classic example of fast-moving operations. However, he had a tendency to outrun his logistics base and was unable to solidify his victories into a strategic advantage. Also, one should remember that the Afrika Korps was a relatively small formation (especially when compared with the units on the Eastern Front). But if one examines Rommel's command of the Seventh Panzer Division during the Battle for France (May–June 1940), it is clear that his performance was superb–he repulsed the British counterattacks at Arras and cut off Allied forces at Cherbourg. His unit

became known as the "Ghost Division" to the British for its ability to penetrate and appear where needed.

RICHARD TAYLOR (January 27, 1826–April 12, 1879)
During the American Civil War (1861–65), he performed superbly in any capacity—ranging from a divisional commander under Stonewall Jackson to a theater commander in Louisiana, Mississippi, and Alabama.

LEWIS BURWELL ("CHESTY") PULLER
(June 26, 1898–October 11, 1971)
Puller was the most decorated Marine in American history, and his performance ranging from the Central American Banana Wars through World War II to Korea made him a living legend. His leadership on Guadalcanal (1942) and later command positions make him one of the best tactical field commanders in history.

ARTILLERY: NAPOLEON BONAPARTE
(August 15, 1769–May 5, 1821)

Before he was Emperor of France, he was an artillery captain; in fact, he received his promotion to general officer because of his superb handling of artillery at the Siege of Toulon (September 4–December 19, 1793). During many of his battles, he personally assisted in the site placement of the "Grand Battery," and he was always interested in proper artillery employment.

RECONNAISSANCE: JOACHIM MURAT
(March 25, 1767–October 13, 1815)

Napoleon's cavalry commander, he was superb in using cavalry for both shock effect and reconnaissance. However, as an independent commander, he was less than mediocre.

REAR GUARD: CHIEF JOSEPH (c. 1840–September 21, 1904)

A Native American chief, he led his tribe (including women and children) in a 1,300-mile fighting withdrawal. It was only when the U.S. cavalry had achieved a numerical superiority of 10 to 1 that he was finally brought to bay.

COMBAT ENGINEER: SEBASTIEN LE PRESTRE DE VAUBAN (May 15, 1633–March 30, 1707)

He was the fortification designer of the 17th century, and his expertise was noted in both offense and defense. His plans for fixed fortifications are still studied as a model of the art.

NAVAL COMMANDER: HORATIO NELSON (September 29, 1758–October 21, 1805)

The finest fighting admiral in history—bar none.

AIR (STRATEGIC): CURTIS LEMAY (November 15, 1906–October 3, 1990)

He was responsible for the strategic bombing offensive over Japan during World War II, and his use of operations research and problem analysis led to field success.

AIR (TACTICAL): ADOLF GALLAND (March 19, 1912–February 9, 1996)

Inspector-General of the Luftwaffe during World War II, he understood the capabilities and limitations of tactical air. He was able to maximize the effort by his pilots, despite being given little support by his national command authority.

UNCONVENTIONAL OPERATIONS: PAUL EMIL VON LETTOW-VORBECK (March 20, 1870–March 9, 1964)

A Prussian Junker, he led a guerrilla campaign in East Africa during World War I. His was the last force to surrender after the Armistice. Interestingly enough, most of his troops were *askaris* (indigenous personnel). Haya Safari!

CIVILIAN INTERFACE: LEV DAVIDOVICH BRONSTEIN (LEON TROTSKY) (October 26, 1879–August 21, 1940)

A Bolshevik revolutionary, he formed the Red Army during the Russian Civil War (1918–21). With no prior background or training, he displayed an exemplary ability to recruit, train, and motivate personnel.

Literary Soldiers

Soldiers are not always committed to a military life; several veterans have become more well known in the field of literature.

1. LEO NIKOLAYEVICH TOLSTOY
(August 28, 1828–November 8, 1910)

Receiving a commission in the Russian Army, he served at the Siege of Sevastopol (1854–55). His major literary works include *War and Peace* and *Anna Karenina*.

2. IAN FLEMING (May 28, 1908–August 12, 1964)

A graduate of the British Military Academy at Sandhurst, he served as a commander in British naval intelligence. His major literary works include the James Bond series—which have become an industry unto themselves. Of course, since James Bond served as an officer during World War II, he is the spryest octogenarian alive, given the later franchise publications.

3. **ROBERT HEINLEIN** (July 7, 1907–May 8, 1988)

He was a graduate of Annapolis whose military career was cut short by tuberculosis. His major literary works include *Starship Troopers* and *Stranger in a Strange Land.*

4. **MIGUEL DE CERVANTES SAAVEDRA (CERVANTES)** (1547–1616)

Author of *Don Quixote*, he had previously served in the Spanish army. Having enlisted in 1570, he fought at the Battle of Lepanto (October 7, 1751), receiving three wounds (two in the chest and one that maimed his left hand).

5. **EDWARD GIBBON** (April 27, 1737–January 16, 1794)

Author of *The Decline and Fall of the Roman Empire*, he held a captain's commission in the Hampshire Grenadiers.

6. **LEWIS (LEW) WALLACE** (April 10, 1827–February 15, 1905)

A Union major general during the Civil War, he wrote a series of novels, the most famous of which was *Ben Hur.*

7. **AESCHYLUS** (525–456 B.C.)

A Greek poet and tragedian, whose 70 plays include *Prometheus* and *Oresteia*, he was also a Greek hoplite at the battles of Marathon, Artemisium, Salamis, and Platea (490–479). His self-composed epitaph notes, "The grove of Marathon, with its glories, can speak of his valor in battle / The long-haired Persian remembers and can speak of it too"; nowhere does it mention his literary accomplishments.

8. GAIUS VALERIUS CATULLUS (CATULLUS) (C. 84–54 B.C.)

A Roman lyric poet, he served as a staff officer for Memmius, governor of Bithynia.

9. QUINTUS HORATIUS FLACCUS (HORACE) (December 8, 65–November 27, 8 B.C.)

A Roman lyric poet, he served as military tribune in Brutus's army, which was defeated by Octavian and Antony at Philippi (42).

10. DECIMUS JUNIUS JUVENALIS (JUVENAL) (C. A.D. 60–40)

A Roman poet and satirist, he served as a Roman officer in Britain and Egypt.

War Correspondents

War correspondents hold a dubious position in combat. They can mythologize or demonize; they can be helpful or they can be a royal pain in the nether regions. How partisan should they be? How partisan are they? Their role has changed over the years, and the role of the media in swaying public opinion in favor of military efforts has increased tremendously.

1. ERNIE PYLE (August 3, 1900–April 18, 1945)

During World War II, he was the "GI's Buddy." His gritty reporting from the perspective of the enlisted combat soldier made him possibly the most beloved combat correspondent of all time. He was killed by a Japanese sniper on Ie Shima.

2. WILLIAM HOWARD RUSSELL (March 28, 1820/1821–February 10, 1907)

The first famous war correspondent, he reported on the Crimean War (1853–56), setting the tone for future newspaper reporters. His epitaph at St. Paul's Cathedral calls him "the first and greatest" war correspondent.

3. **EDWARD R. MURROW** (April 25, 1908–April 27, 1965)

Murrow reported in the media of print, radio, and television. His famous radio reports ("This is London . . . the Blitz") brought World War II into the American living room. As a broadcast journalist, he set the tone for future reporters and news coverage.

4. **WINSTON CHURCHILL**
(November 30, 1874–January 24, 1965)

His coverage of the Boer War for the *London Times* was classic, although his bias was apparent. Churchill had formerly served as an officer in the British Army and was later to serve as Lord of the Admiralty during World War I and prime minister during World War II. His speeches and writings are 20th-century masterpieces.

5. **DAVID HALBERSTAM** (b. April 10, 1934)

A combat reporter for the *New York Times* during the early period of the Vietnam War (1964–73), he shifted from complete acceptance of the official line to a seeking out of what really was happening. Although he was regarded as being against the war, he was really against the inefficiencies of the U.S. Military Command.

6. **BILL MAULDIN** (b. October 29, 1921)

Although not a war correspondent per se, he was a cartoonist for *Stars & Stripes.* His "Willie and Joe" cartoons from the European Theater of Operations in World War II exemplify the combat soldier as nothing has done before or since.

7. **WILLIAM HARDING DAVIS** (April 18, 1864–April 11, 1916)

He was an adventurer whose coverage of the Spanish-American War fit in well with the sensationalism of the times.

8. **ERNEST MILLER HEMINGWAY** (July 21, 1899–July 2, 1961)

Although he was better known as a novelist, his combat reporting from the Spanish Civil War and World War II (especially his take on the liberation of Paris) are classics of the genre.

9. **RICHARD TREGASKIS**
(November 28, 1916–August 15, 1973)

His *Guadalcanal Diary* and other World War II reports merit a place in the pantheon of combat reporting. Sadly, his later reporting from Vietnam was marred by an unwavering acceptance of the U.S. military's official posture.

10. **STEPHEN CRANE** (November 1, 1871–June 5, 1900)

His *Red Badge of Courage* is one of the best novels ever written on men in armed conflict; at the time, he had never been exposed to combat. Later, his reporting on the Spanish-American War showed that his writing expertise was not limited to fiction.

Honorable Mention

WALTER CRONKITE (b. November 4, 1916)

His combat reporting from World War II was superb. However, he made a larger impact as the CBS news anchor during the Vietnam War. When he decided that the war was not winnable after the 1968 Tet Offensive, it was the beginning of the end for Lyndon Johnson and his attempts to mobilize the American population.

BATTLES AND MANEUVERS

Decisive Battles

I n 1851, Sir Edward Creasey defined the *Fifteen Decisive Battles of the World.* Since the initial publication of his epic tome, historians have debated the merits of inclusion and exclusion of particular battles. Since most of the lists in this particular book are in groups of 10, I have the unenviable task of examining almost two additional centuries of warfare and deleting at least five battles originally included. In each case, I have given the justification for my actions.

MARATHON (490 B.C.)

The initial battle in which the Greek city-states defeated the Persian Empire. Reason for deletion: It was only the opening act in a bellicose drama that would last for the next 50 years.

1. PLATEA (NEW) (479 B.C.)

In a seesaw struggle, the Greek city-states and the Persian Empire struggled for supremacy. Numerous battles were fought, but nothing had been decisive. This battle resulted in the complete destruction of a Persian army and the end of Persian threats to the Greek mainland.

SYRACUSE (413 B.C.)

The destruction of the Athenian invasion force at Syracuse marked the beginning of the end for imperial Athens and the rise of Sparta. Reason for deletion: The fall of Athens did not give way to the rise of a Spartan golden age. How much homage do we pay to Spartan culture today? While we know where Athens is located, where on the map is Sparta?

2. GAUGAMELA (October 1, 331 B.C.)

Alexander the Great decisively defeated the Persian army in a final battle. The dominance of Western culture was assured.

3. METAURUS (207 B.C.)

Rome decisively defeated Hannibal's brother, Hasdrubal, in Spain. This battle renewed Roman morale and transferred the strategic initiative to Rome. The dominance for the Mediterranean was determined by this battle, and henceforward, all roads would lead to Rome.

4. TEUTOBURGER WALD (September/October A.D. 9)

Germanic tribes annihilated three Roman legions, thereby placing a limit on Roman expansion. The Rhine River became the boundary of Pax Romanum, and German *kultur* was allowed to develop on its own.

5. CHALONS (A.D. 451)

This was the converse of the Teutoburger Wald in that the barbarian expansion under Attila was decisively halted by the remnants of the Roman Empire.

6. TOURS (October 10, A.D. 732)

Moslem expansion into western Europe was halted by Charles "the Hammer" Martel. While Spain continued to be dominated by

Moorish influences for another 700 years, such influence was unable to cross the Pyrenees.

HASTINGS (October 14, 1066)

William the Conqueror defeated the Anglo-Saxon forces under Harold. The Norman Conquest resulted in a stronger centralized government and began the rise of the British Empire. Reason for deletion: Harold had begun to forge a united nation; his defeat was incurred because he faced too many enemies too quickly. If the Normans had been unsuccessful, England might well have developed on its own anyway.

ORLEANS (October 12, 1428–May 7, 1429)

Joan of Arc led the French army in a victory over English and Burgundian forces. This gave legitimacy to the rule of Charles VII and removed English claims to the European mainland. Reason for deletion: The demographic base of England was too limited to maintain its European claims. Though this battle prevented English domination of Europe, the cross-cultural connections had already been made.

7. SPANISH ARMADA (1588)

A motley collection of English regulars, privateers, and pirates forced Spain to abandon its invasion attempt. This victory resulted in England's becoming a maritime power and beginning its path to a world empire.

BLENHEIM (August 13, 1704)

The Duke of Marlborough and Prince Eugene of Savoy defeated the French, thereby preventing a single nation from dominating the European mainland. Reason for deletion: France had already overextended itself and was economically in trouble before being defeated on the battlefield.

POLTAVA (June 28, 1709)

Charles XII of Sweden was decisively defeated by the Russians. Reason for deletion: Demographics dominated the equation. Sweden and the Scandinavian states simply lacked the population and economic base to dominate eastern Europe.

8. SARATOGA (October 7, 1777)

British forces under General John Burgoyne were forced to surrender to American forces under generals Gates and Arnold. This defeat of British arms allowed the United States to obtain foreign recognition and assistance, thereby paving the way for the fledgling nation to achieve its independence.

VALMY (September 20, 1792)

French revolutionary forces resisted regular Prussian troops. Reason for deletion: While the French exhibited revolutionary fervor, this battle was an extension of a "whiff of grapeshot." The true export of the revolution would have to await a future nation in arms.

9. LEIPZIG (NEW) (October 16–18, 1813)

Napoleon was decisively defeated by the nations of Europe in a concerted action. The allied generals had learned from the French example, and while not as good as Napoleon, were able to defeat him by overwhelming numbers and perseverance. This battle ended the French dream of a unified Europe under French domination.

WATERLOO (June 18, 1815)

Napoleon was decisively defeated by a combined British-Prussian force and forced to abdicate for a second time. Reason for deletion: Assuming that Napoleon had won at Waterloo, there were separate Austrian and Russian armies ready to begin the next battle. Even if

Napoleon at Waterloo, June 18, 1815. Even if Napoleon had managed to win this battle, other Austrian and Russian armies stood ready to fight against him. If that was not enough, the British always had more money ready to finance another coalition.

the French had secured a separate peace, British finances would still have been prepared to finance the next coalition.

10. **KURSK (NEW)** (July 5–17, 1943)

Axis forces were defeated in one of the largest tank battles in history. While the Battle of Stalingrad (August 19, 1942–February 2, 1943) had determined that the Germans could not defeat the Russians, Kursk determined that the Germans would lose the war. Thus, Nazi Germany would be unable to establish a true Festung Europa (Fortress Europe), and its policies of racial genocide would be rejected by the victorious Allies.

Decisive Naval Battles

The decisive naval battles of history are actually easier to define than are decisive battles in general. The reason is that naval battles are rather rare. Until the 19th century, they generally occurred within sight of land. Navies are much more expensive to maintain than are land forces; therefore, nations are reluctant to risk them unless victory is virtually guaranteed. Thus, throughout much of history, the stronger naval power was not challenged until other causes of decay had weakened the naval arm as well.

1. SPANISH ARMADA (1588)

In what is regarded as one of the ten decisive battles of world history, a ragtag group of English regulars, privateers, freebooters, and pirates forced Spain to abandon its invasion attempt. The battle itself was not as decisive as the poor weather, which became a stout English ally and claimed more Spanish ships than did actual battle losses. This was the first serious invasion attempt of the British Isles since the Norman invasion (1066).

2. SECOND BATTLE OF THE VIRGINIA CAPES
(September 5–9, 1781)

The destruction of the enemy fleet, although the normal goal, does not have to be the required end state for a decisive naval battle. When French Admiral Francois de Grasse (1722–88) was able to achieve temporary control of the sea lanes against British Admiral Thomas Graves (1725–1802), the result was the reinforcement of the American army with siege artillery and French troops—all of which proved decisive in the Battle of Yorktown (September 28–October 19, 1781), effectively securing American independence.

3. LEPANTO (October 7, 1571)

The Holy League under Don John de Austria (1547–78) decisively defeated the Turkish navy under Pasha Ali Monizindade. Although the fleets were evenly matched in terms of number, the league's better training, armaments, and wind advantage proved to be the factors in determining victory. Although each fleet was composed of about 300 vessels, only 47 Turkish ships escaped, while the league lost only 13 galleys. Miguel Cervantes (later author of *Don Quixote*) lost his left hand during the battle. This effectively stopped Turkish naval expansion westward into the Mediterranean.

4. TRAFALGAR (October 21, 1805)

British Admiral Horatio Nelson (1758–1805) defeated a combined Franco-Spanish fleet. By relying on the better training of his subordinates, he was able to achieve a decisive victory, thereby averting any possible chance that Napoleonic France would ever be able to mount a serious invasion of Great Britain.

5. **SYRACUSE** (413 B.C.)

The Athenian fleet was defeated in shoal waters by a combined Corinthian-Syracusean fleet. The army was isolated and, without a logistical supply line, was completely defeated. This marked the end of the Athenian dream of empire and led to a temporary Spartan hegemony, although the end result was actually a fragmentation of the Greek city-states that left them ripe for conquest by Alexander the Great and later Rome.

6. **ACTIUM** (September 2, 31 B.C.)

The Rome of the West under Octavian (63 B.C.–A.D. 14) confronted the Rome of the East under Mark Antony (83–30 B.C.) and Cleopatra (c. 69/68–30 B.C.) for supremacy of the nascent empire. Octavian's naval commander, Marcus Vipsanius Agrippa (c. 64/63–12 B.C.), is one of the few ancient naval commanders to be remembered by history. Although the fleets were evenly matched at about 400 triremes each, Agrippa's fleet decisively overwhelmed Antony's center and left.

7. **JUTLAND** (May 31–June 1, 1916)

During World War I, the British Home Fleet under Admiral John Jellicoe (1859–1935) engaged the German High Seas Fleet under Admiral Reinhard Scheer (1863–1928). Although Scheer did better tactically, he disengaged and returned to port, while tacitly conceding strategic control of the seas to the Royal Navy. Both sides expected a decisive battle, and Jellicoe could well have lost the war in an afternoon; the decisiveness of the battle could be appreciated only in retrospect.

8. **TSUSHIMA STRAITS** (May 27, 1905)

Japanese Admiral Heihachiro Togo (1848–1934) decisively defeated the Russian Fleet under Admiral Zinovy Rozhdestvenski (1848–1909) in a classic tactical feat where he crossed the enemy T. The end result was the recognition of Japan as a world power in the 20th century and a negotiated settlement of the Russo-Japanese War.

9. **MIDWAY** (June 4–6, 1942)

In a matter of fortuitous timing, U.S. Admiral Raymond Spruance (1886–1969) decisively ambushed and defeated Japanese Admiral Isoroku Yamamoto (1894–1943) in the classic carrier battle of World War II. The Japanese lost four fleet carriers *(Akaga, Kaga, Soryu,* and *Hiryu)* to the American one *(Yorktown).* Ten minutes decisively changed the initiative of the war in the Pacific, and Japan could never recover from the loss of so many skilled pilots.

10. **LISSA** (July 20, 1866)

Austrian Admiral Count Wilhelm von Tegetthoff (1827–71) defeated Italian Admiral Carlo T. di Persano in the largest ironclad battle of history (and the last battle in which ramming formed an integral battle tactic). Though the national policies of the participants were not decisively affected, the dominance of the ironclad over wooden ships was proven, and all the navies of the world paid careful attention to the lessons learned.

Lopsided Victories: More than 30,000 Casualties

There are decisive battles (e.g., Hastings), there are close-run things (e.g., Waterloo), and then there are pure stomp-'em-in-the-dirt overruns. Surprisingly, many well-known victories do not make this list. But that is because the casualty ratio ran only 4 to 1 or so; in each of the cases below, the ratio is at least 20 to 1. Often, the ratio radically increases as a result of the large number of prisoners taken, but *c'est la guerre.* Battles have been included only where reliable casualty figures exist. Thus, Mongol battle results have been omitted as well as the ancient Egyptian battle against the Hyksos invasions (where the Egyptian armies may well have been annihilated upon their first exposure to the war chariot and the horse).

1. **KUWAIT** (February 24–28, 1991)

Iraqi President Saddam Hussein promised the "Mother of All Battles" against the U.S.-led coalition forces. Instead, his incompetence resulted in one of the largest tactical defeats in history.

> Coalition casualties: 500
> Iraqi casualties: 60,000–100,000 killed/wounded
> 175,000 captured
>
> Ratio: 500:1

2. **GAUGAMELA** (October 1, 331 B.C.)

Despite being outnumbered by more than five to one, Alexander the Great defeated Darius III and the Persian Empire. His tactical adroitness enabled him to see the weakness in the Persian battle line, and by counterattacking toward Darius himself, the Macedonian army completely destroyed their Persian opponents.

> Macedonian casualties: 500
> Persian casualties: 40,000–90,000
> Ratio: 150:1

3. **ISSUS** (October, 333 B.C.)

Alexander the Great's first battle with Darius III. Outnumbered on the battlefield by only three to one, Alexander refused his left flank and his companion cavalry rolled up the Persian left wing. The Macedonian phalanx collapsed the enemy right flank, and Darius fled the battlefield in such haste that he abandoned his mother, his wife, and his children.

> Macedonian casualties: 450
> Persian casualties: 15,000–50,000
> Ratio: 77:1

4. **BARDIA** (January 3–5, 1941)

World War II and Africa immediately conjure visions of Rommel's Afrika Korps. However, a little-known British general almost shut down the African Theater of Operations before it even opened. Lieutenant-General Richard O'Connor seized the initiative against the Italians in North Africa and captured the bulk of the enemy forces in the fortified city of Bardia. His success was so great that the British High Command reduced his force structure to assist other areas. The resulting lack of offensive capability allowed the Axis forces to reinforce North Africa. Sadly, General O'Connor was later captured by the Germans while engaged in a reconnaissance mission. He escaped from Italy after the Armistice in 1943 and served as a British corps commander at D-Day and thereafter in the European Theater of Operations.

> British casualties: 150 killed/350 wounded
> Italian casualties: 38,000 (includes killed, wounded,
>   and captured)
>
> Ratio: 76:1

5. SIDI BARRANI (December 9–12, 1940)

General O'Connor's limited spoiling attack against the Italian army developed into a swirling battle of maneuver and annihilation. His unexpected success was quickly followed up by the attack on Bardia (see number 4).

> British casualties: 624
> Italian casualties: 2,000 killed/wounded
>   38,000 captured
>
> Ratio: 64:1

6. OMDURMAN (September 2, 1898)

General Horatio Kitchener's British army proved that the British square supplemented with modern firepower (including Maxim machine guns) could defeat indigenous troops in the Sudan. The follow-on cavalry charge by the 21st British Lancers was the last such action in British history (and a young lieutenant Winston Churchill was there).

> British casualties: 43 killed/428 wounded
> Dervish casualties: 9,700 killed/16,000 wounded
>   5,000 captured
>
> Ratio: 63:1

7. PYDNA (June 22, 168 B.C.)

Warfare changes over time: yesterday's winning tactics may well be tomorrow's antiquated defenses. Though the phalanx warfare perfected by Alexander the Great proved a great success, it could not withstand the more mobile Roman legion. One hundred and fifty years after Alexander's death, the Macedonians suffered a devastating defeat when their phalanx proved incapable of maneuvering across broken terrain.

> Roman casualties: 500 killed/wounded
> Macedonian casualties: 20,000 killed
> 10,000 captured
>
> Ratio: 60:1

8. PHARSALUS (August 9, 48 B.C.)

Julius Caesar defeated Pompey the Great in the Roman Civil War. Although Pompey actually had the better military reputation, his troops were not as well trained as those of Caesar. Better training and better morale usually emerge the victors.

> Caesar's casualties: 230 killed/700 wounded
> Pompey's casualties: 15,000 killed
> 24,000 captured
>
> Ratio: 41:1

9. PLATEA (479 B.C.)

The Greek city-states under Spartan leadership defeated the Persians in an ungraceful exhibition of phalangial push and shove. Overall, training, equipment, and discipline again outweighed mere numbers.

> Greek casualties: 1,300–2,000
> Persian casualties: 50,000
> Ratio: 33:1

10. **INCHON** (September 15–25, 1950)

This amphibian invasion was possibly Douglas MacArthur's finest tactical battle. It placed United Nations troops behind the lines of the North Korean forces. Surprise was total, and the capture of Seoul cut off the bulk of the North Korean Army.

> U.N. casualties: 5,000
> North Korean casualties: 10,000 killed/wounded
> 125,000 captured
>
> Ratio: 25:1

Lopsided Victories: Fewer than 30,000 Casualties

As in the prior list, these victories were extreme, although the total casualties were of a lesser magnitude.

1. BEDA FROMM (February 5–7, 1941)

General Richard O'Connor's offensives against the Italian army in World War II stand out as classics of armored warfare.

> British casualties: 50
> Italian casualties: 1,500 killed/wounded
>   25,000 captured
> Ratio: 530:1

2. HALIDON HILL (July 19, 1333)

Scottish pikes versus English longbows prove that reaching out and touching someone is much better than engaging in hand-to-hand combat. The Scottish army was destroyed.

> English casualties: 14
> Scottish casualties: 4,000
> Ratio: 285:1

3. **KINSALE** (December 26, 1601)

Outnumbered by more than four to one, English regular forces proved more than capable of defeating rebels supplemented by Spanish troops.

> English casualties: 20
> Rebel/Spanish casualties: 2,500
> Ratio: 125:1

4. **CRÉCY** (August 6, 1346)

Edward III's English longbows decisively defeated the French knights. Chivalry has its merits, but range and accuracy will beat nobility and hand-to-hand every time.

> English casualties: 100
> French casualties: 11,500
> Ratio: 115:1

5. **SHERPUR** (December 23, 1879)

Afghanistan has proved to be a disaster for invaders throughout history. The British had a pattern of disasters in their Afghan wars without really accomplishing anything. But they usually won out in the end. This battle during the Second Afghan War showed how outclassed the locals were when matched against professional and prepared British regulars.

> British casualties: 3 killed/30 wounded
> Afghan casualties: 3,000 killed/wounded
> Ratio: 90:1

6. **JEMMINGEN** (July 21, 1568)

During the War of Dutch Independence (1568–1648), the Spanish regulars succeeded in crushing the Dutch rebels. The Spanish *tercio*

("Spanish Square"), composed of pikemen and arquebusiers (early musketeers), proved itself to be the dominant battlefield formation.

> Spanish casualties: 100
> Dutch casualties: 7,000
> Ratio: 70:1

7. TRENTON (December 26, 1776)

Training and professionalism count; preparedness counts even more. General George Washington led his colonial irregulars across the Delaware River to fall upon the unsuspecting Hessians in a delayed

Washington at the Battle of Trenton, December 26, 1776. Washington's surprise raid on the unsuspecting Hessians claimed over 900 prisoners and boosted the morale of the American revolutionaries.

Christmas gift. Although it was more of a raid than a battle, its success offered a needed morale boost to the American revolutionaries.

> American casualties: 4 killed/12 wounded
> Hessian casualties: 22 killed
> 918 captured
>
> Ratio: 58:1

8. GRANICUS (334 B.C.)

Alexander the Great's Macedonian forces invaded Persia. The Persian local satraps, discounting the Macedonian combat capabilities, hurriedly marched to eliminate the invaders, only to learn that the Greek/Macedonian phalanx was an effective weapons system.

> Macedonian casualties: 115
> Persian casualties: 4,000 killed
> 2,000 captured
>
> Ratio: 52:1

9. KAMBULA (March 29, 1879)

Although the Zulus had secured a significant success in their war against the British at Isandhlwana (January 22, 1879), the *assegai* (spear) could not effectively defeat the breech-loading rifle in an open meeting engagement not marked by surprise.

> British casualties: 29 killed/55 wounded
> Zulu casualties: 2,000 killed/2,000 wounded
> Ratio: 47:1

10. MAJUBA HILL (February 27, 1881)

While the British had made a tradition of beating up indigenes, they had not been compelled to fight European troops since the Crimean War (1854). Their colonial wars had given them an arrogance that led them to discount the fighting abilities of the Boers in South Africa. In seizing a hill at night, the British troop commander forgot the axiom to seize the high ground. When the morning arrived and the mist dissipated, the British troops were fully exposed to Boer sharpshooters—and could do little to ameliorate their predicament.

Boer casualties: 1 killed/5 wounded
British casualties: 90 killed/133 wounded
                58 captured

Ratio: 46:1

Military Upsets

There are victories and defeats in the history of warfare. But occasionally, the odds are turned upside down and the side that was given no chance by any credible observer derives a victory. It may be decisive, it may be *en passant,* but for the participants, it changed their world.

1. **ADOWA** (March 1, 1896)

During the late 19th century, every major European nation had to have a presence in Africa merely to maintain its status as a world power. Italy decided to extend its influence in Abyssinia and used regular troops to confront the indigenous militia. However, the Italian army dispersed its forces in several columns; after all, the locals would not be able to stand up to modern firepower. But the local militia force did stand and defeated the Italians in a shocking affront to imperialism. Following its defeat, Italy was forced to recognize Abyssinian independence.

2. **CRÉCY** (August 23, 1346)

Hubris has its price in the history of warfare. During the Hundred Years' War, the English were retreating, and the French had caught up to them. Prudence suggested that the French organize and begin an assault the following day—but the French nobles demanded an immediate attack. Beginning the attack with their Genoese bowmen (who were ineffectual), the French knights then ran them down as mere fodder in order to close with the English positions. The English longbows were effective long before any French response could be effective. However, instead of regrouping and analyzing the situation, the French continued in a series of separate uncoordinated assaults. Each succeeding assault simply rendered the terrain more unmanageable with its own corpses of man and animal. The cream of French nobility had been decimated by an army one-third its size—and its main offensive weapon had consisted of yeoman stock and not nobility.

3. **MARATHON** (490 B.C.)

In this first battle of the Greek-Persian wars, the Persians expected an easy victory. As a world empire, they did not expect much challenge from a ragtag group of Greek city-states who could never agree among themselves. Instead, the Greeks diverted the Persian cavalry and then used the terrain to cause a double envelopment of the Persian infantry. There is still dispute as to whether the maneuver was deliberate or simply a result of the flanks being stronger than the center, but the end result was that the flanks were victorious and moved forward while the center retreated and caused the Persians to advance. The end result was a truly classic double envelopment and a major victory for the Greek city-states.

4. **LEUCTRA** (July 371 B.C.)

The Spartan infantry had established a reputation for invincibility on the battlefield. No troops known could stand up to the Spartan hoplite attack. Traditionally, better troops were placed on the right of the line of battle since this was more amenable to a right-handed pikeman. Epaminondas, commanding the Theban army, designed a novel attack formation; he overstacked left and echeloned right, thereby refusing a flank. By attacking in echelon instead of all along the line of battle, the Thebans overwhelmed the Spartan right wing by weight of numbers and then wheeled to allow their troops to totally crush the formerly elite Spartan army.

5. **VALMY** (September 20, 1792)

The French Revolution had completely transformed the army. Instead of a small professional cadre, it would utilize the *levee en masse* (conscription) and become a national army. But that was to occur in the future. In this battle, occurring early in the War of the First Coalition (1792–98), the Prussian army planned to sweep aside the French volunteers and simply abort the revolution early in its gestation period. When the two armies met, a cannonade occurred and the professional military thinking assumed that the French irregulars would simply melt away. However, they stood their ground, and instead, the Prussians had to retire because of logistical considerations. As a battle, it was not much; as a psychological operation, it was a victory for revolutionary France.

6. **TENOCHTITLAN** (November 18, 1519–August 13, 1521)

Hernando Cortés (1485–1547) invaded the Aztec Empire with 600 men and 20 horses; the odds were 8,000 to 1. Appealing to indigenous tribes who hated the Aztecs, utilizing the novelty of horses and gunpowder, plus the unintended consequences of biological warfare (i.e., smallpox, measles, and other European diseases) that killed up to 90 percent of the population—all these allowed Cortés to literally conquer an empire in the name of Spain.

7. **PLASSEY** (June 23, 1757)

Robert Clive (1725–74) used 800 British troops and 2,100 Indian infantry to defeat the indigenous Indian military force of 50,000. Though both sides used gunpowder, the British forces were better able to keep their powder dry during an afternoon monsoon. While a British victory would appear to be a major upset to the general population, Clive knew that most of his opponent's subordinates were actively plotting to take over and that their reliability would be questionable during the battle. The end result was that Great Britain began to seize the jewel in the crown of the British Empire in a single afternoon.

8. **RUSSO-FINNISH WAR**
(November 30, 1939–March 12, 1940)

When the Red Army invaded Finland, the Finnish Army consisted of 50,000 regulars and 250,000 reserves. The Soviets committed over 750,000 troops. In numerous battles, the Finns were victorious, but the demographics simply were impossible to counter. When Finland finally surrendered, their losses were 25,000 killed in action; the Soviet losses were in excess of 250,000 killed. The strong showing of the Finnish army encouraged Nazi Germany to consider the Red Army a weak military force and hence materially assisted in the decision to invade the Soviet Union on June 22, 1941.

9. **LEUTHEN** (December 5, 1757)

Frederick the Great (1712–86) made a habit of upset victories. Most of his reign in Prussia was spent fighting multiple enemies on multiple flanks, generally outnumbered. At the Battle of Leuthen, he fought outnumbered almost two to one; tactically, he feinted toward the Austrian right wing. When they responded, he marched the bulk of his army across their front (screened by low hills) to fall upon the enemy left wing. If the Austrians had had any type of forward observation, they would have noticed the movement and been able to attack Frederick in a vulnerable column formation. Instead, this oblique attack forced the disintegration of the Austrian Army.

10. **BLENHEIM** (August 13, 1704)

The Duke of Marlborough (1650–1722) and Prince Eugene of Savoy (1663–1736) combined to decisively defeat the French. Achieving tactical surprise, the Allies pounded the French until the heavy cavalry finally penetrated the French center. At the time, France was considered the dominant military power in Europe; the result of this battle shocked Europe into recognizing the primacy of the English Army as an elite fighting force.

Honorable Mention

TET OFFENSIVE (January 30–February 24, 1968)

Victory is not always achieved on the battlefield. When North Vietnam and the Viet Cong launched their offensive, it came as a surprise to the United States and South Vietnam. However, it was a military disaster for the Viet Cong—they were virtually annihilated throughout South Vietnam. But as for North Vietnam, the operation had two benefits: (1) by eliminating the Viet Cong as a viable political force, it made the war more amenable to control by the North; (2) the psychological impact was devastating to American morale and was largely responsible for the beginning of the end of American support for the war. When Walter Cronkite questioned the conduct of the war on his evening television report, it was clear evidence that the Johnson Administration had lost control.

SIX-DAY WAR (June 5–10, 1967)

There is a major difference between the informed professional and the average citizen when it comes to understanding potential combat results. When Egyptian President Nasser demanded the withdrawal of the United Nations Emergency Force (UNEF) on May 18, 1967, it was clear that war was imminent. What was not clear was the outcome. Given the demographic disadvantage facing Israel, the situation looked grim. Temples and synagogues in the United States held special services of prayer and hope. What they did not realize (and what the professional military did) was that the caliber of the Israeli Air Force was qualitatively better than that of the combined Arab Air Forces. When the Israelis launched a preemptive air strike (June 5, 1967), they established air supremacy, which allowed their ground forces to achieve a major series of victories on all fronts (Syrian, Egyptian, and Jordanian).

Airborne Operations

Vertical insertion—death from above. The concept of airborne operations is almost as old as the viable aircraft. The first parachute jump was made on February 28, 1912, thereby raising that eternal question, Why would you want to jump from a perfectly good airplane? During World War I, Brigadier General Billy Mitchell proposed a plan to seize the then-German city of Metz by "parachute infantry." But the effective use of air-delivered combat troops had to wait for World War II for practical application. In virtually every conflict since World War II, there have been airborne assaults.

1. OPERATION MARKET-GARDEN (September 17, 1944)

The largest airborne operation in history, this was British Field Marshal Bernard Montgomery's masterstroke to end World War II. The plan envisioned a massive airborne assault on five major bridges culminating with Arnhem, Netherlands. As the bridges were seized, a relief column would link up and relieve the lightly armed paratroops and pave the way for the invasion of Germany proper. As Lieutenant General Frederick "Boy" Browning noted, "We might be going a bridge too far" (later the title of an excellent book by Cornelius Ryan and a Hollywood movie). Utilizing the British 1st

Airborne Division, the American 82nd and 101st Airborne Divisions, and later the Polish 1st Parachute Brigade, the Allied elements were defeated in detail, incurring twice as many casualties as on D-Day. This massive loss of elite unit personnel and the failure of the plan revealed the brittle nature of airborne assault and the even more brittle nature of Montgomery's strategic planning abilities—it delayed the crossing of the Rhine for almost six months.

2. **D-DAY** (June 6, 1944)

The British 6th Airborne Division and the two elite American airborne divisions (82nd and 101st) preceded the amphibious invasion of Normandy with a combat assault. Although many troops landed in the wrong areas, the disruption and confusion they engendered among the German defenders justified the mission.

3. **CRETE** (May 20, 1941)

The largest German airborne operation of World War II, this assault was a Pyrrhic success. Although the Germans succeeded in seizing the island, their losses were so high that German paratroopers were never used in an air assault again. Max Schmeling, the former heavyweight champion (who gained his title from Joe Louis and then lost it back to him), was a German paratrooper at Crete.

4. **OPERATION DRAGON ROUGE** (November 23, 1964)

During the chaos of newfound independence in what had been the Belgian Congo, a primitive rebel movement (the Simbas) seized a number of hostages. United States air assets assisted in moving Belgian paratroops from Europe to Africa, where the Belgian First Para-Commando made a combat parachute assault onto the airfield at Stanleyville. After securing the airfield, the paratroops rescued most of the hostages. Losses included 3 dead and 7 wounded as well as 27 dead hostages, but about 2,000 hostages were rescued.

5. **EBAN-EMAEL** (May 10, 1940)

With the demise of the Sitzkrieg ("Phony War"), Nazi Germany began the invasion of France and the Low Countries. In order to pass through Belgium, the Germans would have had to secure the fortress at Eban-Emael. Virtually impregnable to frontal assault and too small in area for a valid drop zone, the fort would be vulnerable only to a hasty assault. The Germans determined that such an assault could best be accomplished by glider troops. As dangerous as airborne operations are, glider operations are more so—which is why there are no glider troops in any nation's inventory today. The assault element (54 men) succeeded in capturing the fortress with minimal losses and captured 1,000 Belgians.

6. **OPERATION TORCH** (November 8, 1942)

As part of the invasion of North Africa, the 509th Parachute infantry Battalion supported the Allied landings in Algeria. This was the longest airborne operation in history—the assaulting element had left from England and flown 1,600 miles to seize the airport in Oran, Algeria, by parachute assault.

7. **SICILY** (July 9, 1943)

As part of Operation Husky (the invasion of Sicily) during World War II, this was the first American parachute combat operation—and it showed. Eighty percent of the parachute troops were dropped in the wrong areas, with errors ranging from 1 to 65 miles; the glider elements released too early, with some gliders falling into the ocean and others into inhospitable terrain. Overall, it could be summed up as a hard-lessons-learned experience.

8. **KANEV** (September 23, 1943)

The concept for the only major airborne assault by the Red Army during World War II was to drop the First Airborne Corps on the western bank of the Dniepr River, thereby cutting off the retreating German army. However, the logistics-poor Soviet army was incapable of providing sufficient airlift; for example, 180 transports were required to airlift the corps, but only 6 were available. Thus, instead of dropping a 10,000-man assault element in a sudden and overwhelming attack, the actual drop penny-parceled out the airborne troops over several days, thereby obviating any potential for success.

9. KOREA (March 23, 1951)

During Operation Tomahawk, a regimental combat team and two ranger companies (about 3,400 men) conducted a paratroop assault at Munsan-Ni, South Korea. This was the last of several air assaults made by American troops during the Korean War.

10. OPERATION JUNCTION CITY (February 22, 1967)

The first airborne assault during the Vietnam War and the first since Korea, this assault was designed to destroy enemy bases in War Zone C. An airborne assault was planned so that a heliborne assault could be made as an immediate reinforcing operation. Out of 780 troops who made the drop, only 11 incurred minor injuries. This was the first combined parachute and heliborne operation in history.

Amphibious Operations

Military doctrine contends that an opposed river crossing is the most difficult operation. An amphibious invasion—crossing not a river, but an ocean—must be even more difficult! Yet an examination of amphibious operations shows that they generally have been successful. This is probably due to the fact that an amphibious invasion is not mounted until the offensive has overwhelming superiority in sufficient areas as to tilt toward success.

1. D-DAY (June 6, 1944)

During World War II, Operation Overlord was the largest amphibious invasion in history. Preceded by an airborne assault of three divisions, 4,000 Allied ships carrying over 175,000 troops were landed in Normandy, France, on five beachheads (Gold, Juno, Sword, Omaha, and Utah). The naval escorts constituted 600 warships. By the first night, five divisions had landed and secured a lodgment in the beginning of the end for the Third Reich.

2. THE PACIFIC ISLAND CAMPAIGNS

During World War II, the U.S. Marine Corps was primarily responsible for securing terrain in an "island-hopping" strategy toward the

Japanese home islands. The amphibious assault doctrine had been promulgated in the 1920s, but during World War II, it was put into effect on a scale never anticipated. Landings were made on Tulagi and Guadalcanal (August 7, 1942), New Guinea (July 2, 1943), Makin Island and Tarawa (November 20, 1943), Kwajalein (February 1, 1944), Saipan (June 15, 1944), Pelelieu (September 15, 1944), Iwo Jima (February 19, 1945), and Okinawa (April 1, 1945). Resistance was heavy, but the U.S. Marines established a reputation of excellence in island fighting.

3. INVASION OF BRITAIN (September 28, 1066)

William of Normandy claimed the English throne and invaded at Pevensey (Sussex). Having allowed the Vikings to bleed the English army, William then defeated Harold at the Battle of Hastings (October 14, 1066). Since Harold had been preoccupied with the earlier invasion, William's force landed unscathed.

4. INVASION OF BRITAIN (August 55 B.C.)

Julius Caesar (100–44 B.C.) landed two legions near Dubra (Dover). The Britons defended the beachhead, but the landing was supported by catapults mounted on the invasion ships. The Roman army forced its way ashore and remained on the island for three weeks. This was the largest invasion across the English Channel until D-Day—almost 2,000 years later.

5. QUEBEC (June 26, 1759)

British General James Wolfe (1727–59) conducted an amphibious assault with 9,000 troops against Orleans Island as a prelude to his final assault against Quebec on the Plains of Abraham (September 13, 1759). The British victory sealed the fate of a continent and allowed North America to develop as a British dependency.

6. **VERACRUZ** (March 9, 1847)

General Winfield Scott (1786–1866) conducted the first major am-phibious operation in U.S. military history. During the Mexican War, he disembarked 10,000 troops in an unopposed landing; the city fell 18 days later. What is more interesting is that this amphibious opera-tion was conducted without any losses and proceeded almost exactly according to plans.

7. **GALLIPOLI** (April 25, 1915)

During World War I, a daring plan was conceived by Winston Chur-chill (1874–1965) intended to force the Dardanelles and drive the Ottoman Empire out of the war. Though the plan could have worked, the British command was too hesitant to follow up its ini-tial success. Instead, the Turkish Army successfully forced the British to evacuate the foothold they had secured (January 9, 1916). Reper-cussions included the dismissal of Churchill from the government as well as the severe loss of personnel among the Australian and New Zealand forces committed during the operation.

8. **OPERATION TORCH** (November 8, 1942)

During World War II, a cross-channel invasion was the ultimate objec-tive of the Allies in order to force Germany to surrender. However, in 1942, there was no way that the Allies had sufficient troops or land-ing craft to accomplish this goal. Instead, they determined to land in North Africa and cut off the Afrika Korps. The landings were a learn-ing experience and proceeded with light to moderate opposition. With some invasion troops debarking directly from the United States, this was the longest amphibious invasion ever performed by the United States—a distance of over 3,100 nautical miles.

9. **INCHON** (September 15, 1950)

The Korean War began with the invasion of South Korea by the North. The U.S. troops had retreated back to the Pusan Perimeter in the southern tip of the Korean peninsula. General Douglas MacArthur (1880–1964) planned a daring amphibious invasion of Inchon, near Seoul. The tides were favorable for an invasion only six hours in a day, thereby lulling the Koreans to discount the possibility of such a landing. The successful invasion resulted in the virtual destruction of the entire North Korean army.

10. FALKLANDS (June 11, 1982)

Argentina, claiming a spurious legal title, seized the Falkland Islands from Great Britain. Forced to scramble an offensive fleet (and resurrect forces and ships previously deemed obsolete), the British responded with an amphibious assault that regained the islands in twenty-four days. Because of the distance between the port of debarkation and the Falkland Islands, this constituted the longest amphibious invasion in history—over 6,800 nautical miles.

Honorable Mention

ANZIO (January 2, 1944)

During World War II, while American and British troops were fighting their way north from the landings at Salerno and Naples, a second amphibious assault was planned at Anzio to pin the German army between the two forces. The landings were initially a success, but General John P. Lucas (1890–1949) was too cautious in exploiting the breakout; this allowed German troops to contain and almost destroy the beachhead. Anzio was sarcastically called the largest prisoner-of-war camp in Europe. The tragedy is that if the troops had been properly utilized, the backbreaking and casualty-inducing drive up the Italian Peninsula might have been avoided.

Last Stands

The "last stand" is an epic of myth; often it serves as a cry of defiance, a call for vengeance. The following incidents are among the best-known last stands of history. The major criterion utilized was that it had to indeed be a final stand; while there may be some survivors, a last stand does not allow the besieged to overcome their enemy (thus, Rorke's Drift, January 22–23, 1879, is not considered a last stand despite the odds, since the British were victorious).

1. **THE LITTLE BIG HORN** (June 25, 1876)

"Custer's Last Stand" is the subject of books, movies, and near-myth. Lieutenant Colonel George Armstrong Custer, formerly a brevet brigadier general during the Civil War, was hoping to secure the Republican presidential nomination; in order to do so, he needed a major victory. Therefore, he split his command into three elements and attacked the Sioux Nation without waiting for reinforcements. His particular element was completely destroyed, with the sole survivor being a cavalry horse (Comanche). Ever since, military students have been taught that dividing one's forces in the face of the enemy is a gross error. Rarely is it pointed out that Custer had previously enjoyed success with just such a maneuver against the

Cheyenne at the Washita River (November 27, 1868) and that Robert E. Lee had secured a major victory at Chancellorsville (May 1–6, 1863) in the same manner.

2. "REMEMBER THE ALAMO!" (February 23–March 6, 1836)

United States citizens had been moving into Texas, at that time part of Mexico. Eventually, the Texicans decided that they wanted independence. When they revolted, the Texicans fortified the Alamo, a little-known religious mission. Mexican General Santa Anna laid siege to the mission with 3,000 troops and slaughtered all the male combatants (women, children, and slaves were released). Such American heroes as William Travis (1809–36), Jim Bowie (1796–1836) and Davy Crockett (1786–1836) died at the Alamo. The cry for vengeance became a rallying cry for both Texas and the United States.

3. MASADA (A.D. 72–73)

During the Judean Revolt, Masada was the last rebellious Jewish stronghold. The Jews committed suicide rather than surrender to the Roman besiegers; over 900 men, women, and children died. Today Israeli armored soldiers take their oath at Masada by declaring that it "will never fall again!" and it has become a symbol of strength, resolution, and defiance.

4. CAMERONE (April 30, 1863)

A company of the French Foreign Legion (three officers and 62 men) defended a homestead for 10 hours against 2,000 Mexican troops; the three surviving Legionnaires were captured. The French commander, Captain Jean Danjou, was killed, but his artificial hand remains one of the most sacred relics of the Legion, and Camerone Day is still celebrated (April 28) by the French Foreign Legion as a symbol of its determination.

5. **THERMOPYLAE** (c. July 480 B.C.)

"Three hundred" Spartans under their king, Leonidas (plus 1,100 other Greek allies) held the pass at Thermopylae against the Persian army under Xerxes. A Greek traitor helped the Persians through the pass, and the Greeks died in place. The Spartans were offered quarter but refused to surrender the body of their king. A memorial was placed on the site: "Tell them in Sparta, passerby, / That here, obedient to their orders, we lie."

6. **DESTRUCTION OF THE SACRED BAND** (August 4, 338 B.C.)

Philip II of Macedon decisively defeated an Athenian-Theban coalition at the Battle of Chaeronea; his son, Alexander the Great, commanded the cavalry in his first major engagement. The Theban elite unit, the Sacred Band, was composed of 150 male couples. They died in place (depending on the source, either all or 254 of them) rather than surrender to the Macedonians. When Philip surveyed their bodies, he said, "Woe to them who think evil of such men." The unit was never re-formed.

7. **THE FETTERMAN MASSACRE** (December 21, 1866)

United States Cavalry Captain William J. Fetterman said, "Give me eighty men and I'll ride through the whole Sioux Nation." He disobeyed an order and rode after some Indians with his detachment of two officers and 78 enlisted men. No one ever returned alive.

8. **ISANDHLWANA** (January 22, 1879)

Discounting the fighting abilities of the Zulu *impi,* Major General Frederick Chelmsford allowed his central column to be ambushed and annihilated. The British forces were surprised at close quarters and could not distribute ammunition quickly enough to fend off the attacking Zulus. This was one of the major disasters of the Victorian era.

9. **THE RESIDENCY AT KABUL, AFGHANISTAN**
(September 5, 1879)

Major Pierre Louis Napoleon Cavagnari (c. 1841–79) was the British resident at Kabul; he and his security staff (drawn from the Corps of Guides) were wiped out at the British Residency in Kabul. The *Far Pavilions* (by M. M. Kaye) offers an excellent fictional treatment of this episode.

10. **ANNIHILATION OF THE VARANGIAN GUARD**
(April 11–13, 1204)

This elite unit was founded in 988 by Emperor Basil II as an imperial bodyguard for the Byzantine Empire. Initially composed of Vikings (one alumnus, Harold the Ruthless, later became king of Norway and was killed at the Battle of Stamford Bridge in England, 1066), it came to include Russians, Anglo-Saxons, and other displaced warriors. The unit was annihilated in its defense of Constantinople against the Fourth Crusade. Although later reconstituted, it became simply another ceremonial unit of Byzantium.

Massacres
(World)

One death is a tragedy; a million deaths is a statistic.

Attributed to Joseph Stalin (1879–1953)

A massacre is defined as "the indiscriminate killing of human beings." But in historical terms, the massacre is a very discriminate form of killing. It may be wanton and inhumane, but it does appear targeted at a particular class. What is more interesting is that famous massacres have ranged from the hundreds to the millions of victims. Genocide is not a new concept; the Assyrians were infamous for their slaughter of subjected peoples and the Romans were not overly concerned for the future of Carthage.

1. THE HOLOCAUST (1942–45)

Under the aegis of Adolf Hitler (1889–1945), Germany, the land of civilization—of Beethoven, Bach, and Schiller—embarked upon one of the most atrocious acts of violence in human history. Military authorities (including the Waffen SS and the Einsatzgruppen) had been exterminating Jewish civilians upon the invasion of the Soviet Union (Operation Barbarossa). However, on January 20, 1942, Reinhard Heydrich (1904–42), head of the SD (Sicherheitsdienst; German Security Service) and the president of Interpol ("the policeman is your friend?"), held a conference at the latter organization's head-quarters in Wannsee, a Berlin suburb, and authorized the *Endlosung* ("The Final Solution")—a plan to make Europe *Judenfrei* (free from Jews). For the rest of the war, the German war machine made the extermination of the Jews a higher priority than the war itself. Approximately 6,000,000 Jewish civilians were exterminated—one-third of the world's Jewish population. And that does not include the other *Untermenschen* (undesireables) of the Third Reich (e.g., homosexuals, Jehovah's Witnesses, Gypsies, etc.).

2. **THE ARMENIAN GENOCIDE** (1915–17)

In the first 20th-century case of "ethnic cleansing," the Ottoman Empire exterminated 1,000,000 Armenians. It employed the military to round up the men and use them as slave labor until they could be eliminated. The women and children were then transported to the Syrian desert and abandoned. To the present day, the modern nation of Turkey has refused to acknowledge the reality of this event, although it has been well documented. But then again, there are those who deny the Holocaust.

3. **SAMARKAND** (June 1220)

The Khwarezm War (in what are now parts of Iran and Iraq) began because Sultan Muhammad II insulted the Mongols; he killed two of their envoys and sent the third back to Genghis Khan (c. 1167–1227) with his beard shaven. The Mongols swore revenge and swept through the major cities of Khwarezm. Genghis Khan and his troops laid siege to this city on the "Silk Road." The Turkish garrison, terrified of the Mongols, betrayed the city. The Mongols then proceeded to drive the population outside the city, deport the artisans to Mongolia, and exterminate 75 percent of the remaining population. The Turkish turncoats were then exterminated as an object lesson. The total casualties exceeded 75,000 men, women, and children. The Sultan fled further into his empire, eventually dying of fear and exhaustion.

4. THE RAPE OF NANKING (December 1937)

After creating the puppet state of Manchuko, Japan invaded China proper on July 7, 1937. On December 13, 1937, Nanking fell to the Japanese, who looted the city for the next three weeks. An orgy of rape, murder, and pillage was not a case of the Japanese Army's losing control of its soldiers; it was obvious that they simply did not care. Estimates of civilian noncombatant casualties range from 50,000 to 300,000. Japan contends that the episode has been exaggerated and was not that serious, but these are the same people who brought you the Bataan Death March and the beheading of the Raiders on Makin Island.

5. MAGDEBURG (May 20, 1631)

After a seven-month siege, this city fell to Johann von Tilly (1559–1632) during the Thirty Years' War (1618–48). Although he had wanted the city as a supply base, Tilly lost control of his troops and they sacked the city for three days and then destroyed it by fire. Twenty-five thousand people were killed out of a total population of 30,000.

6. BADAJOZ (April 6–9, 1812)

During the Napoleonic Wars, the Duke of Wellington's British troops stormed and seized the Spanish-Portuguese border fortress city of Badajoz from the French garrison after a four-week siege. Although the British were allied with Spain and Portugal, the British troops went berserk for three days—looting, raping, and killing—before Wellington could reassert control. This was the worst breakdown of British troop discipline during Wellington's campaigns.

7. CAWNPORE (June 27, 1857—July 15, 1857)

During the Great Mutiny, the British Garrison at Cawnpore agreed to leave under promise of safe escort by Nana Sahib. However, as they proceeded out of the city, the men were massacred (June 27, 1857) and approximately 200 women and children were imprisoned in the *Bibi-Ghar* ("House of the Women"), where they were butchered on July 15, 1857. The massacre of the men was overshadowed by the deaths of the noncombatants; Victorian England was both shocked and vengeful. When the British recaptured the site, they forced each *sepoy* (native) prisoner to lick a square foot of blood-stained floor before being taken out for a "slow" hanging.

8. LIDICE (June 9, 1942)

During World War II, Czech agents under British supervision assassinated Reinhard Heydrich, the Nazi Protector of Bohemia-Moravia (and former deputy chief of the Gestapo). The Germans reacted with reprisals. The small Czech town of Lidice was surrounded and all men and boys over 16 (172) were shot; the women and children were sent to concentration camps. The village was completely razed.

9. DEIR YASSIN (April 9, 1948)

During the Arab-Israeli War of 1948, this Arab village was attacked by elements of the Irgun and the Stern Gang (irregular and terrorist Jewish underground organizations). Although the plan had been to warn the population to flee, few inhabitants heard or heeded the warning. After hard fighting, the village was captured. What then happened is difficult to ascertain—were men simply rounded up and shot? The Jews claimed that 250 out of 400 inhabitants were killed; the Arabs claimed that only 110 of 1,000 survived. The Arabs claimed that the Jews looted, raped, and pillaged; the Jews denied the charges. This incident has become a rallying cry for Arab vengeance over the last 50 years. What has been forgotten is that Deir Yassin was not a peaceful village; the Jewish casualties amounted to 40 percent of the assault force. But perceptions may indeed be more important than reality, and the echoes of this assault reverberate down to the present.

10. **AGINCOURT** (October 25, 1415)

Henry V (1387–1422) defeated the French in a decisive battle of the Hundred Years' War. However, in the midst of the battle, Henry received reports that the French had broken into his rear and were attacking his supply trains. Since he feared that he did not have sufficient forces to both relieve the assault and guard his prisoners, he simply killed his prisoners—up to 5,000 nobles of France were so slaughtered. Aside from the moral implications, Henry also faced the economic loss of their ransom value (which was probably more important to him anyway).

Massacres
(United States)

In its relatively short history, the United States has witnessed a number of massacres either by or against Americans on U.S. and foreign soil. However, it is interesting to note their magnitude—rarely do the losses exceed 500 casualties. While the rest of the world can count its casualties in millions, the United States does so in hundreds, and many of the incidents have been termed "massacres" for political purposes alone.

1. **MALMEDY** (December 17, 1944)

During the initial stages of the Battle of the Bulge (December 16, 1944–January 18, 1945), Lieutenant Colonel Joachim Jochen Peiper's SS troops captured a number of American prisoners from Battery B, 285th Field Artillery Observation Battalion. They were taken to a field and deliberately executed; out of about 150 prisoners, 80 were killed. This was the only organized execution of prisoners of war by either side during the Bulge. The repercussions were twofold: (1) Americans were less likely to surrender; (2) Americans were less likely to accept the surrender of SS personnel. After the war, Peiper was sentenced to death for war crimes, but his sentence was commuted to life, and he was released after 11 years in prison.

2. MY LAI (March 16, 1968)

Second Lieutenant William Calley (b. 1943) was not the "best and the brightest": a college dropout, he received his commission as a "90-day wonder" (through officer candidate school). As a platoon leader, he was substandard; as a combat leader, he was a failure. But he and his platoon killed about 500 men, women, and children located in this Vietnamese village. Few arms were found and even fewer guerrillas. Calley had made a serious mistake—his actions were too visible and were picked up by the American press. At his court-martial, he was convicted of murder (although his sentence was commuted to time served). The higher chain of command was not convicted of any war crimes, although this incident ended the careers of several senior officers. What was of more historical import is the fact that he was charged and convicted at all; such incidents of accountability are all too rare in history.

3. WOUNDED KNEE (December 29, 1890)

This was the final "pacification" of the Plains Indians. They surrendered to the Seventh U.S. Cavalry, but when the Indians argued over details, the cavalry simply answered with massive firepower (including artillery). When it was over, 300 Sioux were dead along with 29 U.S. cavalry, many of whom had been hit by friendly fire. It was so one-sided that the officer on the scene was court-martialed by the military authorities, although he was exonerated by the secretary of war. To the present day, Native Americans regard this as an unjustified slaughter.

4. FORT PILLOW (April 12, 1864)

Confederate Lieutenant General Nathan Bedford Forrest captured Fort Pillow on a raid. Under a flag of truce, he demanded the Union surrender and stated "[S]hould my demand be refused, I cannot be responsible for the fate of your command." The Union commander refused to surrender, and after an assault of the breastworks, the white flag was shown by the Northern troops. However, black troops may have retreated and kept firing; this may have been logical, since they would not have expected humane treatment from a Confederate officer who had been a slavetrader. The end result was that most of the black troops were killed; of the fort's 580-man garrison, 354 were killed or wounded and the remainder captured. The North regarded this as an unjustified massacre; the South saw it simply as within the limits of the rules of war.

5. **LAWRENCE, KANSAS** (AUGUST 21, 1863)

William Quantrill (1837–65) and his Raiders invaded this city ostensibly as representatives of the Confederate Army. However, Quantrill's military affiliation was mere cover for banditry in its worst form (Jesse James and the Younger Brothers were Quantrill alumni). Although the city may have been a valid military target, Quantrill's men proceeded to loot and burn the town. Over 150 men were killed.

6. **FORT DEARBORN** (August 15, 1812)

An American troop column was guaranteed safety by the British and their Indian allies to evacuate Fort Dearborn, Illinois. Consisting of 54 soldiers, 12 militia, 9 women, and 18 children, the Americans were attacked en route, with over one-half of the column being killed.

7. **THE WAXHAWS MASSACRE** (March 29, 1780)

Colonel Banastre Tarleton (1754–1833) was probably the most hated British officer in the rebellious colonies (with the exception of Benedict Arnold). Upon surrounding a group of American militia, he demanded an instant surrender. When the Americans were tardy in their response, Tarleton's Raiders immediately attacked, granting no quarter to surrendering rebels. Of the Waxhaws Militia, 113 were killed, 150 wounded, and 53 taken prisoner.

8. THE CANBY MASSACRE (March 10, 1873)

During the Modoc Indian War (1872–73), General E. R. S. Canby met with Modoc tribal leader Captain Jack at a truce conference. The Indians used the meeting as a pretense for an assault on the negotiators; four of the seven Americans were killed. Several months later, the army captured and unceremoniously hanged Captain Jack for his treachery.

9. BOSTON MASSACRE (March 5, 1770)

A prequel to the American Revolution, this involved a civil-military action. When American colonists engaged in riotous activity, British regular troops replied by firing on the crowd. Five men were killed and six wounded; the British troops were withdrawn from Boston and the principals were tried for the incident. Defended by John Adams (1735–1826), five soldiers were acquitted and two were convicted of manslaughter.

10. NO GUN RI (July 26, 1950)

During the early stages of the Korean War, U.S. military forces were retreating desperately south. There is dispute as to what exactly happened at No Gun Ri; allegations made 50 years later contend that American troops fired on and killed up to 300 South Korean civilians. But were North Korean troops using the civilians as a shield to penetrate American defensive lines; did the "massacre" in fact occur? This particular incident has become a political issue and not a historical one.

Mutinies

M utiny is the breakdown of military discipline; it is the most feared concept to any commander. Yet there have been comparatively few incidents of troops in history refusing to obey orders. Troop cohesion and training often serve to prevent disaffection and insubordination, but when the situation grows bitter, it is often difficult to improve.

1. KRONSTADT (March 1–18, 1921)

The Russian sailors stationed at Kronstadt (near St. Petersburg) had been in the vanguard of the Revolution and the Civil War. However, by 1921, they had grown weary of Bolshevik promises and demanded an end to Bolshevik rule with all power to go to the Soviets (district councils). The Bolsheviks responded with Leon Trotsky (1879–1940) and Mikhail Tukhachevsky (1893–1937) leading loyal Bolshevik troops across the ice to stamp out the insurrection. Most of the mutineers were summarily executed.

2. SPITHEAD/NORE (April 16–June 15, 1797)

In the midst of the wars against Revolutionary France (1792–1802), the British fleet mutinied over poor working conditions and pay.

The Spithead Mutiny was peacefully resolved by May 15, 1797, but the Nore Mutiny required harsh measures and bloodshed to quell. The French Fleet, unaware of the British problem, was unable to take any advantage.

3. HMS *BOUNTY* (April 28, 1789)

In possibly the most famous naval mutiny in history, master's mate Fletcher Christian (1764–92) led a mutiny against Captain William Bligh (1754–1817) and seized the British warship *Bounty*. The mutineers later settled on Pitcairn Island, where their descendants live to this day. The incident is the subject of a classic sea trilogy, *Mutiny on the Bounty* (1932), *Men against the Sea* (1934), and *Pitcairn's Island* (1934) by Charles Nordhoff (1887–1947) and James Hall (1887–1951). The first book has been made into a movie several times (with the 1935 version starring Clark Gable probably being the best).

4. HMS *HERMIONE* (September 21, 1797)

Captain Hugh Pigot was a sadistic commander who finally went too far. He ordered the flogging of the last man down from the rigging; in their haste, three men fell to their deaths, and the captain simply ordered their bodies thrown overboard without ceremony. He and his officers were killed that night in the bloodiest mutiny in British naval history, and the ship sailed to Venezuela and defected to the Spanish. In 1799, HMS *Surprise* recaptured the ship, and most of the mutineers were court-martialed and hanged after a global manhunt over the next eight years.

5. INDIAN MUTINY (May 10, 1857–June 1858)

In the most famous mutiny of British imperial history, native troops *(sepoys)* revolted for a number of reasons: there were rumors that the new cartridges were greased with both pig and beef fat (thus being anathema to Moslems and Hindus, respectively), there was a prophecy that British rule would come to an end, and the *sepoys* were told that they would be shipped overseas despite prior guarantees. Local native rulers took advantage of the discontent, and it took over a year for British troops and loyal *sepoys* to quell the rebellion. The intense fighting was characterized by massacres (Cawnpore, July 1857), atrocities, and looting (Delhi, September 1857), with both sides escalating the violence to new and deeper levels.

6. **THE WESTERN FRONT** (April 21–September 15, 1917)

After almost three years of massive bloodletting with few results, the soldiers of the French Army decided that they had had enough. After the failure of the Nivelle Offensive (April 16–29, 1917), the troops simply refused to take any offensive action. Over one-half of the French Army was affected by the mutiny (68 out of 112 divisions), but the Germans did not learn of the situation until June 30, 1917, when most of the danger had passed. Almost 3,000 soldiers were convicted by court-martial, but succeeding army commander Henri Petain (1856–1951) commuted most of the death sentences.

7. *POTEMKIN* (June 14, 1905)

The crew of this battleship protested against their rations; the ship captain's response was to order a firing squad to execute the ringleaders of the protest. The firing squad refused to obey orders, and the crew then threw the officers overboard. Fearing that they would be attacked by the rest of the fleet, the sailors steered the ship to Romania, where they sought asylum—a foreshadowing of things to come. A classic film, *Battleship Potemkin*, was made by Sergei Eisenstein (1898–1948).

8. ALEXANDER THE GREAT AND HIS ARMY
(c. July 326 B.C.)

After fighting their way across most of the known world for 10 years, Alexander's troops simply told their leader that enough was enough. Although Alexander was a charismatic leader and orator, he could not sway his men; thus, he ceased his invasion of India and began the return home. Upon reaching Opis (north of Baghdad), he faced a second mutiny (this time over the integration of his Persian and Macedonian forces), which he subdued without violence.

9. USS *SOMERS* (1842)

The crew of a U.S. brig, used as a training ship for naval apprentices, suffered from low morale on a voyage to Africa. On the way back to the West Indies, the captain arrested Midshipman Philip Spencer, the son of the secretary of war, charged him with mutiny, and had him and two confederates court-martialed and hanged on December 1, 1842. A naval board of inquiry exonerated the captain for his actions. This was the only mutiny ever noted on a U.S. warship.

10. PORT CHICAGO MUTINY (July 17, 1944)

Two ammunition transport ships blew up in the worst military disaster in the continental United States during World War II. Everything was destroyed within a one-mile radius, and 320 men were killed and 400 injured. Afterwards, the surviving troops refused to load munitions until they were assured that safety conditions had been improved. Most of the troops were black, and the Navy quickly court-martialed 50 of them. All were convicted, dishonorably discharged, and sentenced to lengthy terms of imprisonment (although President Harry S Truman commuted their sentences after the end of the war). It was only 50 years later that the government reconsidered the situation and conceded that racism might well have contributed to the summary action at the time.

(Dis)Honorable Mention

PRAETORIAN GUARD

With the advent of the Roman Empire, the Praetorian Guard soon became a permanent factor in succession to the purple. Payments of salaries in arrears together with additional bonuses often determined who the next emperor would be. Thus, this military institution designed to protect the city of Rome and the throne became in fact an agent of mutiny and dissension.

Honorable Mention

REVOLT OF THE ADMIRALS

With the end of World War II, there was some dispute in the American military and civilian establishments as to what the future organization and budgeting should emphasize. Chief of Naval Operations Louis Denfield was fired by the secretary of defense for publicly opposing proposed plans for a stronger air force. Several other naval officers agreed, and they were regarded as insubordinate and forced to retire (Arleigh Burke was saved only by the direct intervention of President Harry S Truman). Their actions preserved naval aviation for the future. This "revolt" was not a mutiny in the legal sense, but rather a case of military officers willing to sacrifice their careers for what they regarded as the good of the service—an action that has become all too rare in contemporary society.

CURRAGH MUTINY (March 1914)

The commanding officer and 56 other officers of the British Third Cavalry Brigade resigned their commissions rather than force Ulster Protestants to accept Irish home rule. The Chief of the Imperial General Staff (Sir John French, later head of the British Expeditionary Force during World War I) resigned his position as well.

Raids

A raid is a temporary intrusion against an enemy position with a specific intent—either to cause maximum damage or to requisition specified assets (e.g., equipment, loot, or individuals). By definition, it is normally employed against a superior force and entails a greater degree of risk than is normal with military operations.

1. ENTEBBE (July 3–4, 1976)

When Palestinian terrorists hijacked Air France Flight 139, they flew to Entebbe, Uganda, and demanded certain concessions from the State of Israel. Otherwise, they threatened to execute the flight crew and all Israeli and Jewish passengers. An Israeli commando rescue mission was mounted over a distance of 2,200 miles—the longest raid in history. All passengers but one were rescued. Interestingly, many nations condemned Israel for its violation of Uganda's national integrity (despite the fact that Uganda was abetting the terrorists). This has a current impact with the widespread use of international terrorism. Although the United States currently has declared war on terrorism, there are legal problems. "War may be defined as a legal condition of armed hostility between States" (*Field Manual 27-10, Law of Land Warfare*, paragraph 8[a]). Thus, the pursuit of terrorists, even across international boundaries does not constitute an act of war. Since terrorists hold no commission or delegated authority from any state, their actions are not against any particular state, but rather against all of humanity and would constitute piracy. Thus, the practice of nations has allowed any state to have the right to exterminate pirates without any declaration of war, and such "pirates" can be subject to military law even though they do not have the rights or privileges of belligerents.

2. DIEPPE (August 18–19, 1942)

In the early years of World War II, the proper planning and execution of amphibious operations was still in a learning phase. A "dress rehearsal" for later amphibious operations involved the Canadian Second Infantry Division and two British commando units. The Allies took horrendous casualties and seemingly did not accomplish much. However, the lessons learned would be important for the forthcoming invasion of the continent. Overall, the price was possibly too high, but it was the first major land action against Hitler's *Festung Europa* (Fortress Europe).

3. ST. NAZAIRE (March 28, 1942)

In Operation Chariot, British commandos attacked the sub pens and dry docks at St. Nazaire, France. A major goal was to prevent the German battleship *Tirpitz* from relocating from Norway to the Atlantic. HMS *Campbeltown* (a former U.S. Lend-Lease destroyer) was packed with explosives and used with motorboats to lead the assault. The mission was not executed smoothly, although the main objective of the raid was achieved: the destroyer was captured and was being inspected by German officials when the ship detonated, causing many casualties and extensive damage to the docks. However, most of the raiders were killed or captured; five Victoria Crosses were awarded for gallantry.

4. **DOOLITTLE RAID** (April 18, 1942)

Lieutenant Colonel Jimmy Doolittle (1896–1993) led 16 B-25 bombers from the deck of the aircraft carrier *Hornet* to bomb Tokyo, Japan. Although the bombing caused little actual damage, the psychological effect was enormous—giving a morale surge to the United States and shocking the Japanese that their homeland was so vulnerable.

5. **MAKIN ISLAND** (August 17, 1942)

In a counterpart to the European Theater's Dieppe Raid, the Second Marine Raider Battalion ("Carlson's Raiders") performed a landing from two submarines on Makin Island. A Japanese reconnaissance base was largely destroyed, although when the Marines left, they abandoned some of their own men, who were executed by the Japanese defenders. After the war ended, the persons responsible for such executions were hanged as war criminals. (The bodies of the executed Marines were discovered and returned to the United States in 2001.)

6. **GRIERSON'S RAID** (April 18–May 3, 1863)

During the Civil War, Union Colonel Benjamin H. Grierson (1826–1911) led three regiments of cavalry from La Grange, Tennessee, on a successful destructive raid through the entire state of Mississippi to Baton Rouge, Louisiana. The motion picture *The Horse Soldiers* with John Wayne was based upon this historical incident.

7. **MOSBY AT FAIRFAX** (March 9, 1863)

With 29 Rangers, Confederate partisan John S. Mosby (1833–1916) penetrated Union lines and slipped into Fairfax Courthouse, Virginia, where he kidnapped Union General Edwin H. Stoughton (1838–68). "Mosby Country" (the Virginia counties of Fairfax, Loudoun, Fauquier, and Culpeper) continued to offer the guerrilla leader support throughout the Civil War.

8. SKORZENY AND MUSSOLINI (September 12, 1943)

When Benito Mussolini (1883–1945) was removed from power, he was imprisoned at a hotel in Gran Sasso, Italy. SS Officer Otto Skorzeny (1908–75) led a daring and successful glider rescue that temporarily freed the Italian leader.

9. DRAKE AT CADIZ (April 19–20, 1587)

Francis Drake (1541–96) led an English fleet of six ships into the Spanish harbor of Cadiz on a raid for loot and plunder. Immensely successful, the raid disrupted enemy shipping, caused the Spanish to spend more time and effort fortifying their ports, and offered a financial windfall to his investors.

10. THE GERMAN COMMERCE RAIDERS OF WORLD WAR I

German commerce raiders established a reputation for courage and daring during World War I, even if their results were not overly significant. Captain Karl von Muller (1873–1923) led the SMS *Emden,* a light cruiser, on a four-month commerce raiding voyage in 1914 before being sunk by an Australian warship. Count Felix von Luckner (1881–1966) commanded a sailing schooner, the *Seeadler (Sea Eagle)* in commerce raiding for eight months (December 2, 1916–August 2, 1917) in the Atlantic and Pacific Oceans.

Honorable Mention

THE VIKINGS (c. 800–950)

The Norsemen invaded all over Europe in an attempt to seek plunder. Their raids ranged from England (including London) to France (including Paris) to Spain to Russia. No one particular raid has great historical import, but the overall succession of raid following raid determined much of early feudal society (including prayers to preserve oneself from the wrath of the Norsemen).

Sieges

Siegecraft is a dirty, nasty aspect of war, which is dirty and nasty in and of itself. Generally, the besieged suffer from starvation and disease as well as battle casualties, while the besiegers often suffer more casualties. For example, at the Second Siege of Rhodes (June 25, 1522–December 21, 1523), the Turkish army suffered about 100,000 losses while the defending Christians suffered only about 5,000 losses. The Turkish losses, however, were only 50 percent of engaged forces, while the Christians were totally defeated.

1. TROY (C. 1184 B.C.)

The subject of Homer's classic *Iliad,* this 10-year siege of the city of Troy was brought to a successful conclusion by the Greeks only when they resorted to Odysseus's Trojan Horse stratagem. With a supporting cast (e.g., Helen, Paris, Hector, Achilles) known to anyone with a modicum of literacy, this was thought to be a mythical event until the reality of the siege was proved by Heinrich Schliemann's archeological expedition in 1870.

2. **CONSTANTINOPLE** (February–May 29, 1453)

The Byzantine Empire was the descendant of the Roman Empire. However, it was a pale shadow of its past glory. Christian Emperor Constantine XI and 10,000 troops attempted to hold this bastion against Mehmet the Conqueror with his Turkish army of 80,000 plus heavy artillery. Without reinforcements or assistance from Europe, the Byzantine Empire was doomed, and its demise heralded the end of the Middle Ages.

3. **TYRE** (January–July 29, 332 B.C.)

To defeat the Persian Empire, Alexander the Great had to negate their naval capabilities. Tyre, an island, was the principal seaport of Phoenicia and the Persian main base. Alexander had to recruit a navy ab initio; simultaneously, he built several land bridges (called "moles") from the mainland to the island. With a double-pronged assault, the Macedonians stormed the city and razed it. As an example to others who might consider resistance, Alexander crucified 2,000 of the city's defenders and sold 30,000 others into slavery. The artificial mole remains extant to the present.

4. **CANDIA** (June 1647–September 6, 1669)

Little-known today, the Siege of Candia has the dubious distinction of being the longest siege in history. For over two decades, the Venetians defended Candia (present-day Heraklion on Crete) from the Turks. Venetian naval victories held the Turks at bay until eventually lack of reinforcements and continuous Turkish assaults resulted in a city with no options remaining. An evacuation and treaty of peace were the end results of this epic struggle.

5. **LENINGRAD** (September 8, 1941–January 27, 1943)

During Operation Barbarossa, Hitler's Army Group North had the objective of seizing Leningrad, the spiritual capital of the Soviet Union and the prior capital of the Russian Empire. During the winter, the Soviets were able to reinforce the city over the frozen Lake Ladoga by ersatz roads and railroads. This epic struggle of 900 days resulted in a German defeat; however, Soviet civilian casualties were horrific during the siege. Dimitri Shostakovitch wrote his *Seventh Symphony (Leningrad Symphony)* to commemorate this struggle. The city itself received the Order of Lenin (1945) and the title Hero City of the Soviet Union (1965). Today, it is once again St. Petersburg.

6. **MALTA** (May 18–September 8, 1565)

The "Great Siege" occurred between the Turkish Empire and the Christian Knights of St. John. The knights held out until relieved in an epic struggle against seemingly overwhelming odds. The Turks suffered from a triumvirate of command, and both sides had an interesting facet in that the commanding officers were over 70 years old.

7. **SEVASTOPOL** (October 8, 1854–September 9, 1855)

A combined Anglo-French force invested this Russian Crimean city in a siege noted for poor leadership, poor planning, and poor execution. The famous Charge of the Light Brigade occurred during this siege (October 25, 1854). Altogether, the mismanagement by the British and French forces was one of the worst in history—only to be outdone by sheer Russian incompetence.

8. **VICKSBURG** (May 19–July 4, 1863)

Union General U. S. Grant invested this Mississippi city and gradually closed in, utilizing both siege artillery and gunboats. The Confederate defenders and the civilian population sought refuge in caves but finally surrendered on the Fourth of July—a date that was not celebrated in that city again until 1944. With the Union victories at Gettysburg and Vicksburg on the same day, the Confederacy was faced with the beginning of the end.

9. **PORT ARTHUR** (May 25, 1904–January 2, 1905)

This Russian naval base (now known as Lushunkou, a Chinese naval base closed to foreigners) was located in the Manchurian Peninsula. When hostilities seemed imminent, the Russian Empire discounted the threat capabilities of the empire of Japan. However, the Japanese had learned from the past and had modernized both their army and navy. After a hard-fought siege, the Russian forces surrendered and evacuated the area.

10. **LILLE** (August 14–December 11, 1708)

The Austrians under Eugene of Savoy and the British under the Duke of Marlborough defeated the French in this "impregnable" fortress city. This siege represents the apex of siege warfare. The city's defenses were designed by Marshal Sebastien Le Prestre de Vauban (1633–1707), who was acknowledged to be the master at fortifications in both offense and defense. However, there is no city that can be considered impregnable.

Honorable Mention

DIEN BIEN PHU (November 20, 1953–May 7, 1954)
Following World War II, France attempted to reassert control over its colonial empire. In its battle against the Vietminh, French forces attempted to lure their enemy into an ill-fated assault. Thus, the French defended a village and airstrip in what is now northern

Vietnam. However, proving that the spirit of Napoleon was buried, the French effort resulted in their entrapment. Vietminh artillery pieces were moved to surrounding mountains, and the French forts fell one by one. Although the Vietminh took horrendous losses, the French were compelled to surrender, thereby ending their control of Vietnam. Also, many of the French defenders were Foreign Legionnaires (a number of whom were former members of the German Army during World War II). Some have called this siege the final battle of the *Wehrmacht.* This was different from the sieges listed above; it was a siege of purely military dimensions—there were no pesky civilians to defend.

Retrograde Operations

W hile the best defense in football may be a strong offense, the same is not true in the art of warfare. An army may not have the strength to assume the offensive or it may need to retrench for a future day. Throughout history, certain retrograde maneuvers have established themselves as exemplars of the genre—on both land and sea.

1. LONG MARCH (1934–35)

The Chinese Nationalist Forces under Chiang Kai-shek (1887–1975) were victorious in the campaigns against the Chinese Communist forces in 1934. The Communist First Front Army (with political commissar Mao Tse-tung, 1893–1976) executed a 6,000-mile fighting retreat to Yenan in order to start anew. This was the longest and fastest sustained march ever made under combat conditions by infantry. Of the 86,000 who began the march, only 4,000 finished—a survival rate of 4 percent. But the survivors became the cadre for a new and stronger Chinese Communist Army—and the stuff of myth and legend.

2. *THE ANABASIS* (401–400 B.C.)

While fighting as mercenaries in a Persian civil war under Cyrus the Younger, the Greeks found themselves isolated when Cyrus was killed in the Battle of Cunaxa. Xenophon then led the Greeks in a fighting withdrawal over 1,000 miles of hostile terrain. Xenophon's "Ten Thousand" participants became immortal through his memoirs (*The Anabasis*, "March Upcountry"), although only 4,000 actually survived.

3. DUNKIRK (May 21–June 4, 1940)

With the fall of France, the British Expeditionary Force was threatened with total destruction. However, with the Germans slowing down their advance to the Channel ports and the defense of Calais, the Royal Navy managed to evacuate 338,000 troops (one-third of whom were French or Belgian). The British had to abandon their heavy equipment and armored vehicles, but they were able to preserve the army for later use.

4. QUINTUS FABIUS MAXIMUS VERRUCOSUS (*CUNCTATOR*, "THE DELAYER") AND THE SECOND PUNIC WAR (217–203 B.C.)

After Hannibal had defeated the Romans at the Battle of Lake Trasimene (April 217), Fabius (266–203 B.C.) took command and engaged in a guerrilla campaign against the Carthaginians. His tactics of refusing to meet the Carthaginian army in open battle were successful; however, the Romans became impatient and removed him from command. The result was the Battle of Cannae (August 216 B.C.)—one of the worst Roman defeats in history. He then was appointed to command Rome's military forces once again and resumed his campaign of maneuver and attrition.

5. CHIEF JOSEPH AND THE NEZ PERCE (June 17–September 30, 1877)

Rather than move onto a reservation, Chief Joseph (c. 1840–1904) began an epic retreat with his entire tribe, seeking freedom in Canada. Pursued by U.S. cavalry, Chief Joseph led a classic fighting withdrawal across 1,300 miles. He finally surrendered on September 30, 1877, when he was only 30 miles from the Canadian border ("From where the sun now stands, I will fight no more forever").

6. NAPOLEON IN RUSSIA (June 24–December 18, 1812)

When Napoleon's Grand Armée invaded Russia, it was the most powerful army in the world. The Russians were not capable of facing this force in open battle and determined to trade space for time. Under Mikhail Barclay de Tolly (1761–1818) and Mikhail Kutuzov (1745–1813), the Russian strategy prevailed when "General Winter" arrived. Time, distance, and logistical difficulties forced Napoleon to begin a catastrophic retreat out of Russia.

7. THE UNITED STATES MARINE CORPS AND THE CHOSIN RESERVOIR (November 27–December 9, 1950)

When the Chinese intervened in Korea, they caught the American military completely by surprise. The First Marine Division consolidated around the Chosin Reservoir, surrounded by eight Communist divisions. Marine Major General Oliver Smith stated that the Marines were not retreating but were "attacking in another direction." The running fight ended when the Marines linked up with the Third Marine Division near Hungnam; they had executed their movement in good order, and carried out their equipment, their wounded, and their dead.

8. THE FRENCH CAMPAIGN OF 1814

After Napoleon's defeat at the Battle of Leipzig (October 16–18, 1813), it was apparent that the French were decisively beaten. However, the French Emperor proved that he had not lost his famous ability to "see" the battlefield. In the Battles of Champaubert (February 10, 1814), Montmirail (February 11, 1814), and Vauchamps (February 14, 1814), he defeated Blucher's Prussians despite being severely outnumbered. His tactical operations still bear study, although in a strategic sense, it was impossible for him to prevail and he was forced to abdicate (April 6, 1814).

9. THE FLIGHT OF THE *GOEBEN* AND *BRESLAU*
(August 3–10, 1914)

With the onset of World War I, the German battle cruisers *Goeben* and *Breslau* were ordered to sail the breadth of the Mediterranean to Turkey. It was hoped that their arrival would persuade Turkey to enter the war as a Central Power. Sailing over 1,000 miles while being relentlessly (albeit somewhat incompetently) pursued by a British task force, the Germans finally entered Constantinople and turned over both ships (now renamed as *Yavuz Sultan Selim* and the *Midili*) to the Turkish Navy. Two months later (October 30, 1914), Turkey did enter the war as a German ally.

10. THE PURSUIT OF THE *GRAF SPEE*
(August 21–December 17, 1939)

This German "pocket battleship" left Germany on August 21, 1939, and began its career as a commerce raider on September 30, 1939. After sinking almost 50,000 tons of merchant shipping, it was brought to battle by a British task force. Though the battle was inconclusive, the German ship sought temporary refuge in the neutral port of Montevideo, Uruguay, to effect repairs. On December 17, 1939, the ship was scuttled after leaving the harbor; this was one of the first British successes of World War II.

Revolutions

Ostensibly, a revolution is a successful attempt to seize power, overthrow a government, or become independent. Where a revolution ended and a civil war began may be a question to be determined by a political scientist, but the following revolutions have changed history—for better and worse.

1. UNITED STATES (1775–83)

The Founding Fathers, in an attempt to avoid "taxation without representation," provided a list of grievances to the legitimate government, and when the response was not deemed adequate, determined to found a new nation on the North American continent, composed of the 13 British colonies. Thanks to French support (supplied simply to tweak the English and not because the French supported the ideals and goals of the revolutionaries), the United States secured its independence from Great Britain.

2. FRANCE (1789–1802)

With the lofty ideals of the American Revolution acting as a catalyst, the French people decried the ancien régime and declared a republic, executing their former king and many of his entourage in the interim. Eventually, the Revolution fed on itself and settled for a new ruler—Napoleon.

3. RUSSIA (1917–18)

Actually, there were two revolutions. Alexander Kerensky established a provisional government when Tsar Nicholas II abdicated in February/March. Eight months later, the Bolsheviks seized power in a second and final revolution that established the "dictatorship of the proletariat" for the next 75 years.

4. MEXICO (1911–19)

In an ongoing civil war, revolt, and revolution, the various leaders of Mexico attempted to achieve control of the government. However, the violence of the revolution left most of the dominant leaders dead, and the revolution simply ran out of energy, although the ruling party had established the seeds of its domination of the nation for the next 70 years.

5. IRAN (1979)

Shah Muhammad Rez Pahlavi (1919–80) was deemed too autocratic by liberals and too Western by conservatives. He was replaced by the Ayotollah Ruhollah Khomeini (1901–89), who founded the Islamic Republic of Iran, a religious fundamentalist state that has been responsible for the rebirth and export of a religious right that has endangered moderate Muslim states and Western democracies worldwide.

6. ALGERIA (1954–62)

Although formally a department of France, Algeria sought independence. A bitter, hard-fought war against France resulted in formal independence after eight years of conflict.

7. THE REVOLUTIONS OF 1848 (FRANCE, GERMANY, ITALY, AUSTRIA-HUNGARY)

Most of western and central Europe revolted for more liberal governments based upon the principles of the Enlightenment. The separate monarchies and governments were terrified and offered a number of concessions. However, the concessions were small enough to be ignored later when the established governments had regained control of their constituents. Interestingly enough, these revolutions, albeit successful in the short term, all failed to achieve their ultimate goals and actually engendered a retrenchment of conservatism.

8. CUBA (1956–59)

Fidel Castro (b. 1926) overthrew the corrupt regime of Fulgencio Batista (1901–73). He later established a Communist government and attempted to export Communism to Latin America for the next four decades—thereby providing a continuous source of aggravation to the United States.

9. ENGLAND (1688)

The ruling house of Stuart just did not get it. Following the execution of Charles I, his grandson announced his plans to convert England to Catholicism and acted arrogantly, unaware of the unrest within the population. "Invited" to leave England, he was replaced by his daughter and son-in-law (William and Mary of Orange) in a bloodless revolution, the Glorious Revolution.

10. RUSSIA (1905)

In a precursor to the more violent revolutions of 1917 (see number 3), the general population demonstrated against Tsar Nicholas II. Leon Trotsky's Soviet (council) of Workers' Deputies and the Constitutional Democrats (Kadets) arose to claim power. The Tsar allowed a *duma* (national assembly) but later reestablished autocratic control.

Honorable Mention

CHINA (TAIPING REBELLION) (1850–64)

In one of the longest and most violent rebellions in history, an apocalyptic religious sect challenged the power of the ruling Manchu dynasty. The rebellion would probably have succeeded but for the Western Powers, who decided that they needed to prop up the Manchus to have better markets for opium.

Civil Wars

The mere definition of a civil war is fraught with confusion and misunderstanding. Generally, it may be regarded as a result of competing interests vying for sovereign power or an attempt to secure political, civil, or religious freedom. The following are those civil wars that have had the greatest impact.

1. UNITED STATES (1861–65)

The U.S. Civil War pitted North against South in a struggle over states' rights, slavery, preservation of the Union, economic self-interest—take your pick of any and all of them. But what is most intriguing is the legal aspect: nowhere in the Constitution of the United States is a state prohibited from leaving the Union. Of course, the War of Northern Aggression or the War to Preserve the Union has definitively interpreted the illegitmacy of unilateral withdrawal.

2. ENGLAND (1642–51)

Actually three separate civil wars and insurrections running head-on, this civil war determined that the king had to rule with the consent of Parliament and not by fiat. Although the ruling monarch

(Charles I, 1600–49) was executed and replaced by Oliver Cromwell (1599–1658), the throne was eventually restored, albeit with restrictions.

3. **ROME** (49–44 B.C.)

Rome had a civil war every 20 years or so. This particular war, the Great Civil War, had Julius Caesar (100–44 B.C.) representing the popular interest against Pompey the Great (106–48 B.C.), who represented the vested interests of the senatorial party. Of course, the rival sides were not as distinct as that, because Caesar's ultimate victory set the foundation of the empire, which restricted both popular and senatorial power.

4. **RUSSIA** (1918–24)

After the Bolsheviks seized power from the Kerensky government in 1918, a civil war resulted with virtually every coloration of interests being involved. The Reds represented the Bolshevik and Left Social Revolutionaries (until the latter were purged); the Whites ranged from Imperialists to Kadets to democratic libertarians. And if that was not enough, the peasantry (Greens) often decided to protect their own interests against all outsiders. Although the chances of anything other than a Red victory were nonexistent by 1921, the war dragged on in various segments of the former Russian Empire until at least 1924, and separate incipient revolts flared up even later.

5. **CHINA** (1945–49)

With the end of World War II, the Chinese Communists resumed their war against the Nationalists (which had been fought between 1930 and 1934, with an intermission declared only because of Japanese aggression). Although supported by the United States, the Nationalist Chinese had lost popular support and had to flee to Formosa, where they established the Republic of China. This two-China entity has lasted to the present day, although the People's Republic considers the Nationalist regime illegitimate.

6. SPAIN (1936–39)

In a foreshadowing of things to come, the Fascist Party, supported by the military, staged a coup. The legitimate government was left of center and quickly supported by Stalin; the fascists were supported by Hitler. Soviet Russia and Nazi Germany sent equipment and troops to field-test both hardware and doctrine. The actual results were less important to these powers, but the lessons learned were applied during World War II.

7. IRELAND (1921–23)

After Ireland had secured partition and become the Irish Free State, the resulting nation had to face its own internal conflict. In order to secure independence, the Irish had to agree to abandon the northern province of Ulster. It took two years and much internecine warfare before the Free State could begin to act as a united nation. But then in 1968 the dispute flared up again, and it has continued to the present day.

8. GREECE (1944–49)

Supported by Communist interests from the Soviet Union and the Balkans, the leftist interests determined to seize control of the state with the conclusion of World War II. The centrist government was supported by American interests and troops and defeated the insurgents. This was one of the first defeats of Communist insurgent movements.

9. CONGO (1960–68)

With the declaration of independence of the Republic of the Congo, both tribal conflict and mutinous armed forces led to a prolonged period of unrest. White mercenaries, Belgian paracommandos, and U.S. air assets intervened in a forlorn attempt to bring order to the nation. It was only when one side ultimately defeated all rivals that peace came to the Congo—and only temporarily.

10. **CAMBODIA** (1970–75)

Spillage from the Vietnam Conflict contributed to the fragility of the government of Cambodia. The Communist Khmer Rouge eventually secured control of the nation (which was renamed Kampuchea). Under the Khmer Rouge, intellectuals and urban citizens were exterminated in a national genocide that exceeded the Holocaust in percentage of population. The civilized nations took no action, regarding this as an internal matter.

LITERATURE AND ENTERTAINMENT

War Movies: Operational

War movies inspire passion. Everyone has his or her favorite, and this list will be sure to inspire both anguish and derision. The basis for inclusion is visceral and arguable: Was the movie moderately accurate? Did it engage the viewer? Was there something that made it stand out?

1. *ZULU* (1964)

This movie did a superb job of re-creating the Battle of Rorke's Drift, the battle where the most Victoria Crosses were won in a single engagement (January 22, 1879). Every long-suffering spouse can recite with dread the exact moment that the Zulu *impis* begin their song of warfare only to be answered with "Men of Harlech." The movie had an added feature—"and introducing Michael Caine."

2. *A BRIDGE TOO FAR* (1977)

Operation Market-Garden was treated in an accurate and entertaining fashion. Field Marshal Montgomery's flawed airborne drop came alive with a large supporting cast. Although some have criticized this film as disjointed, it did re-create the different and disconnected problems faced by the various airborne formations in the actual battle.

3. *THE LONGEST DAY* (1962)

Yes, everyone in Hollywood somehow did manage to make an appearance in this film, but that was not a fatal flaw. It is still an excellent historical portrayal of the D-Day invasion (June 6, 1944).

4. *BATTLE OF BRITAIN* (1969)

The aerial warfare of the Battle of Britain (August 8–October 12, 1940) was caught in an engaging production with portrayals from both sides.

5. *TORA! TORA! TORA!* (1970)

This film re-creation of the Japanese surprise attack on Pearl Harbor (December 7, 1941) seems to improve with age; it emphasizes historical, not political, correctness.

6. *MIDWAY* (1976)

This film is an interesting re-creation of the battle that swung the tide of battle in the Pacific Theater of Operations.

7. *LIGHT HORSEMEN* (1987)

A personal favorite, this was a fine cinematic telling of the Australian Light Horse's charge against Turkish Ottoman forces in Beersheba, Palestine (October 31, 1917), one of the last uses of cavalry in British history.

8. *WATERLOO* (1971)

Although this was not Napoleon's finest hour, and although Rod Steiger seems to be playing Rod Steiger playing Napoleon, the battle scenes of the French cavalry and British squares mandate this inclusion.

9. *GALLIPOLI* (1981)

This is an excellent treatment of the flawed landing in the Dardanelles. Churchill's operational plan had its merits, but the field commanders were incapable of proper execution.

10. *DAM BUSTERS* (1954)

This is an interesting film that approaches the bombing of the Ruhr dams in World War II from the British perspective. The actual bombing did not generate any decisive results.

War Movies: nonoperational

These films are not necessarily based on a single historical incident, or they cover a time span longer than a particular battle.

1. *DESERT FOX* (1951)

James Mason was Erwin Rommel. This biography of the Desert Fox during World War II was both masterful and engaging.

2. *THE ENEMY BELOW* (1957)

Although not historical, this cat-and-mouse engagement between an American destroyer and a German U-boat set a high standard. Robert Mitchum as the American commander and Curt Jurgens as the U-boat skipper gave sympathetic portrayals of both sides.

3. *ALL QUIET ON THE WESTERN FRONT* (1930)

World War I in all of its glory, this movie should be required viewing in all high schools and military academies. Strictly from the German perspective, this adaptation from the classic novel was not limited to a side, but was more universal in nature.

4. *PATHS OF GLORY* (1957)

As long as one is discussing the futility of war, Stanley Kubrick's treatment of French élan and discipline during World War I illustrated the moral bankruptcy of the High Command.

5. *THE CROSS OF IRON* (1976)

Director Sam Peckinpah was known for his choreography of violence. Here, he painted a visual picture of life on the Russian Front during World War II. Although the ending was disappointing, the film itself brought home the dread of the artillery barrage and the brutality of the war.

6. *BLUE MAX* (1966)

This portrays superb aerial combat coupled with Junker morality and the new concept and practice of war during World War I.

7. *LAWRENCE OF ARABIA* (1962)

A young British officer leads the Arab revolt against the Ottoman Empire. Superbly filmed and acted, this was a classic study of an ancillary theater during World War I.

8. *SAVING PRIVATE RYAN* (1998)

Stephen Spielberg's homage to the American GI during World War II was commendable. The first 20 minutes established a new parameter in cinematic combat, and while the rest of the film could not maintain that standard (e.g., the Normandy *bocage* [the hedgerow terrain] looks suspiciously non-French), it was still good enough.

9. *TAKE THE HIGH GROUND* (1953)

Richard Widmark and Karl Malden were drill sergeants in this classic film of basic training during the Korean War. While the film was stereotypical, the stereotypes did have some truth. As a private who endured basic training in 1970 and later as an operations officer of a drill sergeant battalion, I can state that much of this film was indeed accurate.

10. TWELVE O'CLOCK HIGH (1949)

This study of the men of Bomber Command during World War II is still utilized as a training tool by the U.S. Air Force—not for its history but for its treatment of men under the stress of combat and command.

Honorable Mention

The following two films are recommended not because they are war movies, but because they portray the results of war.

MRS. MINNIVER (1942)

Greer Garson portrayed a British housewife simply trying to live life with her family during the darkest days of the evacuation of Dunkirk and the Battle of Britain. Life goes on even during war, and this film gave an excellent picture of "normal" life.

THE BEST YEARS OF OUR LIVES (1946)

When the war is over, the returning veterans have to readjust to civilian life. This movie showed how three different men with different problems had to weather their adjustment to a world returned to normalcy. The period covered was post–World War II, but the events in the movie are applicable to any society that has undergone conflict.

Exception to Policy

THE BRIDGE ON THE RIVER KWAI (1957)

As you scratch your head wondering why your favorite movie wasn't listed, this Oscar winner comes to everyone's mind. This was my father's favorite war movie of all time; I was never able to convince him of its flaws. While based on an actual incident, it was actually a tale of collaboration and futility. As a former judge advocate, I would have been happy to prosecute the British commanding officer for his misdeeds. His redeeming destruction of the bridge—is it deliberate or happenstance? Either way, it is too little too late. Therefore, this classic film may be an epic of psychological conflict, but I do not regard it as a classic of warfare.

War Movies: Testosterone

There are certain war movies that one can watch again and again. They may lack historical accuracy, they may lack decent acting, but what they offer is a visceral thrill. Whether it is a cavalry charge or a three-rank volley, there is something that holds the viewer, and often he can recite the dialogue and entire scenes (much to his spouse's chagrin).

1. *ZULU* (1964)

Although this also serves as one of the best war films ever done, it embodies the testosterone experience. The cinematic treatment of the Battle of Rorke's Drift (January 22, 1879) is well developed, but what gives the visceral thrill is the scene when Lieutenant John Rouse Merriot Chard (1847–97) listens to the Zulu war chants and then asks one of his soldiers if he couldn't do better. The soldier replies that the Zulus have a good bass section but "lack a top tenor." As the British respond with "Men of Harlech," the Zulus continue their war chant in a contrapuntal exposition of martial fervor, which ceases only when the Zulus charge the British positions. As the British ranks volley fire, one becomes totally enveloped in the experience.

2. *THE GREEN BERETS* (1968)

John Wayne was responsible for this Vietnam War movie, which glorified the Green Berets. At the time of filming, the Pentagon found it too gung-ho and offered little support; at the time of release, the nation seemed to have moved left of center, and its support for the actual war in South Vietnam had waned. But while many of the contemporary Vietnam War movies have faded as historical curiosities, this film keeps gaining fans. The sun may occasionally rise in the west, and the plot may be more akin to a World War II movie, but it still is engaging. At Fort Bragg, North Carolina, when this is played on local television, the noise level in Moon Hall drops to a respectful level.

3. *THEY DIED WITH THEIR BOOTS ON* (1941)

Errol Flynn is George Armstrong Custer—from West Point to the Little Big Horn. Although the historical accuracy of this film is more than dubious, the climactic scene of Custer standing his ground against the entire Sioux Nation as "GerryOwen" plays in the background is unforgettable.

4. *THE GREAT ESCAPE* (1963)

Based on the largest Allied escape from a German prisoner-of-war camp during World War II, this film glories in the ingenuity of the prisoners and follows their attempts to secure their freedom. The soundtrack has remained a classic and lends a certain panache to the film.

5. *THE CHARGE OF THE LIGHT BRIGADE* (1936)

Errol Flynn once again leads a unit into annihilation and everlasting glory. Here, Major Geoffrey Vickers is an officer of the 27th Lancers.

He intentionally leads his cavalry unit into the face of the Russian guns at Balaklava because he knows that Surat Khan, the man responsible for the massacre of the unit's dependents at Chukoti in 1856, is standing with the Russians. As the unit is decimated ("Into the valley of Death / Rode the six hundred," Tennyson), Vickers hurls his lance into Khan with his dying breath. With an inspiring musical score from Max Steiner and direction from Academy Award–notable Michael Curtiz, this film stands out—despite its ludicrous version of history. The Charge of the Light Brigade actually occurred on October 25, 1854; the Indian Mutiny occurred in 1856–57.

6. *PATTON* (1970)

This tells the story of General George Patton (1885–1945) during World War II, from North Africa to the end of the war. Though it mythologizes of his actual career, its dynamism and breadth made this one of the most successful war films ever done.

7. *STRIPES* (1981)

Two slackers join the army since it is so much like a health spa. As reality sets in, the conflict between the slacker and the professional drill sergeant results in the former's becoming a leader of men. His platoon's performance of close-order drill ("That's a Fact, Jack") has become part of the military ethos, and the background music is standard marching fare at any basic training post ("Na na naa naa, na na naa naa, hey heeeyy, good-bye").

8. *TRIUMPH OF THE WILL* (1934)

This is not a war movie, but its martial undertones create an evil splendor that can still attract and fascinate, much as one may feel while looking at an attractive but poisonous coral snake. Film Director Leni Riefenstahl knew how to successfully use the film medium as a propaganda tool, and this film of the 1934 Nazi Party Congress

in Nuremberg remains one of the most powerful celluloid state-
ments in history.

9. *THE ALAMO* (1960)

John Wayne is Davy Crockett in a larger-than-life portrayal of the
last stand of the Alamo in 1836. Although the baby boomers may
think of Disney's Fess Parker as the quintessential Crockett, Wayne's
extravaganza lives on as a jingoistic display of questionable taste
that one is loath to admit ever watching.

10. *TOP GUN* (1986)

Tom Cruise is a hot-shot F-14 Tomcat pilot who learns the value of
teamwork and cooperation at the Top Gun school. Eventually, he
puts his training to good use against Libyan fighters. This is a war
movie without a war. While its estrogen content is also high
("You've Lost That Loving Feeling" and its own theme song), the film
has become the anthem of fighter jocks.

Honorable Mention

FINAL COUNTDOWN (1980)

The carrier *Nimitz* is transported back in time to December 1941.
The attack on Pearl Harbor, while imminent, has not yet occurred.
Does the captain order an assault on the Japanese strike fleet even
though war has not yet been declared? The film cops out, and the
contemporary carrier returns to the present before confronting the
final question. But everyone who has seen the film just keeps mut-
tering "a few more hours, a few more hours." This is similar to ask-
ing oneself, "What if Napoleon had had tanks?" or "What if Hitler
had had the atomic bomb?"

War Movies: Estrogen

There are certain "military movies" that appeal strongly to women. Men may be dragged unwillingly to view these cinematic wonders, but rarely will a military veteran admit to enjoying the experience.

1. *THE ENGLISH PATIENT* (1996)

Winning the Oscar for best picture of the year, one knew that this would be a difficult experience when it was lauded for its lyricism and complexity, in moral and emotional terms. Told by flashback, it is the story of a Hungarian mapmaker employed by the British (the real-life patient on whom the character was based was actually a German SS officer)—his love affair, his betrayal, and the nurse who cares for him.

2. *CAPTAIN CORELLI'S MANDOLIN* (2001)

Telling the story of a sensuous affair between the Italian commander of a garrison on a Greek island and a woman engaged to a Greek soldier, this picture makes the Italian occupation of Greece during World War II appear as a romantic idyll until interrupted by German savagery.

3. *yanks* (1979)

The British had a common expression for what was wrong with the Americans stationed in Great Britain during World War II—"overpaid, oversexed, and over here." This film delves into the romantic relationships between the American troops and the English inhabitants of a rural town about 1943–44.

4. *HANOVER STREET* (1979)

An American army pilot falls in love with a British nurse, but she is already married. He discovers this and learns that his mission involves working with the woman's husband. Will they work together to survive? Does anyone really care?

5. *PEARL HARBOR* (2001)

In this the politically correct version of the surprise attack on Pearl Harbor (December 7, 1941), the "day which will live in infamy" is subservient to a triangular tale of love among two pilots and their girlfriend. In effect, this became the *Titanic* of war movies.

6. *COMING HOME* (1979)

Jane Fonda plays the wife of a captain stationed in Vietnam. But when she volunteers at a veterans hospital, she falls in love with a wounded veteran. There are critical life decisions to be made in this two- to three-handkerchief film.

7. *D-DAY THE SIXTH OF JUNE* (1956)

A terribly mislabeled film, it involves two officers remembering their affair with the same woman as they are transported to Normandy on June 5, 1944. The actual battle segment is confined to the last 15 minutes of the picture. There are many baby boomers who remember being dropped off for a Saturday matinee, looking eagerly forward to a real war movie, only to end up suffering an afternoon of dreary romance.

8. *BORN ON THE FOURTH OF JULY* (1989)

The seriousness of this biography of Ron Kovic, a paralyzed veteran and antiwar activist, was undercut by Tom Cruise's casting.

9. *I WAS A MALE WAR BRIDE* (1949)

Cary Grant plays a French Army captain in postwar Germany who fell in love with an American WAC officer. When his wife is recalled to the United States, he must seek entry as a "war bride."

10. *OPERATION PETTICOAT* (1959)

During World War II, a submarine captain has to enter combat with five nurses in his submarine—and it has been painted pink by accident. Once again, Cary Grant stars in a film endeavor that proved as a leading man, he produced more estrogen than a hormone prescription.

Honorable Mention

THE FRENCH LIEUTENANT'S WOMAN (1981)

A film within a story, the underlying tale of a 19th-century affair contrasted with the actors involved in the film has absolutely nothing to do with anything remotely military. This does not prevent it from being named by men as an "estrogen" film.

Television Shows

In 1961 Federal Communications Chairman Newton Minow characterized television as a "vast wasteland." It is shocking to see how right he was when we consider war and the military as seen on the small screen. In over 50 years of television, there have been fewer than 30 programs that fit this category. While everyone has a favorite war movie, there are few television programs that have engendered such passion.

1. *VICTORY AT SEA* (1952–53)

A documentary series of 26 half-hour programs on World War II in the Pacific. This series is still being televised and remains eminently viewable to this day. The musical score by Richard Rodgers is superb and remains a consistent musical seller.

2. *M*A*S*H* (1972–83)

Adapted from the 1970 movie about a Mobile Army Surgical Hospital during the Korean War, this was not as dark a treatment. The show was intensely popular, and its final episode still holds the record as the most watched television program in history. Although it tended toward political correctness, there were still enough genuine moments to render this program one of the best. Its treatment of Regular Army officers versus reservists and intelligence operatives (Colonel Flagg) versus the rest of the military establishment has become part of army lore.

3. *TWELVE O'CLOCK HIGH* (1964–67)

Adapted from the 1949 movie, this show was a fictional treatment of a World War II U.S. Army Air Corps bomb group (918th Bomb Group). It emphasized the perils and responsibilities of command.

4. *COMBAT* (1962–67)

Vic Morrow was platoon sergeant Chip Saunders in this tale of the European Theater of Operations during World War II. One of the longer-lasting shows, it tended to be trite but did have an impact on its viewers. During the Battle for Hue in Vietnam, street fighting was occurring in the old Imperial City. The Marine Corps had ceased to teach urban operations, and a sergeant supposedly told his men to just do what the soldiers had done on Combat. It worked!

5. *77TH BENGAL LANCERS* (1956–57)

A Kiplingesque television show of the British Army during the Imperial Raj. Fascinating in its acceptance of British mores in India, it was an entertaining diversion.

6. *THE GRAY GHOST* (1957)

A fictional treatment of the career of John Singleton Mosby's guerrilla operations during the American Civil War. Tod Andrews played Mosby, although he was from New York.

7. *THE WORLD AT WAR* (1974)

Narrated by Sir Laurence Olivier, this was a documentary series on World War II.

8. *RIN TIN TIN* (1954–59)

Set in the American West after the Civil War, this was a classic children's show of cavalry versus Indians. A boy and his dog could win the West. While it may not stand the test of time, it had a deep influence on the baby boomers.

9. *CAPTAIN GALLANT OF THE FOREIGN LEGION* (1955–57)

This was another children's show, this time set in the North African milieu of the French Foreign Legion.

10. *BOOTS AND SADDLES* (1957–59)

Featuring the Fifth Cavalry in the Old West, this fictional treatment of cavalry and Indians was entertaining, albeit unrealistic.

Honorable Mention

The following were not regularly scheduled seasonal television programs. However, they made a big enough impact to require their inclusion herein.

DAVY CROCKETT (1954–55)

Anyone over the age of 50 can probably hum the "Ballad of Davy Crockett" ("Born on a mountaintop in Tennessee . . ."). This three-part series produced by Walt Disney became one of the classic fads in television history. In a mythical biography of Davy Crockett (1786–1836), Fess Parker was the famed frontiersman in the Creek Wars, the riverboat races, and the Alamo. Some of us still remember our coonskin caps and buckskin regalia.

THE SWAMP FOX (1959–60)

Another Disney production, this was a mythologized tale of Francis Marion (1732–95), the South Carolina guerrilla leader during the

Revolutionary War. Although not as memorable as *Davy Crockett*, the program remains a childhood favorite for those who remember watching it live—and Francis Marion was played by Leslie Nielsen!

(Dis)Honorable Mention

RAT PATROL (1966–68)
Supposedly based on the exploits of the British Long Range Desert Group, this transformed the protagonists into American soldiers fighting Rommel's Afrika Korps during World War II. In effect, the British armored cars were changed into American jeeps/dune buggies that were able to outmaneuver and outwit the Germans every week. Jeep versus *Panzerkampfwagen III*—who are you going to bet on?

JAG (1995–)
Commander Harm and the naval Judge Advocate Corps are seeking to vanquish enemies of the United States both inside and outside the courtroom. There are so many flaws with this program that it is difficult to know where to begin. As an adventure saga, it is entertaining; as a reflection of the military, it is abysmal. In order to become a JAG, an officer must be a member of a state bar; in the show, an ensign is attending law school at night. Any resemblance between military law and/or the manual of courts-martial is purely coincidental. When the show premiered, a group of naval JAGs sat down to watch it. Anytime someone saw an error, he would down a beer; after 20 minutes, the group stopped—everyone was becoming too inebriated to continue.

Music: Classical Compositions

If music "has charms to soothe the savage breast," it also is capable of arousing the savage breast. From the first recorded history, music has been used to establish a martial mood in soldiers as well as to serve as a signaling device. Only with the advent of the classical movement (c. 1750) did musical composition begin to create a "martial spirit" for listening pleasure.

1. *1812 OVERTURE* (1880)

Composed by Peter Ilyich Tchaikovsky (1840–93) to commemorate the defeat of Napoleon in Russia, it is probably the most famous classical martial music ever written. It was intended for outdoor performance, with cannon fire enhancing the battle musical scene as the French Grand Armée is defeated by the Russians.

2. *WELLINGTON'S VICTORY* (1813)

This was composed by Ludwig van Beethoven (1770–1827) to commemorate the British victory over the French at the Battle of Vittoria (June 21, 1813) in Spain. More of a novelty piece than a great musical composition, it is still entertaining.

3. SEVENTH SYMPHONY *(LENINGRAD)* (1941)

This was composed by Dimitri Dimitrievich Shostakovich (1906–75) to symbolize the Russian will to defeat the Nazi invasion during World War II, specifically the indomitable fighting spirit of the besieged city of Leningrad. The threatening and somber Germanic melody is overcome by the Russian response in a contrapuntal motif.

4. MASS NO. 11 *(NELSON)* (1798)

The mass was composed by Franz Joseph Haydn (1732–1809) to commemorate the threat of Napoleon. In Latin, this is known as the *Missa in Angustiis (Mass in Straitened Times)*. It was associated with Admiral Nelson's victory over the French fleet at the Battle of the Nile (August 1, 1798), although it was in fact completed before news of the British victory even reached the composer.

5. *RADETZKY MARCH,* OP. 228 (1840)

This was composed by Johann Strauss (1804–49) to honor Austria-Hungary's leading military figure, Josef Radetzky (1766–1858).

6. *MARCHE SLAV* (1876)

The piece was composed by Peter Ilyich Tchaikovsky (1840–93) as an orchestral march for a benefit program for wounded Serbian troops in a conflict with Turkey.

7. SYMPHONY NO. 3, OP. 55 *(EROICA)* (1805)

Composed by Ludwig van Beethoven (1770–1827), it is commonly thought to have been written as a tribute to Napoleon, with the dedication removed when Napoleon crowned himself emperor, but there is no clear evidence of this. Still, it remains a great symphony.

8. *ALEXANDER NEVSKY*, CANTATA OP. 78 (1938)

Composed by Sergei Prokofiev (1891–1953), this was the background music for Sergei Eisenstein's movie *Alexander Nevsky* (1938), which commemorated the victory of the Russians over the Teutonic Knights at the Battle of Pskov (April 4, 1242).

9. *WARSAW CONCERTO* (1942)

Composed by Richard Addinsell (1904–77), this is not even a concerto (since it has only one, and not three, movements). Released for a grade-B British war movie (*Dangerous Moonlight*, released in the United States as *Suicide Squadron*), it has become synonymous with resistance to tyranny and oppression.

10. SYMPHONY NO. 100 *(MILITARY)* (1794)

Composed by Franz Joseph Haydn (1732–1809), it was one of the first classical pieces to utilize a bass drum. Commonly used more for military purposes than for musical ones, the bass drum gave this work a radical and threatening tone. Today, it seems quite mild.

Music: Popular Compositions

Popular music has generated its share of martial songs. The United States has generated the bulk of such memorable music in two wars—the American Civil War (1861–65) and World War II (1939–45). In both cases, the war lasted for a substantial period and maintained a popular appeal (unlike the Vietnam Conflict). The pieces directly concern combat itself, although some were parodies or not written during any conflict. The unforgettable World War II ballads (e.g., "The White Cliffs of Dover," Dick Todd, 1941; "Lili Marlene," Lale Andersen/Marlene Dietrich, 1939/1942; "We'll Meet Again," Vera Lynn, 1941; "When the Lights Go On Again," Vaughan Monroe, 1942) are recommended for listening pleasure, but they are not martial music.

1. "BATTLE HYMN OF THE REPUBLIC"
(Julia Ward Howe, 1861)

The marching song of the Union Army during the Civil War, it has become an American standard.

2. "REMEMBER PEARL HARBOR" (Eddy Howard, 1942)

During World War II, this was a cry for vengeance and number one on the Hit Parade. "Remember Pearl Harbor, as we go to meet the foe...."

3. "COMIN' IN ON A WING AND A PRAYER"
(the Golden Gate Quartet, 1943)

During World War II, a bomber hits its target and returns home, damaged by flak, "on a wing and a prayer."

4. "PRAISE THE LORD AND PASS THE AMMUNITION"
(Kay Kyser, 1942)

Religion and patriotism merge in this World War II tune as we "swing into position."

5. "MARCHING THROUGH GEORGIA"
(Henry Clay Work, 1865)

This was a Civil War song commemorating Union General William T. Sherman's 1864 campaign from Atlanta to Savannah. Although it is still memorable today (although one should not be singing it below the Mason-Dixon line), Sherman himself grew to hate it.

6. "BALLAD OF THE GREEN BERETS" (Barry Sadler, 1966)

Special Forces Staff Sergeant Barry Sadler composed and sang this song, which became a top hit in 1966. It remains the anthem of SpecOps and may always be heard somewhere at Fort Bragg, North Carolina—either in music or by soldiers chanting it as they march.

7. "DER FÜHRER'S FACE" (Spike Jones, 1942)

Spike Jones and his City Slickers had a fine parody of Nazi personages and philosophy ("Are we not the master race? Yes, we are the master race") during World War II. With its Bronx cheer and raspberry responses, it made clear Jones's position on the issues.

8. "BATTLE OF NEW ORLEANS" (Jimmy Driftwood, 1958)

Not done during a war, this song commemorated the Battle of New Orleans (January 8, 1815), in which Andrew Jackson (1767–1845) defeated the British regulars—after a peace treaty had already ended the War of 1812.

9. "SNOOPY VERSUS THE RED BARON"
(The Royal Guardsmen, 1967)

A tongue-in-cheek song, this hit portrayed the dog Snoopy (from *Peanuts,* a cartoon strip by Charles Schulz) in his World War I flying ace persona taking on the Red Baron, Manfred von Richthofen (1892–1918). "Ten, twenty, thirty, forty, fifty or more, The bloody Red Baron is rolling up the score...."

10. "WENN WIR FAHREN GEGEN ENGELAND" (1940)

English-speaking nations did not have a monopoly on songs commemorating warfare. This tune sprang quickly to the top on Radio Berlin during the Battle of Britain in World War II. Literally translated, it means "When We Drive against England," and it is probably as politically correct as singing "Marching through Georgia" at the annual convention of the Sons of the Confederacy.

Entertainers

The idea of entertainers going out to the troops is a relatively recent concept. With the advent of mass media and mass transportation, it became feasible for a star to literally go to the front and put on a show. Such entertainment was generally light fare, composed of song, dance, and attractive women.

1. **BOB HOPE** (b. May 29, 1903)

In every conflict from World War II (1939–45) through the Gulf War (1990–91), Bob Hope was the quintessential entertainer. He spent more time in the front lines than many men who have earned the combat infantryman's badge. But his ceaseless dedication to the American soldier no matter where he is located has created an immortal legend of care. He brought the stars to the troops and he will never be forgotten. "Thanks for the Memory."

2. **MARTHA RAYE** (August 27, 1916–October 19, 1994)

Initially part of Bob Hope's USO shows, she became so much more. She was famous for her shows in World War II, Korea, and Vietnam. In the Vietnam Conflict, she had a special relationship with

During a USO show in Vietnam, General William C. Westmoreland, *right,* thanks Bob Hope for his many years of entertaining American troops in the field.

the Special Forces and became known as "Colonel Maggie." When she died, a special exception was made to allow her burial at the Fort Bragg Military Cemetery.

3. **JERRY COLONNA**
(September 17, 1904–November 21, 1986)

Bob Hope's sidekick during World War II and Korea, this comic was known for his bulging eyes and handlebar moustache.

4. **BETTY GRABLE** (December 18, 1916–August 2, 1973)

Her pinup poster graced footlockers and walls throughout the U.S. Armed Forces; her legs were the stuff of dreams. She was often on tour with Bob Hope during the Second World War.

5. **VERA LYNN** (b. March 20, 1917)

A British torch singer known as the "Forces Sweetheart," she went anywhere that His Majesty's Forces were. She performed her signature song, "We'll Meet Again," from France to New Zealand and all points in between.

6. **ANDREWS SISTERS** (LaVerne Sofia, July 6, 1911–May 8, 1967; Maxene Angelyn, January 3, 1916–October 21, 1995; Patty [Patricia] Marie, b. February 26, 1918)

This trio performed some of the top vocal hits of World War II (e.g., "Boogie Woogie Bugle Boy," "Don't Sit under the Apple Tree," "Rum and Coca-Cola"), and they often appeared with USO tours.

7. **AL JOLSON** (May 26, 1886–October 23, 1950)

This burlesque singer-entertainer, perhaps best known for his starring role in the early talking picture *The Jazz Singer,* was also a frequent USO trouper who spent much of World War II in the field entertaining the troops.

8. **RAQUEL WELCH** (b. September 5, 1940)

A sex siren of the 1960s, she accompanied Bob Hope on many of his USO tours during the Vietnam Conflict.

9. **JOEY HEATHERTON** (b. September 14, 1944)

A platinum blonde actress and mattress spokesperson, she was best known for her appearances with Bob Hope during the Vietnam Conflict.

10. **JAY LENO** (April 28, 1950)

A stand-up comic who later became host of the Tonight Show, he was quick to volunteer to entertain the troops during the Gulf War (1990–91).

(Dis)Honorable Mention

JANE FONDA (b. December 21, 1937)
While many entertainers were risking their lives in order to enter-tain the troops during the Vietnam Conflict, she did the same—only for the other side! "Hanoi Jane" earned an enduring reputation of derision and contempt from the American military for her visits to and endorsements of North Vietnam.

The Basic
Military Library

Deciding upon 10 books to form a library covering 3,000 years of history is an exercise in omission. The recommended books are merely a starting point for an overview of military events; all are currently available from any reputable bookseller, and the latest editions and retail prices are noted. Where possible, the hardback version has been listed.

General

1. *THE HARPER ENCYCLOPEDIA OF MILITARY HISTORY FROM 3500 B.C. TO THE PRESENT*

R. Ernest and Trevor N. Dupuy, Harper & Row (4th edition; 1993) ($80.00): The starting point for all inquiries, it literally covers the world.

2. *A CONCISE HISTORY OF WARFARE*

Montgomery of Alamein, Wordsworth Editions (2000) ($12.00, paper). This is an excellent survey of military history until 1860; thereafter, the field marshal's views grow ever more "unusual." I really regret omitting J. F. C. Fuller, *A Military History of the Western World,* Da Capo (1988) ($14.00/volume). However, it is in three volumes and has the same flaw as Montgomery's, that is, the post–1865 period is subject to question.

Ancient

3. WARFARE IN ANTIQUITY

Hans Delbruck, University of Nebraska Press (1990) ($29.95, paper). Almost a century old, this history of ancient warfare still stands out as a classic treatise. The footnotes sometimes overwhelm the text, but the author is careful to explain his analysis of the battles.

Medieval

4. MEDIEVAL WARFARE

Hans Delbruck, University of Nebraska Press (1990) ($29.95, paper). Again, Delbruck provides the best analysis of this period of warfare. Oman's *Art of War in the Middle Ages,* Greenhill Press (1991) ($29.95/volume) may be more detailed, but it is in two volumes.

Napoleonic

5. CAMPAIGNS OF NAPOLEON

David Chandler, Macmillan (1973) ($85.00). With the thousands of books written on Napoleon, Chandler remains the first choice, especially when coupled with the atlas below.

6. *A MILITARY HISTORY AND ATLAS OF THE NAPOLEONIC WARS*

Vincent Esposito and John Elting, Greenhill Books (1980) ($80.00). This features superb maps coupled with an excellent text on the major battles of the period.

American Civil War

7. *BATTLE CRY OF FREEDOM*

James M. McPherson, Oxford University Press (1988) ($49.95}. This is the best one-volume history of the American Civil War—bar none.

8. *THE WEST POINT ATLAS OF AMERICAN WARS: 1689–1900,*

Vincent J. Esposito, Henry Holt (1995) ($75.00). The maps coupled with McPherson give a complete picture of the American Civil War; as a bonus, maps and text are included on other aspects of American military history up to 1900 (e.g., American Revolutionary War, Spanish-American War).

Modern

In addition to omitting Asian military history almost in its entirety, the list has given short shrift to modern European history. The rise of the European national state in the 16th to 18th centuries and the rise of the Prussian state in the 19th century can be gleaned only from the perspectives of the 20th-century world wars.

9. *THE WEST POINT ATLAS OF AMERICAN WARS: 1900–1918*

Vincent J. Esposito, Henry Holt (1995) ($75.00). This completely covers the major aspects of World War I, and not just the American perspective. Sadly, Volume II used to cover 1900–1953, but obviously, the publisher has now decided to add a third (and possibly a fourth volume). There is not a really great textual source that covers the First World War, although one may be forthcoming (Hew Strachan's *The First World War: To Arms,* Oxford (2001), the first volume of a projected trilogy, has been published). An additional caveat: There is a new school of thought concerning the conduct of the war on the Western Front. John Mosier's *The Myth of the Great War,* HarperCollins (2001), best exemplifies this approach and should be considered by anyone interested in the period.

10. *A WORLD AT ARMS: A GLOBAL HISTORY OF WORLD WAR II*

Gerhard L. Weinberg, Cambridge University (1994) ($69.95). This is a complete integrated analysis of World War II—both European and Pacific Theaters. Detailed and comprehensive, it offers a coherent picture of the war on economic, political, and military levels.

Memoirs

Attempting to choose only 10 memoirs in 3,000 years of history has been a challenge. I have divided the selections by general officer, company grade officer, and enlisted soldiers. Each type has its own perspective and its strengths and weaknesses. It was only after I had made my choices that I noted that World War I dominated the company grade officers. There is a reason—the First World War has been ignored to a large extent in the United States, and yet it established the parameters of Western European civilization in a fashion that is still having an impact. The societal changes and the demographic changes of that war will not be fully recognized for another two centuries.

General Officer

1. *PERSONAL MEMOIRS*, ULYSSES S. GRANT
(April 27, 1822–July 23, 1885)

The former President of the United States, the former General in Chief of the Union Armies was dying of cancer, and he was financially destitute. To leave some legacy to his wife, Grant penned his memoirs, finishing a mere nine days before his death. And yet his memoirs are "the best of any general's since Caesar" (Mark Twain). Actually, they are probably better, since they did not have an agenda other than to tell it simply and directly. With ex-presidents currently receiving in excess of $10 million for their memoirs, Grant's tome is frank, unpretentious, and open.

2. *COMMENTARIES ON THE GALLIC WAR,* JULIUS CAESAR (July 12/13, 100–March 15, 44 B.C.)

At one time (and not that long ago), virtually every school child knew the beginning of this work—"Omnis Gallia est divisa in tres partes . . ." ("All Gaul is divided into three parts"). Caesar's treatise on his experiences leading the Roman legions in Gaul has survived millennia. When first published, the memoir was ridiculed—it lacked the flowery rhetoric common to "good" Latin literature, and Caesar habitually referred to himself in the third person. But it had a direct simplicity that has survived and flowered. The major flaw is that Caesar had his own agenda—he was a professional politician, and in some aspects, this memoir is too self-serving. Overall, however, it has shown a resilience unanticipated by his contemporaries.

3. *THE ANABASIS,* XENOPHON (c. 430–c. 355 B.C.)

A Greek mercenary leader fighting in the midst of a Persian civil war found himself and his army cut off and isolated. *The Anabasis* ("going out") is literally the story of how he was able to extricate himself and his troops in a classic retrograde operation through 1,000 miles of enemy terrain. Aside from the sheer improbability of such an operation, Xenophon was probably the writer most akin to contemporary tastes—his writing is direct and understandable.

4. *FIRST AND THE LAST,* ADOLF GALLAND
(March 19, 1912–February 9, 1996)

After entering the German Air Force (Luftwaffe) in 1934, he became a general officer by 1940 and head of the Fighter Arm. Because of his candor, he was relieved of command and ended World War II as a jet squadron commander. His memoirs, published soon after the war (1954), give a passionate rendition of the rise and fall of the Luftwaffe during the Second World War.

Company Grade Officer

5. *GOOD-BYE TO ALL THAT,* ROBERT GRAVES
(July 24, 1895–December 7, 1985)

Aside from his poetry and his novels (e.g., *I Claudius*), his memoir as a company grade officer in the Royal Welsh Fusiliers during World War I stands out as literature. Decrying the society that has been destroyed by the carnage of the conflict, Graves writes as an excellent observer and participant in this "War to End All Wars."

6. *SEVEN PILLARS OF WISDOM,* T. E. LAWRENCE
(August 15, 1888–May 13, 1935)

Lawrence of Arabia writes of his desert experience tempered with a philosophical bent; his participation and leadership in the Arab Revolt are clearly and succinctly drawn.

7. *STORM OF STEEL,* ERNST JUENGER
(March 29, 1895–February 17, 1998)

Juenger was the last recipient of the Pour le Merite (Germany's highest decoration for courage under fire), and his war journal is reminiscent of Graves's in that both men transform a war journal into literature. Juenger was a commander of shock troops in the trenches during World War I, and his narrative is one of the best ever done on combat.

8. *COMPANY COMMANDER,* CHARLES B. MACDONALD
(November 23, 1922–December 4, 1990)

A war memoir that could have been written only by an American, this details MacDonald's experience as a company commander during World War II. Frank and direct, it presents lessons that are still being confronted today. This book remains mandatory reading for young combat arms officers.

Enlisted Soldiers

9. *FORGOTTEN SOLDIER,* GUY SAJER (b. 1926)

An enlisted soldier with the Gross Deutschland Panzer Grenadier Division during World War II (1939–45), Sajer explains the unromantic, dreary, and dangerous side of war, especially on the Eastern Front. There has been some dispute as to whether Sajer's experiences were real, but the consensus seems to be that the memoirs are factual.

10. *WITH THE OLD BREED,* EUGENE BONDURANT SLEDGE
(November 4, 1923–March 2, 2001)

Sledge delineates the U.S. Marine Corps and its Pacific island-hopping campaigns from the view of the common rifleman. But the rifleman was not common; he was the best that America had to offer, and his sacrifices are rendered in plain view.

War Novels

The novel, a fictional tale, is a relatively recent literary phenomenon—only about 350 years old. There have been sagas of folklore that have passed down from generation to generation, but the concept of the war novel has matured within the last 150 years.

1. *THE ILIAD* (Homer/c. 1000 B.C.)

This was not a novel, but rather an epic poem, made to be told and retold. However, it has been reduced to writing, and with translations that modernize the prose, it has become the first "novel" that delineates the grand scale of the war in which the Greek city-states successfully defeated Troy. The intervention of the gods, the passions on both sides—all contribute to form a complex and fascinating tale of war, vengeance, and just bad luck.

2. *THE RED BADGE OF COURAGE* (Stephen Crane/1895)

This is a novel of a young boy "seeing the elephant" (facing combat for the first time) during the American Civil War. Crane had no previous military experience, and yet he wrote the most descriptive narrative of combat ever done. The book is brief and an easy read, but it is also unforgettable.

3. *WAR AND PEACE* (Leo Tolstoy/1869)

An epic of literature, it details the Napoleonic invasion of Russia (1812). With a large cast of characters and a larger panorama of war, from the perspectives of the unknown individual to the Emperor Napoleon, this is a long book, but well worth the read.

4. *ALL QUIET ON THE WESTERN FRONT* (Erich Maria Remarque/1929)

Perhaps the best antiwar novel ever written, this follows a number of German youths from their classroom to the front trenches of World War I. Patriotism, cowardice, the futility of war—all are present.

5. *CATCH-22* (Joseph Heller/1961)

This deals with the basic insanity of war as portrayed in an Army Air Corps unit during World War II. The "Catch-22" is that one can be relieved of combat missions only if he is crazy, but a crazy person would not ask to be relieved; therefore, if a pilot asks to be relieved, he is a priori not crazy. A cast of unforgettable characters (e.g., the capitalist Milo Minderbender, Major Major Major)—all contribute to an environment that only the military bureaucracy could create. I have to admit that the first time I tried to read this book, I just didn't get it; then I went to basic training. Afterwards, I found it one of the funniest books I had ever read.

6. *ONCE AN EAGLE* (Anton Myrer/1968)

A saga of an American officer from World I through the beginning of Vietnam, this book *is* the American military experience of the 20th century. It covers honor, duty, and country versus careerism and bureaucratic infighting; right does not always prevail.

7. *THE CRUEL SEA* (Nicholas Monsarrat/1951)

A description of the World War II experiences of a British corvette on antisubmarine patrol, this novel portrays the lives of the officers and men both ashore and at sea. It offers a complete picture of what the duty must have been—at times boring, dangerous, and seldom conclusive. As literature, it is never boring or dangerous but it is conclusive. An interesting mirror image is that of the German U-boat perspective (cf. Lothar-Gunther Buchheim's *Das Boot*).

8. *BATTLE CRY* (Leon Uris/1953)

In the U.S. Marines during World War II, a regiment's leaders and a company's men experience the highs and lows of combat and the island-hopping campaigns.

9. *THE YOUNG LIONS* (Irwin Shaw/1948)

Three enlisted men—two American and one German—experience World War II in their own ways. Their lives interconnect, but they each experience war on their own terms.

10. *THE KILLER ANGELS* (Michael Shaara/1974)

This is a historical narrative of the Battle of Gettysburg (July 1–3, 1863), from perspectives as disparate as the opposing commanders, selected regimental commanders, and some troops. Overall, it is more like a history than a novel, but still an unforgettable read.

And Why Not...

A FAREWELL TO ARMS (Ernest Hemingway/1929)

Does anyone really read Hemingway other than those students compelled to do so in an academic environment? Symbolic and pretentious, this novel of a wounded veteran after World War I has the intrinsic appeal of a VD ward.

FROM HERE TO ETERNITY (James Jones/1951)
This is an interesting literary work that explains the mindset of the pre–World War II army, but the war does not begin until the novel's conclusion.

THE NAKED AND THE DEAD (Norman Mailer/1948)
This describes men in combat, but its main attraction when published was the "realistic" dialogue ("fug" as a literary breakthrough does not yield immortal literature).

THE LAST OF THE MOHICANS
(James Fenimore Cooper/1826)
Possibly the first American war novel, it has literary merit, but its use of authentic dialect does not succeed.

Military Fiction Series

There are dozens of series of novels on various periods of military history. The ones listed here are all currently available or in the process of being reprinted. Interestingly enough, British 19th-century military history dominates the list.

1. HORATIO HORNBLOWER (C. S. Forester, 1937/11 volumes)

One of the first and definitely one of the best, this series covers a British naval officer during the Napoleonic Wars. He never served in a fleet action, but the action sequences of his single-ship engagements are extremely well done.

2. HARRY FLASHMAN
(George Macdonald Fraser, 1969/11 volumes)

Superb historical research coupled with humor characterizes this ongoing saga of a liar, cheat, and coward who dishonestly receives virtually every award for valor between the Afghan and Boer Wars (1842–1900). There are volumes in this series that cannot be read without laughing out loud.

3. **RICHARD SHARPE** (Bernard Cornwell, 1982/16 volumes)

This recounts the adventures of a British soldier, from private in India under Arthur Wellesley (later to become the Duke of Wellington) to field grade officer commanding a rifle battalion through the Napoleonic Wars.

4. *BROTHERHOOD OF WAR* (W. E. B. Griffin [William E. Butterworth], 1982/9 volumes)

A saga covering three military officers from the conclusion of World War II through the Vietnam era, this series is one of the best ever done on the American Army in the period 1945–60.

5. **THE CORPS** (W. E. B. Griffin [William E. Butterworth], 1986/8 volumes)

This is a subsequent series on the U.S. Marine Corps during World War II from the perspective of a number of protagonists.

6. **RICHARD BOLITHO** (Alexander Kent [Douglas Reeman], 1968/24 volumes)

Telling the story of a British naval officer during the Napoleonic Wars, this actually begins during the American Revolution. The series is at its best when Bolitho is a frigate captain; when he achieves flag rank, the novels become darker and more disjointed.

7. **LORD RAMAGE** (Dudley Pope, 1965/18 volumes)

The protagonist is a titled British naval officer during the Napoleonic Wars. Many of the books in the series were published in Great Britain only and are finally being reprinted in the United States.

8. **CASCA** (Barry Sadler, 1979/22 volumes)

Written by the same staff sergeant famous for his classic "Ballad of the Green Berets," this series covers a Roman legionnaire who was cursed with immortality at the crucifixion of Jesus. Subsequent volumes find him in every major (and often minor) military engagement over the next two millennia. Though the writing is pedestrian, the books are a quick read.

9. **ALEXANDER SHERIDAN**
(Vivian A. Stuart, 1964/5 volumes)

This is a series about a British army officer during the Crimean War and the Indian Mutiny. As literature, it is not superb, but as history, it is first-rate (much of the verbiage seems to have been liberally borrowed from firsthand accounts).

10. **AUBREY/MATURIN** (Patrick O'Brian, 1970/20 volumes)

One of the most popular series, this covers a British commander and the ship's medical officer during the Napoleonic Wars. Written in a very dry British style, it is more of a period piece than a naval history. It seemed dull to me, but it remains one of the best-selling sets of novels.

Military Science Fiction

There has always been an affinity between military subjects and science fiction. Since so much science fiction occurs with an expansion of humanity toward the stars or alternate histories, the logical nexus between exploration and alien contact is often a military one. The following books and/or series are among the best of the genre, and are all currently available.

1. *STARSHIP TROOPERS* (Robert A. Heinlein, 1959)

This is an interesting book about the infantry of the future, with a concept that bears consideration—only those who are willing to defend the nation can earn the right to vote. The movie (1997) was more of a Gen-X "shoot-'em-up."

2. *ENDER'S GAME* (Orson Scott Card, 1977/4 volumes)

Beginning as a novelette, this expanded into a fascinating story of the military training of a young boy and how his expertise would become the only hope of humanity in an interstellar war.

3. *FOREVER WAR* (Joe Haldeman, 1974)

One of the first science fiction novels done by a Vietnam combat veteran, it is about the soldiers fighting on an interstellar war's front lines and how technology changes affected the battlefield.

4. *HONOR HARRINGTON*
(David Weber, 1992/9 volumes, 3 ancillary volumes)

"Captain Horatio Hornblower in space," this ongoing space saga is about a dynamic woman who becomes the best admiral of her world in a struggle against an aggressive revolutionary rival empire (led by no less than Rob S. Pierre; during the French Revolution, Maximilien Robespierre, 1758–94, was the most important member of the Committee of Public Safety and largely responsible for the Terror).

5. *GUNS OF THE SOUTH* (Harry Turtledove, 1993)

Time-traveling South Africans supply the Army of Northern Virginia with AK-47s during the Battle of the Wilderness. The war changes and history adjusts accordingly.

6. *LORD KALVAN OF OTHERWHEN* (H. Beam Piper, 1965)

When a Pennsylvania state trooper is transported to an alternative feudal world, his knowledge of gunpowder and military tactics becomes invaluable.

7. *HAMMER'S SLAMMERS* (David Drake, 1987/6 volumes)

This is one of the best space mercenary series ever done; the author was a combat veteran of the Vietnam War.

8. **STEN** (Chris Bunch and Alan Cole, 1982/8 volumes)

A tough orphan becomes the prime special operative of a far-flung space empire; the series matures into a story of the corruption of absolute power and the struggle of the protagonist to establish a more democratic state.

9. **LOST REGIMENT** (William Forstchen, 1990/8 volumes)

Colonel Andrew Keane and the 35th Regiment (taken liberally from Joshua Chamberlain and the 20th Maine) are transported from the American Civil War to a world where they must struggle against a Mongol-like alien horde by inventing military technology up to and including a primitive aircraft carrier.

10. **MARCHING THROUGH GEORGIA**
(S. M. Stirling, 1982/3 volumes)

When British Loyalists flee the United States, they settle in South Africa, where they become the Domination of the Draka. One hundred and fifty years later, this alternate World War II posits a Drakan invasion of Russia in a struggle against both Nazi and Soviet forces.

Mandatory Mention

"ALAMAGOOSA" (Eric Frank Russell, 1955)
For anyone who has ever served in the military, the annual general inspection (AGI) is a term of terror. This short story of an interstellar ship called in for a property book inspection rings all too true in terms of what can happen. It has been reprinted numerous times and should be mandatory reading for all junior officers.

War Games: Paper

The traditional war game dates back to the origins of chess. However, the commercial paper war game available to the general public dates back only to the 1950s. Virtually every single period of history has been simulated, from ancient to future conflict. Generally, the game mechanics utilize a geographic map with overprinted hexagons to regularize movement. Force-on-force multipliers determine combat and a die result is utilized for a randomization factor. The games listed below (by designer/year of publication/publisher) represent classic designs, which have often served as exemplars for future products.

1. *SQUAD LEADER* (John Hill/1977/Avalon Hill)

Simulating tactical level on the Eastern Front during World War II, this design fostered a number of descendants, each of which added complexity and chrome. The *Advanced Squad Leader* iteration has become a way of life to some players; it is generally easy to determine such players—their water bills are suspiciously low.

2. *PANZERBLITZ* (James F. Dunnigan/1970/Avalon Hill)

Simulating armored warfare on the Eastern Front during World War II, this design was marred by what was called the "Panzerbush syndrome," in which players flitted from blocked terrain to blocked terrain without incurring opportunity fire. However, it was the first and most popular of its genre.

3. *THIRD REICH* (John Prados/1974/Avalon Hill)

While more recent designs have expanded on the concept, this was the first operational/strategic war game to cover the entire European Theater of Operations.

4. *DIPLOMACY* (Allan B. Callamer/1961/Games Research)

A game of maneuver and diplomacy in pre–World War I Europe, this product emphasizes player interactions.

5. *ACE OF ACES*
(Alfred Leonardi and Douglas Kaufman/1980/Nova)

A totally innovative concept, this game utilizes two booklets of World War I fighters with a series of vignettes on each page with maneuvers listed at the bottom. Each player maneuvers and then turns to a page that is the result of the interaction of both players. In effect, this is equivalent to a paper computer simulation. Unique and interesting.

6. *WOODEN SHIPS & IRON MEN*
(S. Craig Taylor/1974/Battleline)

This simulates tactical ship-to-ship combat in the age of Nelson (about 1792–1815). It is moderately easy to learn, fun to play, and historically fascinating.

7. *WE THE PEOPLE* (Mark Herman/1993/Avalon Hill)

This is a design covering the American Revolutionary War utilizing card-driven events as randomizers to reflect political, diplomatic, and military actions. Serving as the basis for a still-developing genre (*For the People*, 1998, simulates the American Civil War), it was a welcome innovation in its ease of play and recognition of political control.

8. *A HOUSE DIVIDED*
(Frank Chadwick/1981/Games Design Workshop)

An earlier Civil War design, this offers an easier combat system albeit a less realistic conceptualization. Still, it remains playable and offers some insights into the problems faced by both sides.

9. *NAPOLEON'S LAST BATTLES*
(Kevin Zucker/1976/Simulations Publications, Inc.)

A quad-game offering the Battles of Ligny, Wavre, Quatre-Bras, and Waterloo (June 16–18, 1815) either separately or in combination. Since it is easy to learn and provides friendly game mechanics and a challenge to both players, this remains a favorite.

10. *PANZERGRUPPE GUDERIAN*
(James F. Dunnigan/1976/Simulations Publications, Inc.)

This simulation of the German drive on Smolensk in 1941 offers mechanics that have continued to be seen in games ever since—including untried units, divisional integrity, etc.

War Games: Computer

The computer war game arrived only in the late 1970s. For the first few years, this was a niche market. Today, war and strategy games outgross Hollywood revenues. From the 48 K Apple and Atari to the mega-RAM PC, designs have matured to an extent that the military services seriously review such products. The games listed herein are not always playable on contemporary machines; however, any list of computer games would be obsolete before being reduced to print. If the reader is interested in a more detailed examination, I would suggest my personal Web site (*http://www.pressroom.com/~meb*), which lists every computer war game design ever done. However, that is clearly beyond the scope of this book.

1. *CIVILIZATION* (Sid Meier/1991/MicroProse)

The progress of civilization from 4000 B.C. to A.D. 2100, this was not overly historical, but it established a benchmark in game design. The technological development tree gave emphasis to the growth of nations and their military prowess.

2. *EASTERN FRONT* (Chris Crawford/1981/APX)

The Russian Front during World War II, this early eight-bit game design for the Atari computer set parameters that have become standard in computer game design. They included changing geography due to seasonal effects, simultaneous movement, and mouse/joystick input. This game alone was responsible for many gamers' changing over to the computer.

3. *HARPOON* (Larry Bond/1988/Three Sixty Pacific)

A simulation of contemporary naval warfare, this was a conversion from Mr. Bond's previous paper/miniatures design. The computer could now do the bookkeeping and allow the player to concentrate on tactical and operational warfare. This is a superb design that has been republished to keep abreast of computer technologies.

4. *KAMPFGRUPPE*
(Gary Grigsby/1985/Strategic Simulations, Inc.)

Akin to the paper *Squad Leader,* this was the first playable computer game of armored warfare (Eastern Front, World War II). Initially made for eight-bit machines, it has been updated by the designer via his *Steel Panthers* designs for contemporary machines.

5. *RED BARON* (Damon Slye/1991/Dynamix)

Simulating World War I in the air, this product was renowned for its dynamic campaigns. The player began as a novice pilot early in the war, and as he developed his talents, the planes increased in capability, as did his responsibilities in the command structure. Good flight dynamics, good gameplay, and historical background made this a product that hooked the player for hours at a time.

6. *CLASH OF STEEL*
(Martin Scholz/1993/Strategic Simulations, Inc.)

A game covering the entire European Theater of Operations in World War II, its strengths were its playability coupled with economic considerations (not so much guns-or-butter but rather which types of guns).

7. *CIVIL WAR GENERALS II* (Steve Grammont and Doug Gonya/1997/Sierra)

Presenting the American Civil War on an operational level, this product was interesting because of its innovations in determining victory. In addition to traditional geographic areas, victory was also determined by who controlled the most fought-over terrain, thereby rewarding operational combat success.

8. *COMBAT MISSION: BEYOND OVERLORD* (Charles Moylan and Steve Grammont/2000/Big Time Software)

In this game of World War II on the Western Front, the multiple-terrain views allow the player to adopt different perspectives as each turn develops in 60-second increments. Terrain folds and ridges can be properly accessed only at the "you-are-there" perspective, and reconnaissance by fire coupled with proper combat maneuver is essential for successful gameplay.

9. *PANZER GENERAL* (Paul Murray/1994/Strategic Simulations, Inc.)

Featuring World War II "lite," this game of operational combat was buttressed by an interesting campaign system. Although the system's concept of combined arms was fatuous, it was commendable for attracting nonwar gamers to the field. Numerous sequels have since superseded it.

10. *RAINBOW 6* (Carl Schnurr and Brian Upton/1998/Red Storm)

This simulation of contemporary special operations gave special emphasis to preplanning in order to properly execute tactical missions. This served as the basis for other more military-based models (e.g., *Delta Force*).

MISCELLANEOUS

Debunking
Military Myths

Like urban legends, there are military myths. Everyone "knows" that certain events happened, yet the reality may be completely different.

1. "LAFAYETTE, WE ARE HERE!"

A lofty statement usually attributed to General John J. Pershing, commander of the American Expeditionary Force, when American troops first landed to support the Allies during World War I. However, this was actually the creation of one of his staff officers: "It is with loving pride we drape the colors in tribute of respect to this citizen of your great republic. And here and now in the presence of the illustrious dead we pledge our hearts and our honor in carrying this war to a successful issue. Lafayette, we are here." (Colonel Charles E. Stanton in a speech at the tomb of American Revolutionary War General Marquis de Lafayette, July 4, 1917.) But perhaps an anonymous infantryman said it best after the Battle of Soissons (May 27, 1918) with his quintessential response: "We've paid off that old fart, Lafayette. What Frog son-of-a-bitch do we owe now?" (quoted in Don

Mabry, *Historical Text Archive.* December 1, 2001. <*http://historicaltext archive.com/sections.php?op=viewarticle&artid=35*>)

2. "THE OLD GUARD DIES, BUT NEVER SURRENDERS"

At the Battle of Waterloo (June 18, 1815), General Pierre Cambronne (1770–1842), when asked to surrender, supposedly replied, "The Old Guard dies, but never surrenders." The "mot de Cambronne" was more prosaic—he answered a simple "Merde!" (i.e., "Shit!"). Of course, that was difficult to render into the history books, so a more elegant riposte had to be developed.

3. "PECCAVI"

In 1843, General Charles James Napier (1782–1853) conquered the nation of Sind (in what is now Pakistan). He supposedly sent this telegram to the British Foreign Office announcing his success; from the Latin, it may be translated as "I have sinned." Though British officers may have studied Latin, they generally were not the souls of wit. The story derives from a cartoon in the British humor magazine *Punch,* published a few months after the action.

4. "DON'T GIVE UP THE SHIP"

On June 1, 1813, a naval engagement occurred between HMS *Shannon* and the USS *Chesapeake* off Boston. Though the ships were roughly equivalent in firepower, the *Shannon* had an extremely well-trained crew, while the *Chesapeake*'s crew was inexperienced. This proved to be decisive. Although mortally wounded American captain James Lawrence uttered his famous "Don't give up the ship" as he was being carried below, the ship was captured shortly afterwards. The wounded British captain, Philip Vere Broke, recovered to become both a baronet and a rear admiral. But American history books to the present rarely give the results of the battle.

"Don't give up the ship!" In this idealized 1856 engraving, Captain James Lawrence, *center, being carried,* of the USS *Chesapeake* implores his crew to keep fighting during the naval battle of June 1, 1813. In reality, the mortally wounded Lawrence was carried below after uttering his famous words and the ship was soon captured by the British.

5. "SEND US MORE JAPS"

Shortly after Pearl Harbor (December 7, 1941), Japanese forces began assaults on various American outposts in the Pacific Theater of Operations. The Marine contingent on Wake Island held out until December 23, 1941. According to legend, when Pearl Harbor asked if there was anything they could provide, the Marine defenders radioed back this defiant message. However, it was untrue; after the war, Major James Devereaux, commander of the Marine defenders, said that the last thing they needed was more Japanese and that if anything, they would have been glad to send the Japanese somewhere else. But it was a boost to American morale at the time.

6. "SIGHTED SUB SANK SAME"

In one of the more famous combat radio reports of World War II, First Class Naval Aviation Pilot (NAP) Donald F. Mason claimed credit for the destruction of a German U-boat (January 28, 1942). The problem—he missed! Interestingly enough, Mason did sink a U-boat (U-503) two months later (March 15, 1942), for which he received a Distinguished Flying Cross.

7. THE HITLER JIG

One of the more famous newsreels from World War II shows Adolf Hitler dancing an "obscene jig" (as the narration usually reports) on his way to accept the French surrender at Compiègne (June 21, 1940). The problem is that it may not have occurred at all. The *Washington Post* noted that the "famous film of Hitler dancing with glee at the surrender of France was a Western propaganda fraud" (Henry Allen, October 10, 1999). British film editors simply edited the footage of Hitler walking—one of the great psychological operations in military history.

8. SOVIET PARATROOPS—NO CHUTES

There have been various stories about Russian paratroopers being dropped without parachutes into snowbanks during the Russo-Finnish War (1939–40). One version has the troops landing head-first because the weight of their equipment caused them to turn over during their free fall, while the other version has the wily Finns simply painting a rock face white to have the Soviets drop into a true "hard landing." The problem is that neither version can be corroborated! It is an interesting military myth, but probably not much more.

Far from dancing an "obscene jig" after the French surrender in June 1940, Hitler went on a short tour of Paris. This was his only visit to the French capital during the four years of German occupation.

9. THE PANZERS

During World War II (1939–45), the German army (Wehrmacht) used the combined arms doctrine of blitzkrieg ("lightning war") to initially conquer most of Europe. Most people think that the

Wehrmacht was dominated by its Panzers (armored divisions). However, in fact, the German Army was more dependent on hay than gasoline. On June 22, 1941, when the Germans invaded the Soviet Union, they had 750,000 horses—a number 150,000 greater than the number of total vehicles possessed by the Army. As the tide of war turned, the Germans were forced to rely on more horsepower rather than less. The only two all-mechanized armies of World War II were those of the United States and Great Britain (and even they utilized mules and horses in certain situations).

10. NAPOLEON'S HEIGHT

It is a truism that Napoleon was short. Some psychologists have attributed his ambition to his feelings of inadequacy over his height. But Napoleon was not short. Historical records show him to be 5′ 2″—*but* that was in the French measurement. If his height were measured according to English measures, he would have been 5′ 6″—an average height for a Frenchman in the early 19th century. A century of British propaganda has mistakenly convinced much of the world that Napoleon was undersized.

Revolution in Military Affairs

With the end of the Cold War, the U.S. military establishment put its faith in technology. The buzz words rapidly became the "revolution in military technology." The qualitative differential of the new paradigm constituted a quantum break with the past. Military professional academicians "proved" this time and time again. But aside from intellectual snobbery, what are the 10 inventions/adaptations that have constituted a true revolution in military affairs?

1. **BOW** (C. 19,000 B.C.)

The bow was the first true invention that allowed a stand-off capability and acted as a force multiplier. Though the spear does have a stand-off capability, it lacks the range to permit multiple rounds before close combat ensues.

2. **HORSE** (C. 7000 B.C.)

The domestication of the horse allowed military units to move faster. Such accelerated movement allowed one to have the option of when and where to engage against an enemy lacking such assets.

3. **STIRRUP** (C. A.D. 300)

It took a long time to develop the stirrup. This was a quantum leap and not a mere improvement. It allowed the user of cavalry to develop that arm as a shock force and not merely as a form of transportation. Though previous cavalry had been used against troops, the lack of the stirrup prevented maximum speed and shock.

4. **GUNPOWDER** (C. A.D. 919)

This allowed force multiplier to accelerate in both lethality and efficiency. Early muskets were cumbersome and actually slower and less lethal than the English longbow. However, they had the advantage of being easier to learn, and eventually their lethality increased to become the primary means of battlefield damage.

5. **CANNED GOODS** (C. 1804)

Napoleon knew that logistics were the key to effective military employment. Instead of relying on forage and the local environment, he offered a prize to anyone who could develop a method to preserve meat. In 1804, Nicholas Apel invented the first "tin goods." This invention freed military units from the logistical nightmare of local supply and allowed units to develop a professional commissary.

6. **RAILROAD** (C. 1832)

The advent of the railroad has probably been the harbinger of the modern world. Aside from being responsible for time itself (time zones were developed because of railroad speeds; heretofore, no one needed exact times), the railroad allowed troops to be mobilized and transported to the area of need. This was particularly evident during the American Civil War and the Franco-Prussian War.

7. **MACHINE GUN** (c. 1862)

The technological challenge to individual heroism, this invention literally swept the board clean. Although established military hierarchies did not understand its use, improved firepower and effectiveness dominated the battlefield by World War I.

8. **RECOILLESS ARTILLERY/FIRE DIRECTION CONTROL** (c. 1870)

The use of recoilless artillery and improved fire direction control allowed artillery to become the "king of battle." By World War I, it had become the major producer of casualties—both on land and at sea.

9. **WIRELESS** (c. 1923)

The ability to converse with subordinate units quickly and easily has revolutionized the concept of command control and use of military formations. Though such communications can be intercepted and "turned," the advantage is worth the risk—unless the command control becomes so stultified that subordinate commanders are removed from decision making.

10. **ATOMIC BOMB** (1945)

A quantum leap in technology, it rewrote the book on tactics. Weapons of mass destruction made society at large the theater of war. In the 1950s, atomic military theory dominated force analysis, although some strange concepts were developed (e.g., the Davy Crockett, the American atomic cannon, had a range less than its lethality radius—i.e., fire and die). Atomic weaponry has made deterrence a definitive goal in warfare.

Honorable Mention

AIRPLANE (1903)

While its advent made war into a fully three-dimensional space, its use has been limited to reconnaissance and weapons delivery. It is an improvement to existing technology. With the use of space platforms, aerial reconnaissance and weapons delivery may be rendered obsolete.

COMPUTER (1948)

The use of the computer has accelerated current trends—target acquisition, cryptology, and logistical management. As artificial intelligence develops, it may create a quantum differential in the applications of warfare.

Elite Troop Formations

Certain military units have established a reputation for excellence that has echoed through history. Often, such units began initially as the security element for a commander; they evolved into a combat formation that maintained its combat edge through much of its existence. Sometimes, these units are long-lived; at other times, their tenure can be measured in months. However, one can always say that they reflected the best of the martial experience.

1. THE OLD GUARD

The elite of the Imperial Guard, this formation derived from Napoleon's security detachment, the Guides. By 1814, the Imperial Guard had reached a strength of over 110,000, but the Old Guard still maintained its high standards of requiring veterans of five years of military service and two campaigns. The veterans were referred to as *grognards* (i.e., grumblers), a term that contemporary war gamers have adopted as their own. At the Battle of Waterloo (June 18, 1815), General Pierre Cambronne (1770–1842), when asked to surrender, supposedly replied, "The Old Guard dies, but never surrenders." The "mot de Cambronne" was more prosaic—he answered a simple "Merde!" (i.e., "Shit!").

2. THE COMPANIONS

This was an elite cavalry formation made up of Macedonian noblemen. They served as the shock force of Alexander the Great (356–323 B.C.) in his campaigns against the Persian Empire.

3. SACRED BAND

A group of 150 homosexual pairs founded in 375 B.C., they were the elite shock troops of Thebes. They were undefeated until their annihilation by Alexander the Great at the Battle of Chaeronea (338 B.C.).

4. TENTH LEGION

This was the favorite legion of Julius Caesar (100–44 B.C.). He utilized them as special shock troops and an example to the other legions in his army.

5. JANISSARIES

An elite formation in the Ottoman Empire, it was composed of young Christian prisoners. Forcibly converted to Islam, they became the shields of the sultans for almost 500 years. By 1826, having transformed into both a hereditary and an untrustworthy unit, they were eliminated.

6. IRONSIDES

Oliver Cromwell (1599–1658) founded and led this elite cavalry formation (a double regiment of 14 troops). It particularly distinguished itself at the Battle of Marston Moor (1644) and served as the basis for the New Army during the English Civil War.

7. SWISS GUARD

Since the early 16th century, the Vatican State has hired Swiss mercenaries to provide papal security. Since they were not "locals," it was anticipated that they would not become involved in Roman politics. This formation now consists of about 100 men recruited from Switzerland; Michelangelo designed their distinctive parade uniform (tunic, breeches, and stockings). They are one of the only mercenary units in history to have remained faithful to their patron.

8. PREOBRAZHENSKY REGIMENT

A Life Guards regiment founded by Tsar Peter the Great, this unit supported the Russian imperial throne from its founding in the early 18th century through the end of the Romanov dynasty. It was particularly useful in breaking the power of the Streltsy, a unit more devoted to inner-Kremlin machinations.

9. STONEWALL BRIGADE

The foot cavalry of Stonewall Jackson during the Civil War, this unit was famous for its Valley Campaign. It fought through the entire war, although only 210 men survived from its original muster; five of its seven commanders were killed in action. Because of its reputation, it was the first Confederate unit to march through the Federal lines at Appomattox.

10. IRON BRIGADE

Founded in the fall of 1861, this unit from Wisconsin and Indiana was distinguished by its black felt hat and canvas gaiters. Initially referred to as the Black Hat Brigade, its first combat saw it destroy one-third of the Stonewall Brigade (August 28, 1862). Major General Joseph Hooker referred to the unit as his "iron brigade." At the battles of Antietam and Gettysburg, the unit distinguished itself but lost over 75 percent of its strength.

Horses

The horse was the primary mobility enhancer for over 2,000 years of military history. While the cavalry has gone in and out of fashion several times during this period, commanding officers have still often utilized the horse as a primary method of travel. Several of these mounts have been retained in historical memory.

1. BUCEPHALUS

Ridden by Alexander the Great (356–323 B.C.). Supposedly no one was able to ride this horse until Alexander realized that the horse shied at its own shadow; when Alexander used blinders to obstruct the horse's vision, he created a model war horse.

2. TRAVELLER

Ridden by General Robert E. Lee (1807–70) during the American Civil War.

3. CINCINNATI

Ridden by General U.S. Grant (1822–85) during the American Civil War.

4. **LITTLE SORREL**

Ridden by Lieutenant General Thomas "Stonewall" Jackson (1824–63) during the American Civil War.

5. **RIENZI**

Ridden by General Philip H. Sheridan (1831–88) during the American Civil War. Stuffed after death, the horse is currently on display at the Smithsonian Museum (Washington, D.C.).

6. **MARYLAND**

Ridden by Major General "Jeb" Stuart (1833–64) during the American Civil War. Stuart also was known to ride a horse named Virginia.

7. **HERO**

Ridden by Lieutenant General James Longstreet (1821–1904) during the American Civil War.

8. **COPENHAGEN**

Ridden by the Duke of Wellington (1769–1852) during the Napoleonic Wars.

9. **MARENGO**

Ridden by Napoleon (1769–1821) and named after his famous victory there (June 14, 1800).

10. **COMANCHE**

Ridden by Captain Myles Keogh, he was the only survivor from the Seventh Cavalry at Custer's Last Stand (June 25, 1876).

Honorable Mention

XANTHUS

Ridden by Achilles, according to Greek legend.

Cavalry Charges

The cavalry is a military arm that requires extensive training and time. Until the invention of the stirrup, the shock value of cavalry was limited. Thereafter, it became the dominant form of military action. However, many of its historically noted affairs concern the choreography of erroneous employment or last stands rather than successful victories.

1. CHARGE OF THE LIGHT BRIGADE (October 25, 1854)

The most famous cavalry charge in history, not because of its historical impact, but because of Alfred Lord Tennyson's poem "The Charge of the Light Brigade" ("Into the valley of Death / Rode the Six Hundred"). During the Crimean War, the British Light Brigade attacked a Russian artillery position. The actual orders to attack were a mishmash of confusion and error; the movement required a charge across one and a half miles of open terrain covered from the left by Russian artillery on the Fedioukine Heights and on the right by the Causeway Heights. A total of 678 men began the charge; 195 returned (a casualty rate of 78 percent). French General Pierre Bosquet observed the charge and commented, *"C'est magnifique mais ce n'est pas la guerre"* ("It is magnificent, but it is not war").

2. **ADRIANOPLE** (August 9, 378)

The Roman legions attempted to defeat the Goths in a traditional deployment (i.e., legions as center of mass with cavalry on the flanks). However, the Gothic cavalry routed the Roman cavalry on the left and the remaining Roman cavalry fled the battlefield. The legions were left unsupported and were annihilated—even the Emperor Valens was killed. With their use of the stirrup, the Goths were able to magnify the shock impact of their cavalry. This was the first victory of heavy cavalry over infantry, and it ushered in the 1,000-year supremacy of the mounted arm.

3. **GAUGAMELA** (October 1, 331 B.C.)

Alexander the Great's Companion Cavalry was used to decisively thrust through the Persian center. Creating a giant wedge, the Macedonian cavalry drove straight for Darius, who fled the battlefield in a panic. His troops emulated his example, and the Persian army fell apart.

4. **WATERLOO** (June 18, 1815)

The main French infantry advance during the battle occurred about 1:30 P.M. in an advance against the farm complex of La Haye Sainte. When the infantry was stopped by British artillery and infantry fire, Wellington ordered his cavalry forward. Both light and heavy brigades of cavalry routed the French columns. However, the cavalry exceeded their orders and continued to advance, whereupon a French cavalry counterattack threw them back. Lady Elizabeth Butler (1846–1933) commemorated the British charge in her painting of the Scots Greys advancing *(Scotland Forever)*. By 4 P.M., Marshal Michel Ney led the first of several massive cavalry charges into the British positions. The British infantry formed defensive squares, and the British artillerymen sought refuge within the squares as the

French advanced. Luckily, the British artillerymen took their limbers with them so the French could not drag away the artillery, and even luckier for the British, the French had neglected to bring nails to spike the guns. Thus, although the French cavalry swirled around the guns, they could not remove them or render them inoperable. Without a combined arms assault (using cavalry to pack the enemy into dense squares, artillery to render the squares into a killing zone, and infantry to mop up), the French assault was doomed—and so was the battle itself.

5. **BRANDY STATION** (June 9, 1863)

Union Major General Alfred Pleasanton's cavalry crossed the Rappahannock River and surprised Jeb Stuart's Confederate cavalry still in its cantonments. In the largest cavalry action of the Civil War (12,000 Union and 10,000 Confederate), an indecisive result was achieved. But this showed that the Union cavalry was learning and that the Confederate mounted arm could no longer rely on its field superiority.

6. **VON BREDOW'S DEATH RIDE** (August 16, 1870)

During the Franco-Prussian War, the last major successful cavalry charge occurred in western European warfare. At the Battle of Mars-la-Tour, the Prussian cavalry was ordered to attack the French artillery positions in order to relieve the German left wing. Major General Friedrich von Bredow's 12th Cavalry Brigade executed a classic charge into the guns; the six squadrons were fortunate enough to be able to use a depression to conceal their approach until they burst out within a few hundred yards of the French. However, the casualty rate was about 62 percent (194 of 500 men returned to their own lines). This charge was used by cavalry proponents as a justification for the retention of cavalry on the modern battlefield.

7. **YELLOW TAVERN** (May 11, 1864)

During the Battle of Spotsylvania (May 8–18, 1864), Major General Philip Sheridan's cavalry corps raided toward Richmond. Although Jeb Stuart's cavalry tried to blunt the advance, the Confederates were decisively defeated and Stuart himself killed. With Stuart's death, the Confederate cavalry lost its most dynamic leader, and it never recovered from the loss.

8. **OMDURMAN** (September 2, 1898)

The final charge of the regular cavalry in British history was another glorious chapter in unnecessary pageantry and risk. British forces in the Sudan engaged the Dervishes in a defensive execution of machine gun against spear. In the main assault, no Dervish even approached within 500 yards of the British lines. However, the 21st Lancers were the only cavalry regiment in the British army to lack a battle honor (it was mockingly said that their motto should have been "Thou Shalt Not Kill"); their commander ordered a charge against an unknown number of hostiles on unknown terrain, whereupon his unit was almost destroyed. Such gallantry did earn three Victoria Crosses, and a young British lieutenant's presence guaranteed the charge an immortality all its own: his name was Winston Churchill.

9. **THE AUSTRALIAN LIGHT HORSE** (October 31, 1917)

During World War I, the Allied Desert Mounted Corps assaulted Turkish positions at the Battle of Beersheba (also known as the Third Battle of Gaza). The Australian Light Horse charged through the Turkish positions into Beersheba itself. This was the last major cavalry charge in British history and the subject of a fine film.

10. **THE POLISH CAVALRY CHARGE** (1939)

Any pseudohistory of World War II narrates the famous tale of Polish lancers charging German armor. For example, in 1989, the Marshall Islands issued the first of their stamps commemorating the 50th anniversary of World War II, one in which the Polish cavalry was superimposed on German tanks. The problem is that such an attack never occurred. The Poles may have been outnumbered, outgunned, and lacking support, but they were not stupid. On September 1, 1939, two squadrons of Polish cavalry did attack a German infantry battalion near Krojanty; German armored cars came to the relief of the infantry, and the cavalry retreated. There were several other cavalry charges during the short campaign, some of which were tactical successes, but these all involved actions against infantry or dismounted troops. The legend may have derived from German General Heinz Guderian's memoirs, in which he stated that the "Pomorska Cavalry Brigade, in ignorance of the nature of our tanks, had charged them with swords and lances and had suffered tremendous losses" (Guderian, *Panzer Leader*, p. 53). But in reality, there were tanks in the Polish army, and the cavalry was somewhat familiar with their operating capabilities.

Battle Cries

The individual battle cry probably predates the first war. As man confronted man on the field of battle, it is likely that harsh words (or even grunts) were spoken in anger. Eventually, things became organized, and entire armies adopted a rallying cry that could be used to both raise friendly morale and strike fear into the enemy.

1. THE REBEL YELL

During the American Civil War, Confederate troops often entered battle using a loud, reverberating yell. Veterans of the conflict described it differently (anything from a "yip-yip-yip" to a "yoe-woe-woe"), and it was different depending on the geographic region from which the troops had been recruited. It was probably derived from rural hailing customs, and the modern equivalent is probably the pig call ("Sooey, sooey, pig-pig-pig").

2. REMEMBER THE ALAMO! REMEMBER GOLIAD!

Derived from the Texas War of Independence (1836), this was a cry for retribution and vengeance. At Goliad, about 300 Texans who had surrendered to the Mexicans were summarily executed (March 27, 1836); at the Siege of the Alamo (February 23–March 6, 1836), 188

Texans died, with Mexican General Santa Anna refusing to take any prisoners. When the Texans under Sam Houston (1793–1863) defeated the Mexicans at the Battle of San Jacinto (April 21, 1836), they used both names as a rallying cry. While Goliad has been largely forgotten today, the Alamo remains as an American rallying cry.

3. REMEMBER PEARL HARBOR

When the Japanese Navy attacked Pearl Harbor by air on December 7, 1941, precipitating American entry into World War II, President Franklin Delano Roosevelt addressed Congress and said in a rhetorical flourish, "December 7, a date which will live in infamy. . . ." The desire to seek retribution for the sneak attack became both a ubiquitous rallying cry and a number one record ("Let's remember Pearl Harbor, as we go to meet the foe / Let's remember Pearl Harbor, as we did the Alamo").

4. BANZAI

An abbreviated version of *tenno heika banzai* ("may the Emperor live for 10,000 years"), this was the battle cry of Japanese Imperial troops during World War II.

5. CAMERONE

The defiant cry of the French Foreign Legion, it commemorates the battle (April 30, 1863) in which 65 Legionnaires fought more than 2,000 Mexicans in a famous last stand. It is still used when the Legion enters into close combat.

6. "DO YOU WANT TO LIVE FOREVER?"

This exhortation from a leader to his own troops has two separate derivations. Frederick the Great (1712–86), Prussian monarch, noticed that his troops were reluctant to advance at the Battle of Kolin (June

18, 1757). He yelled at them "Rascals, do you want to live forever?" In the U.S. Marine Corps, the question has a separate genesis. Two-time Medal of Honor recipient Dan Daly (1873–1937) was at the Battle of Belleau Wood (June 4, 1918) and yelled to his troops, "Come on, you sons of bitches! Do you want to live forever?"

7. GERONIMO

The shout used by American paratroopers as they exit the plane, it has become an American battle cry for "Let's go." The origin of the phrase is unknown, although at least two possible derivations exist (1) At Fort Sill, Oklahoma, Geronimo supposedly galloped down a cliff on horseback to escape pursuing cavalry, yelling his name. The paratroopers later adopted the cry as their own. (2) The paratroopers happened to see a movie with Geronimo as the principal character and adopted it. Both stories are equally implausible.

8. FOR HARRY AND SAINT GEORGE

The battle cry of English troops at the Battle of Agincourt (October 25, 1415), it honored both their monarch, Henry V (1387–1422), and the patron saint of England. It was rendered in Shakespeare's *Henry V* as "Cry 'God for Harry! England and Saint George!'"

9. GOTT MIT UNS

Literally meaning "God (is) with us," it was used as a battle cry by the Teutonic Knights at the Battle of Tannenberg (July 15, 1410) against Poland, where it was conclusively proven that He was not, and later by the troops of Gustavus Adolphus (1594–1632) during the Thirty Years' War (1618–48). Adopted by many other armies over the centuries, it received a negative connotation when it was used on military belt buckles during the Second World War (1939–45) by Nazi Germany.

10. HAKKAA PÄÄLLE

Another battle cry by Gustavus Adolphus's troops, it was used in the midst of close combat by his Finns and means "Smash them down!"

Honorable Mention

NIAMA!

African explorer and newspaper columnist Henry Stanley (1841–1904) ("Dr. Livingston, I presume?") was not overly solicitous of the indigenous population in Africa. As he traversed the Congo River, he merely blasted his way though the locals. Some of the tribes, partaking in the local custom of cannibalism, used this as their battle cry; it means "meat"—surely a battle cry that could strike fear into its opponents.

Prisoner-of-War Camps

Retention of prisoners of war for a long period is a relatively recent event. The standard treatment for captured prisoners used to be either death or slavery. Few societies would be bothered with the care and feeding of enemy combatants. Under the Geneva Conventions (promulgated in the 19th and 20th centuries), a basic standard of care was established. How effectively such care has been administered is open to question.

1. ANDERSONVILLE (AMERICAN CIVIL WAR)

Possibly the most famous prisoner-of-war camp in history, this Georgia facility was established to hold 10,000 men; as a result of overcrowding in 1864–65, it held as many as 32,000. Over 12,000 Union prisoners of war died, and the camp commander, Henry Wirz, was hanged as a war criminal by the United States. MacKinlay Kantor's Pulitzer Prize–winning novel *Andersonville* (1955) has made this camp a byword for tragedy.

2. ELMIRA (AMERICAN CIVIL WAR)

The Union counterpart of Andersonville, this New York prisoner-of-war camp was designed for 5,000 but held as many as 9,400;

approximately 3,000 prisoners died in this camp. While the Confederacy could say that poor conditions were partially due to a lack of availability of shelter and foodstuffs, the Union had no such excuse.

3. HANOI HILTON (VIETNAM WAR)

The derisive nickname for the Hoa Loa prisoner-of-war camp located in Hanoi. American pilots were held here for several years in an atmosphere of brutal conditions and inhumane treatment. Senator John McCain of Arizona was an alumnus of this facility.

4. STALAG LUFT III (WORLD WAR II)

A prisoner-of-war camp for Allied fliers run by the Luftwaffe, it was the subject of a mass escape on March 24–25, 1944. Seventy-six prisoners escaped, and Hitler was so infuriated that he had fifty of the recaptured prisoners executed by firing squad. A book *(The Great Escape)* by Paul Brickhill (1950) was later made into a classic movie by the same name (1963).

5. KANCHANABURI (WORLD WAR II)

Better known as the River Kwai, this was the camp where 100,000 Asian laborers and 16,000 Allied prisoners of war died building a railroad bridge. Located 130 miles west of Bangkok, it remains a tourist attraction, and served as the inspiration for the Academy Award–winning film *The Bridge on the River Kwai* (1957).

6. COLDITZ (WORLD WAR II)

Officially known as Oflag IVC (an abbreviation for *Offizierslager*, i.e., "officer's camp"), this was established in a castle atop a mountain. Designed to be escape-proof, it was used to hold Allied officers who had shown a penchant for escape. What this did was to concentrate the best escape artists in Europe. Attempts were made to tunnel through rock and even to build a glider to fly to freedom. The war ended before the glider could become operational. Patrick Reid's book *Colditz* (1953) details life in this facility.

7. SON TAY (VIETNAM WAR)

Located 23 miles north of Hanoi, this prisoner-of-war camp earned its fame not because of its prisoners but because of a failed rescue attempt. On November 21, 1970, Army Rangers air assaulted this facility to free the prisoners. The raid was a tactical success but a strategic failure; all of the prisoners had been moved elsewhere four months earlier.

8. CABANATUAN (WORLD WAR II)

The subject of Hampton Sides's book *Ghost Soldiers* (2001), this facility also earned its reputation for a rescue attempt. On January 28, 1945, 121 Army Rangers liberated 511 American and British prisoners of war from this Japanese camp in the Philippines.

9. HAMMELBURG (WORLD WAR II)

General George Patton ordered a rescue attempt on the prisoner-of-war camp at Hammelburg, 60 miles behind German lines. The Hammelburg Raid (March 26–28, 1945) encountered elements of three German divisions, and although Task Force Baum was able to fight its way to the camp, it was unable to return. Patton's son-in-law was a prisoner there, and some have questioned Patton's motives for ordering the raid so late in the war.

10. **SPANDAU (WORLD WAR II)**

This facility was used at the conclusion of World War II to hold high-ranking officers and political leaders of the Third Reich. Following the Nuremburg Trials, it became the prison facility for certain Nazis convicted of war crimes. It remained in use until its last prisoner, Rudolf Hess, died on August 17, 1987. It was then razed so that it would not serve as a shrine for neo-Nazi sympathizers.

Military Clothing

Military clothing has often made a fashion statement. There are popular styles of clothing that trace back to military clothing as well as military clothing named after military figures.

1. SAM BROWNE BELT

A belt with a sash running from right to left, this was designed to help carry the weight of a holstered pistol. It was named after General Sir Samuel J. Browne (1824–1901) of the British Army in India.

2. EISENHOWER JACKET

A tailored military tunic worn in the U.S. Army from World War II to the mid-1960s, it was named after General Dwight D. Eisenhower (1890–1969).

3. RAGLAN SLEEVE

A sleeve extending to the neck without shoulder seams (somewhat resembling a batwing), it was named for FirtzRoy James Henry Somerset (First Baron Raglan) (1788–1855). He was the commander of British troops in the Crimean War (1853–56).

4. CARDIGAN SWEATER

This is a heavy sweater, named after James Thomas Brudenell, the Seventh Earl of Cardigan (1797–1868). He was the commander of the British Light Cavalry during the Crimean War when they made their famous charge (October 25, 1854). While the Crimean War proved to be a disaster for military arms, it established a record in fashion trends.

5. WELLINGTON BOOTS

Heavy military (and later work) boots, which rose to almost knee height, they were named after the Duke of Wellington (1769–1852).

6. PEA COAT

This is a heavy overcoat, initially issued to sailors for working in inclement weather, and now a civilian-type work coat.

7. BELL BOTTOMS

Naval trousers with wide flared legs, which allowed sailors to roll them up for wading ashore or climbing rigging. "Bell Bottom Trousers" became a popular song hit for Guy Lombardo during World War II, and the pants themselves became a fashion statement in the 1960s for civilian wear.

8. PONCHO

A plasticized material with a hole cut through for one's head, it was utilized as military raingear, and now has assumed a ubiquitous status for civilian raingear as well.

9. KHAKIS

In 1846, Sir Harry Lumsden adopted Indian pajamas in lieu of the heavier worsted British white trousers as a work uniform. He colored the pants with mud and *mazari,* a local plant, and called them *khaki* (Hindu for "dust"). Khakis had the advantage of being cooler than the normal British field uniform and blended in with the local terrain. The uniform was adopted by the British Army in 1884 and by the United States by 1898. It has since become standard civilian wear for men and women, while retaining its military usage.

10. BOMBER JACKET

During World War II, heavy bombers had to attain a high altitude to avoid enemy antiaircraft fire. Hence, a leather jacket with a fur collar was adopted by the pilots to allow both warmth and flexibility. The jacket has since become a popular, albeit expensive, civilian accoutrement.

Honorable Mention

CAMMIES

The American Army olive drab (OD) green uniform was modified during the Vietnam War. Special Forces and other units adopted a camouflage pattern that blended in with the jungle (e.g., tiger stripes). By the 1980s, the army adopted a black-and-green pattern for normal use (known to the troops as "artichoke suits") and a tan-and-black pattern for desert use (known to the troops as "chocolate chips"). Both patterns have entered the civilian market in items from pants to book bags.

Courts-Martial

Trial by court-martial requires an extensive commitment to the law. Throughout history, the usual method of punishment for disobedience of military orders has been summary (and often fatal). As there has been a greater commitment to the rule of law, the judicial record of military law has grown ever more expansive.

1. **ALFRED DREYFUS** (September 9, 1859–July 12, 1935)

The most famous court-martial in history, it came close to destroying the French Republic. Dreyfus, a French Army captain who was Jewish, was accused and convicted of spying for Germany. His conviction was due as much to his religion as it was to the evidence. He was sentenced to life imprisonment on Devil's Island (a penal colony in South America), and his case initially aroused anti-Semitism in France. However, Lieutenant Colonel Georges Picquart, an Army intelligence officer, concluded that Dreyfus had been framed (Picquart's motivation was to protect France from further espionage, and he had little sympathy for Dreyfus himself). The French Army did not want to reopen the case, and Picquart was transferred to Tunisia. World-famous novelist Émile Zola published a denunciation of this miscarriage of justice *("J'accuse!")* and eventually the case was reopened. The Army, the Right, and the Church stood opposed to the secularists, the Liberals and the Left. At a new court-martial, Dreyfus was again convicted, but he was pardoned by the president of France (1899). Only in 1906 was he restored to military duty. This case was a landmark in the history of anti-Semitism.

2. **BILLY MITCHELL** (December 29, 1879–February 17, 1936)

An early proponent of air power, he was an American brigadier general who was court-martialed for insubordination after he accused the War and Navy Departments of incompetence and criminal negligence. Convicted in December 1925, he resigned from the Army in 1926, still maintaining that his theories of air power were correct. In 1946, he was awarded a posthumous Special Congressional Medal of Honor.

3. **MICHEL NEY** (January 10, 1769–December 7, 1815)

One of Napoleon's marshals, he was referred to as "the Bravest of the Brave." He did a superb job of commanding the rear guard during the Moscow retreat (1812), but at Waterloo (1815) he misused the cavalry and did not utilize a combined arms assault against the British. He was condemned to death by a court-martial for treason against the Bourbon Restoration. At his execution, he gave the orders to his own firing squad.

4. **HARRY HARBOARD "BREAKER" MORANT** (December 9, 1864–February 27, 1902)

An English emigrant to Australia, he served as an officer with the Bushveld Carbineers during the Boer War. Tried for war crimes (i.e., atrocities committed against prisoners), he was convicted by a British court-martial and shot to death. The trial itself had been conducted irregularly, and his case has become a symbol of Australian nationalism. The film *Breaker Morant* (1980) does an excellent job of pointing out the moral ambiguities of this case.

5. JOHN BYNG (1704–March 14, 1757)

A British admiral, he was acquitted of disaffection and cowardice but convicted of "neglect of duty in battle." His trial and conviction were political, in that his adherence to the Fighting Instructions did not justify any form of neglect of duty. He was executed on the deck of his flagship by firing squad. Voltaire noted in *Candide* that it was sometimes found necessary in England to occasionally shoot an admiral *"pour encourager les autres"* ("to encourage the others").

6. EDDIE SLOVIK (February 18, 1920–March 31, 1945)

He was the last American soldier to be executed for desertion under enemy fire, and his sentence was personally approved by General Dwight D. Eisenhower as a deterrent to others. Many people think that he was the only U.S. soldier to be executed during World War II, but this is not true—at least 50 other service members were executed, usually for the crimes of rape and/or murder.

7. JOHN ANDRÉ (May 12, 1751–October 2, 1780)

A captain in the British Army, he was an aide-de-camp to General Henry Clinton. Serving as the intermediary between Benedict Arnold and General Clinton, he was caught by the New York militia and hanged for espionage.

8. HENRY WIRZ (1822–November 10, 1865)

A captain in the Confederate army, he was the commanding officer of Andersonville prison camp (in Georgia). After the war, he was tried, convicted, and sentenced to death for ill treatment accorded the prisoners under his care.

9. WILLIAM CALLEY (b. June 8, 1943)

On March 16, 1968, as a second lieutenant in the Americal Division, he led his platoon into My Lai, South Vietnam, where they massacred about 500 men, women, and children. At a military court-martial, he was convicted of murder and on March 29, 1971, was sentenced to life imprisonment. In 1974, President Richard Nixon commuted his sentence to time served.

10. **JEFFREY MACDONALD** (b. October 12, 1943)

A physician and captain in the Green Berets, he was accused of murdering his wife and two children at Fort Bragg, North Carolina, on February 17, 1970. Although the investigation was sloppy, he was convicted by a military court-martial. Joe McGinnis wrote a best-seller about the event *(Fatal Vision)*. When he began writing, he thought MacDonald innocent, but his research convinced him otherwise. The case was appealed to the Supreme Court, and MacDonald was eventually granted a new trial, whereupon he was convicted once again. He maintains his innocence to this day.

Web Sites

W eb sites are transient by definition. Here today, gone tomorrow may well be the watchword of the Internet resources.
The ones listed below have shown a certain endurance in their specific areas of coverage. But by no means are they the end result;
they may serve as a beginning portal into an infinite source.

1. GOOGLE *(HTTP://WWW.GOOGLE.COM)*

An excellent search engine, which yields surprisingly good results
without a lot of extraneous baggage.

2. MILITARY BOOKS On-LINE
*(HTTP://MEMBERS.aoL.COM/VONRANKE/MILITARYBOOKS.
HTML)*

A superb source for military history books; separated by era and
linked to Amazon.com for orders, it is a good starting place to add
to one's library.

3. **USMA MAP LIBRARY** *(HTTP://WWW.DEAN.USMA.EDU/HISTORY/DHISTORYMAPS/ MAPSHOME.HTM)*

The West Point atlases of history displayed on-line—and many of these are not even available in printed format elsewhere.

4. **HISTORY CHANNEL** *(HTTP://WWW.HISTORYCHANNEL.COM)*

A general site useful for "all things history."

5. **FIND A GRAVE** *(HTTP://WWW.FINDAGRAVE.COM)*

While it is not specifically dedicated to military history, its information on various historical figures is among the best on the Internet. There are short biographical sketches for most decedents, along with photographs and locations of their final resting place.

6. **VETERANS AND MILITARY WEB SITES** *(HTTP://MEMBERS.AOL.COM/VETERANS/WARLIB6.HTM)*

A useful site for finding other sites dedicated to military matters.

7. **WORLD WAR I** *(HTTP://WWW.WORLDWAR1.COM)*

Good detail on World War I, divided by subject matter.

8. **NATIONAL ARCHIVES** *(HTTP://WWW.NARA.GOV/NARA/SEARCHNAIL.HTML)*

The search engine of the U.S. National Archives. It is surprising how much data are available by on-line access.

9. SPECIAL EVENTS IN HISTORY
(HTTP://WWW.VAXXINE.COM/MGDSITE/HISTORY.EHT)

Good for determining what historical events occurred on a particular day.

10. M. EVAN BROOKS HOME PAGE
(HTTP://WWW.PRESSROOM.COM/~MEB/)

A Web site dedicated to computer military gaming; and if you want to contact the author, so be it.

Bibliography

A bibliography of over 4,000 years of military history must necessarily be an extensive listing. Sources marked with an asterisk (*) were heavily utilized; in addition, the advent of the Internet has substantially assisted in the accumulation of facts that would otherwise have required months in a university library. While professors and other academicians may regard the encyclopedia with horror, I must admit that the 1960 edition of the *Encyclopedia Britannica* was more useful than I ever anticipated in terms of verifying dates. Finally, these sources are a beginning, and not all of them are gospel (e.g., Hanson's *Soul of Battle,* while useful for ancient warfare, arrives at conclusions that I cannot regard as justifiable).

General

Alexander, Bevin. *How Great Generals Win.* New York: Avon Books, 1995.

Ashley, Leonard R. N. *Ripley's Believe It or Not Book of the Military.* New York: Pocket Books, 1970.

Asprey, Robert B. *War in the Shadows.* 2 vols. Garden City, N.J.: Doubleday, 1975.

Bison, Ben. December 1, 2001. <*http://www.fortunecity.com/rivendell/rhydin/111thebes.htm*>

Blumenson, Martin, and James L. Stokesbury, *Masters of the Art of Command.* Boston: Houghton Mifflin, 1975.

Chandler, David G. *Military Maxims of Napoleon.* New York: Macmillan, 1988.

*Creasey, Edward. *Fifteen Decisive Battles of the World.* London: Oxford University Press, 1915.

Dodge, Theodore A. *The Great Captains.* New York: Barnes and Noble, 1995.

*Dupuy, R. Ernest, and Trevor N. Dupuy. *The Encyclopedia of Military History.* New York: Harper and Row, 1977.

Dupuy, Trevor N. *The Harper Encyclopedia of Military Biography.* Edison, N.J.: Castle Books, 1995.

Durschmeid, Erik. *The Hinge Factor.* New York: Arcade, 1999.

——. *The Weather Factor.* New York: Arcade, 2000.

Encyclopedia Britannica. Chicago: William Benton, 1960.

Fortschen, William R., and Bill Fawcett, eds. *It Seemed Like a Good Idea.* New York: Quill, 2000.

*Fuller, J. F. C., *A Military History of the Western World.* 3 vols. New York: Da Capo, 1987.

Hanson, Victor Davis. *The Soul of Battle.* New York: Free Press, 1999.

Heller, Jonathan, ed. *War and Conflict.* Washington, D.C.: National Archives, 1990.

Jones, Archer. *The Art of War in the Western World.* Urbana: University of Illinois, 1987.

Keegan, John. *The Face of Battle.* New York: Viking, 1976.

——. *The Mask of Command.* New York: Viking, 1987.

——. *History of Warfare.* New York: Knopf, 1993.

*Kohn, George C. *Dictionary of Wars.* New York: Anchor, 1986.

L1 News. December 1, 2001. <*http://www.lineone.net/express/99/09/28/ features/ fcolcomment1-d.html*>

Lanning, Michael Lee. *The Military 100.* Secaucus, N.J.: Citadel, 1996.

Liddell Hart, B. H. *The Great Captains Unveiled.* London: W. Blanchard and Sons, 1927.

Mabry, Don. *Historical Text Archive.* December 1, 2001. <*http://www. historicaltextarchive.com/sections.php?op=viewarticle&artid=35*>

May, Herbert G, and Bruce M. Metzger, eds. *The Oxford Annotated Bible with the Apocrypha.* New York: Oxford University Press, 1965.

*Montgomery of Alamein. *A History of Warfare.* New York: William Morrow, 1983.

*Perrett, Bryan. *The Battle Book.* London: Arms and Armour, 1996.

Seymour, William. *Yours to Reason Why.* New York: Da Capo, 1986.

Smith, Robert Barr. *Men at War.* New York: Avon Books, 1997.

Southworth, Samuel A. *Great Raids in History.* New York: Sarpedon, 1997.

Tsouras, Peter G. *The Greenhill Dictionary of Military Quotations.* London: Greenhill, 2000.

Van Crevald, Martin. *Command in War.* Cambridge, Mass.: Harvard University, 1985.

Vaughn, Dr. Leroy. *Hatshepsut.* December 1, 2001. <*http://www.ccds.charlotte. nc.us/vaughn/Diversity/hatshepsut.htm*>.

Weir, William. *Fatal Victories.* New York: Avon Books, 1993.

Woods, W. J. *Leaders and Battles.* Novato, Calif.: Presidio, 1984.

Ancient

Arrian. *The Campaigns of Alexander.* New York: Penguin Books, 1971.

Bury, J. B. *History of the Later Roman Empire.* 2 vols. Mineola, N.Y.: Dover Publications, 1958.

Connolly, Peter. *Greece and Rome at War.* London: Greenhill Books, 1998.

Delbruck, Hans. *The Barbarian Invasions.* Lincoln: University of Nebraska Press, 1975.

*——. *Warfare in Antiquity.* Lincoln: University of Nebraska Press, 1975.

Dodge, Theodore A. *Hannibal.* New York: Da Capo, 1995.

——. *Alexander.* New York: Da Capo, 1996.

——. *Caesar.* New York: Da Capo, 1997.

Field Manual 27-10. *The Law of Land Warfare.* Washington, D.C.: Department of the Army, July 1956.

Fuller, J. F. C. *The Generalship of Alexander the Great.* New York: Da Capo, 1960.

——. *Julius Caesar: Man, Soldier and Tyrant.* London: Wordsworth, 1998.

Gibbon, Edward. *The Decline and Fall of the Roman Empire.* 3 vols. Modern Library Series. New York: Random House, 1995.

Goldsworthy, Adrian. *Roman Warfare.* London: Cassell, 2000.

Graetz, H. *History of the Jews.* 6 vols. Philadelphia: Jewish Publication Society of America, 1891.

Grant, Michael. *The Army of the Caesars.* New York: Scribners, 1974.

———. *Julius Caesar.* New York: Barnes and Noble, 1997.

*Hackett, John. *Warfare in the Ancient World.* New York: Facts on File, 1989.

Hammond, N. G. L. *The Genius of Alexander the Great.* Chapel Hill: University of North Carolina Press, 1997.

Hanson, Victor Davis. *The Western Way of War.* New York: Knopf, 1989.

*Herzog, Chaim, and Mordechai Gichon. *Battles of the Bible.* London: Greenhill Books, 1997.

James, Peter, and Nick Thorpe. *Ancient Inventions.* New York: Ballantine, 1994.

Josephus. *The Jewish War.* New York: Penguin Classics, 1981.

Kagan, Donald. *The Outbreak of the Peloponnesian War.* Ithaca, N.Y.: Cornell University Press, 1969.

———. *The Archidamian War.* Ithaca, N.Y.: Cornell University Press, 1974.

———. *The Peace of Nicias and the Sicilian Expedition.* Ithaca, N.Y.: Cornell University Press, 1981.

———. *The Fall of the Athenian Empire.* Ithaca, N.Y.: Cornell University Press, 1987.

Liddell Hart, B. H. *Scipio Africanus.* New York: Da Capo, 1994.

Montagu, John Drogo. *Battles of the Greek and Roman Worlds.* London: Greenhill, 2000.

Orlinsky, Harry M. *Ancient Israel.* Ithaca, N.Y.: Cornell University Press, 1967.

Polybius. *The Rise of the Roman Empire.* New York: Penguin Classics, 1979.

Rodgers, W. L *Greek and Roman Naval Warfare,* Annapolis, Md.: Naval Institute Press, 1964.

———. *Naval Warfare under Oars.* Annapolis, Md.: Naval Institute Press, 1967.

Sachar, Abraham Leon. *A History of the Jews.* New York: Knopf, 1963.

Strauss, Barry S., and Josiah Ober. *The Anatomy of Error.* New York: St. Martin's, 1990.

Xenophon. *The Persian Expedition.* New York: Penguin Classics, 1986.

Medieval

Bradford, Ernie. *The Great Siege: Malta 1565.* London: Wordsworth, 1999.

Chambers, James. *The Devil's Horsemen.* London: Phoenix, 1979.

Delbruck, Hans. *The Dawn of Modern Warfare.* Lincoln: University of Nebraska, 1975.

*———. *Medieval Warfare.* Lincoln: University of Nebraska, 1975.

Hildinger, Erik. *Warriors of the Steppe.* New York: Sarpedon, 1997.

Kinross, Lord. *The Ottoman Centuries.* New York: Morrow Quill, 1979.

Newby, P. H. *Saladin in His Time.* London: Phoenix, 1983.

Norwich, John Julius. *A Short History of Byzantium.* New York: Knopf, 1997.

Oman, Charles. *The Art of War in the Sixteenth Century.* London: Greenhill, 1987.

*———. *The Art of War in the Middle Ages.* 2 vols. London: Greenhill, 1991.

Runciman, Steven. *The Crusades.* London: Cambridge, 1995.

Seward, Desmond. *The Hundred Years War.* New York: Atheneum, 1978.

Modern

Allen, Charles. *Soldier Sahibs.* New York: Carroll and Graf, 2000.

Allen, George H. *The Great War, Causes of and Motives For.* Philadelphia: George Barrie's Sons, 1915.

Alvarez, Jose E. *The Betrothed of Death.* London: Greenwood, 2001.

Ambrose, Steven. *Citizen Soldiers.* New York: Simon & Schuster, 1997.

Asprey, Robert B. *The German High Command.* New York: William Morrow, 1991.

Baldwin, Hanson W. *Battles Lost and Won.* New York: Avon, 1968.

*Barnett, Correlli. *The Desert Generals.* New York: Berkley Medallion, 1962.

———, ed. *Hitler's Generals.* New York: Quill, 1989.

Bell, J. Bowyer. *Terror Out of Zion.* New York: Avon, 1978.

Bennett, Martyn. *Historical Dictionary of the British and Irish Civil Wars.* Lanham, Md.: Scarecrow, 2000.

Bergerud, Eric M. *Touched with Fire.* New York: Viking, 1996.

———. *Fire in the Sky.* Boulder, Colo.: Westview, 2000.

Black, Jeremy. *War and the World.* New Haven, Conn.: Yale University Press, 1998.

Blair, Clay. *Ridgway's Paratroopers.* New York: Quill, 1985.

———. *The Forgotten War.* New York: Doubleday, 1997.

———. *Hitler's U-Boat War.* 2 vols. New York: Random House, 1998.

Botchkareva, Maria. *Yashka: My Life as Peasant, Officer and Exile.* New York: Frederick A. Stokes, 1919.

Boyington, Gregory. *Baa Baa Black Sheep.* New York: Bantam, 1977.

Buell, Thomas. *The Warrior Generals.* New York: Crown, 1997.

Carr, Caleb. *The Devil Soldier.* New York: Random House, 1992.

*Carver, Sir Michael. *The War Lords.* Boston: Little, Brown, 1976.

———. *Twentieth Century Warriors.* New York: Weidenfeld and Nicolson, 1987.

Catton, Bruce. *The Army of the Potomac.* 3 vols. New York: Doubleday, 1953.

Chalfont, Lord. *Waterloo.* New York: Knopf, 1979.

Chandler, David. *The Campaigns of Napoleon.* New York: Macmillan, 1966.

———. *The Art of Warfare in the Age of Marlborough.* New York: Hippocrene, 1976.

———. *Dictionary of the Napoleonic Wars.* New York: Macmillan, 1979.

———. *Napoleon's Marshals.* New York: Macmillan, 1987.

———. *The Oxford History of the British Army.* Oxford: Oxford University Press, 1996.

Clark, Alan. *The Donkeys.* New York: Award Books, 1965.

Cloud, Stanley, and Lynn Olson. *The Murrow Boys.* Boston: Houghton Mifflin, 1996.

Cross, Milton. *Encyclopedia of the Great Composers.* 2 vols. New York: Doubleday, 1962.

Davies, Norman. *White Eagle, Red Star.* London: Orbis, 1983.

Davis, Burke. *Marine! The Life of Chesty Puller.* New York: Bantam, 1968.

Delderfield, R. F. *Napoleon's Marshals.* New York: Stein and Day, 1980.

Deutscher, Isaac. *Trotsky: The Prophet.* 3 vols. New York: Vintage, 1963.

Dodge, Theodore A. *Napoleon.* 4 vols. Boston: Houghton Mifflin, 1935.

———. *Gustavus Adolphus.* London: Greenhill, 1996.

Doubler, Michael D. *Closing with the Enemy.* Lawrence: University Press of Kansas, 1994.

Duffy, Christopher. *The Military Experience in the Age of Reason.* London: Wordsworth, 1998.

Dunnigan, James F., and Albert A. Nofi. *Victory at Sea.* New York: William Morrow, 1995.

Dupuy, T. N. *A Genius for War.* Englewood Cliffs, N.J.: Prentice-Hall, 1977.

Eicher, David J. *The Longest Night.* New York: Simon & Schuster, 2001.

Eisenhower, John S. D. *So Far from God.* New York: Random House, 1989.

——. *Agent of Destiny.* New York: Free Press, 1997.

Ellis, John. *Social History of the Machine Gun.* Baltimore: Johns Hopkins, 1986.

——. *Brute Force.* New York: Viking, 1990.

Elting, John R. *Swords around a Throne.* New York: Free Press, 1988.

Esposito, Vincent J. *West Point Atlas of American Wars.* 2 vols. New York: Praeger, 1972.

Esposito, Vincent J., and John R. Elting. A *Military History and Atlas of the Napoleonic Wars.* New York: AMS, 1978.

Erickson, John. *The Road to Stalingrad.* Boulder, Colo.: Westview, 1975.

——. *The Road to Berlin.* Boulder, Colo.: Westview, 1983.

——. *The Soviet High Command.* Boulder, Colo.: Westview, 1984.

Farwell, Byron. *Queen Victoria's Little Wars.* London: Allen Lane, 1973.

——. *The Great Anglo-Boer War.* New York: Harper and Row, 1976.

——. *The Gurkhas.* New York: Norton, 1983.

——. *Eminent Victorian Soldiers.* New York: Norton, 1985.

——. *The Great War in Africa.* New York: Norton, 1986.

——. *Armies of the Raj.* New York: Norton, 1989.

Figes, Orlando. *A People's Tragedy.* New York: Viking, 1997.

Foote, Shelby. *The Civil War.* 3 vols. New York: Random House, 1974.

Freeman, Douglas S. *Lee's Lieutenants.* 3 vols. New York: Scribners, 1944.

Freidel, Frank. *The Splendid Little War.* New York: Dell, 1962.

Friedrich, Otto. *Blood and Iron.* New York: HarperCollins, 1995.

Glantz, David M. *Kharkov 1942.* Lawrence: University Press of Kansas, 1998.

——. *Stumbling Colossus.* Lawrence: University Press of Kansas, 1998.

——. *Zhukov's Greatest Defeat.* Lawrence: University Press of Kansas, 1999.

Glantz, David M., and Jonathan House. *When Titans Clashed.* Lawrence: University Press of Kansas, 1995.

——. *The Battle of Kursk.* Lawrence: University Press of Kansas, 1999.

Goerlitz, Walter. *The German General Staff.* New York: Praeger, 1967.

Graber, G. S. *Caravans to Oblivion.* New York: Wiley, 1996.

*Griess. Thomas E., ed. *The West Point Military History Series.* 10 vols. New York: Avery, 1985.

Griffith, Paddy. *Battle Tactics of the Western Front.* New Haven, Conn.: Yale University Press, 1994.

Guderian, Heinz. *Panzer Leader.* New York: Ballantine Books, 1972.

Hamilton, Nigel. *Monty.* 3 vols. New York: McGraw-Hill, 1987.

Hattaway, Herman, and Archer Jones. *How the North Won.* Urbana: University of Illinois, 1983.

Haythornthwaite, Philip J. *Die Hard.* London: Cassell, 1996.

Hoare, Mike. *Mercenary.* New York: Bantam, 1979.

Hirsch, Phil, ed., *Fighting Generals.* New York: Pyramid, 1960.

Hofschroer, Peter. *1815: The Waterloo Campaign.* 2 vols. London: Greenhill Books, 1999.

*Holmes, Richard. *Epic Land Battles.* Secaucus, N.J.: Chartwell Books, 1976.

Hopkirk, Peter. *Setting the East Ablaze.* New York: Kodansha International, 1984.

——. *The Great Game.* New York: Kodansha International, 1992.

——. *Like Hidden Fire.* New York: Kodansha International, 1994.

Horne, Alistair. *How Far from Austerlitz?* New York: St. Martin's, 1996.

Howard, Michael. *The Franco-Prussian War.* London: Methuen, 1971.

Howarth, David. *Waterloo: Day of Battle.* New York: Galahad Books, 1968.

James, Lawrence. *The Rise and Fall of the British Empire.* New York: St. Martin's, 1996.

Johnson, J. E. *Full Circle.* New York: Ballantine, 1964.

Keegan, John. *Fields of Battle.* New York: Vintage Books, 1997.

——. *The Second World War.* New York: Viking, 1990.

——, ed. *Churchill's Generals.* New York: Quill, 1991.

Kennedy, Paul M. *The Rise and Fall of British Naval Mastery.* London: Ashfield, 1983.

——. *The Rise and Fall of the Great Powers.* New York: Random House, 1987.

Kennett, Lee. *Marching through Georgia.* New York: HarperPerennial, 1995.

Knightley, Phillip. *The First Casualty*. New York: Harcourt Brace Jovanovich, 1975.

Kurzman, Dan. *Genesis 1948*. New York: Signet, 1970.

Leckie, Robert. *Strong Men Armed*. New York: Bantam, 1963.

Lincoln, W. Bruce. *Red Victory*. New York: Simon & Schuster, 1989.

Luckett, Richard. *The White Generals*. London: Routledge and Kegan Paul, 1987.

Macdonald, Lynn. *1915: The Death of Innocence*. New York: Henry Holt, 1995.

McElwee, William. *The Art of War: Waterloo to Mons*. Bloomington: Indiana University Press, 1974.

McLynn, Frank. *Villa and Zapata*. New York: Carroll and Graf, 2001.

McMaster, H. R. *Dereliction of Duty*. New York: HarperCollins, 1997.

McPherson, James M. *Battle Cry of Freedom*. New York: Oxford, 1988.

Macksey, Kenneth. *From Triumph to Disaster*. London: Greenhill, 1996.

Manchester, William. *American Caesar*. Boston: Little, Brown, 1978.

Mansoor, Peter R. *The GI Offensive in Europe*. Lawrence: University Press of Kansas, 1999.

Massie, Robert K. *Dreadnought: Britain, Germany and the Coming of the Great War*. New York: Random House, 1991.

Mawdsley, Evan. *The Russian Civil War*. Boston: Allen and Unwin, 1987.

Mellenthin, F. W. von. *Panzer Battles*. New York: Bantam, 1971.

Messenger, Charles. *The Blitzkrieg Story*. New York: Scribners, 1976.

Meyer, Karl E., and Shareen Blair Brysac. *Tournament of Shadows*. Washington, D.C.: Counterpoint, 1999.

Miller, Charles. *Battle for the Bundu*. New York: Macmillan, 1974.

Miller, Francis T., ed. *History of World War II*. Philadelphia: John C. Winston, 1945.

Miller, Nathan. *Broadsides*. New York: Wiley, 2000.

Mitcham Jr., Samuel W. *Hitler's Legions*. New York: Dorset, 1985.

Mitchell, Joseph B. *Decisive Battles of the Civil War*. New York: Fawcett, 1962.

Morelock, J. D. *Generals of the Ardennes*. Washington, D.C.: National Defense University, 1994.

Morris, Donald R. *The Washing of the Spears*. New York: Simon & Schuster, 1965.

Morrison, Samuel Eliot. *The Two-Ocean War.* New York: Ballantine, 1974.

*Mosier, John. *The Myth of the Great War.* New York: HarperCollins, 2001.

*Murray, Williamson, and Allan R. Millett. *A War to Be Won.* Cambridge, Mass.: Belknap, 2000.

Nevins, Allan. *War for the Union.* 4 vols. New York: Konecky and Konecky, 1971.

Nofi, Albert A. *The Spanish-American War, 1898.* Conshohocken, Pa.: Combined Books, 1996.

Overy, Richard. *Why the Allies Won.* New York: Norton, 1995.

——. *Russia's War.* New York: TV Books, 1997.

Padfield, Peter. *Maritime Supremacy and the Opening of the Western Mind.* Woodstock, N.Y.: Overlook, 1999.

Palmer, Michael A. *Lee Moves North.* New York: Wiley, 1998.

Parkinson, C. Northcote. *Britannia Rules.* Worcester, Mass.: Sutton Publishing, 1997.

Parrish, Michael, ed. *Battle for Moscow.* Washington, D.C.: Brassey's, 1989.

Parrish, T. Michael. *Richard Taylor: Soldier Prince of Dixie.* Chapel Hill: University of North Carolina Press, 1992.

Parry, Albert. *Russian Cavalcade.* New York: Ives Washburn, 1944.

Payne, Robert. *Lawrence of Arabia.* New York: Pyramid, 1962.

Perrett, Bryan. *At All Costs!* London: Arms and Armour, 1994.

——. *Impossible Victories.* London: Arms and Armour, 1996.

Perret, Geoffrey. *A Country Made by War.* New York: First Vintage, 1989.

——. *There's a War to Be Won.* New York: Ballantine, 1992.

Perry, James M. *Arrogant Armies.* New York: Wiley, 1996.

Pipes, Richard. *Russia under the Bolshevik Regime.* New York: Vintage, 1995.

Porch, Douglas. *The French Foreign Legion.* New York: HarperPerennial, 1992.

——. *The French Secret Services.* New York: Farrar, Straus & Giroux, 1995.

Pratt, Fletcher. *The Civil War.* New York: Cardinal, 1960.

Prochnau, William. *Once Upon a Distant War.* New York: Times, 1995.

Ready, J. Lee. *Arrogance on the Battlefield.* London: Arms and Armour, 1996.

Richelson, Jeffrey T. *A Century of Spies.* New York: Oxford University Press, 1995.

Ropp, Theodore. *War in the Modern World*. Baltimore: Johns Hopkins University Press, 2000.

Rotundo, Louis, ed. *Battle for Stalingrad*. Washington, D.C.: Brassey's, 1989.

Ryan, Cornelius. *A Bridge Too Far*. New York: Simon & Schuster, 1974.

Schindler, John R. *Isonzo*. Westport, Conn.: Praeger, 2001.

Scott, Jay. *Marine War Heroes*. New York: Monarch Books, 1963.

*Shukman, Harold, ed. *Stalin's Generals*. New York: Grove, 1993.

Spahr, William J. *Stalin's Lieutenants*. Novato, Calif.: Presidio, 1997.

Spector, Ronald H. *Eagle against the Sun*. New York: Vintage, 1985.

——. *At War at Sea*. New York: Viking, 2001.

Steven, Stewart. *The Spymasters of Israel*. New York: Ballantine, 1980.

Stone, Norman. *The Eastern Front: 1914–1917*. New York: Scribners, 1975.

Strachan, Hew. *The First World War: To Arms*. Oxford: Oxford University Press, 2001.

Taylor, Richard. *Destruction and Reconstruction*. New York: Bantam, 1992.

Thomas, Lowell. *Count Luckner, the Sea Devil*. Garden City, NY: Garden City Publishing, 1927.

Toland, John. *No Man's Land*. New York: Ballantine, 1980.

Trotter, William R. *A Frozen Hell*. Chapel Hill, N.C.: Algonquin Books, 1991.

Trulock, Alice Rains. *In the Hands of Providence*. Chapel Hill: University of North Carolina Press, 1992.

Volkman, Ernest. *Spies*. New York: Wiley, 1994.

Volkogonov, Dmitri. *Trotsky*. New York: Free Press, 1996.

*Warner, Ezra J. *Generals In Blue*. Baton Rouge: Louisiana State University Press, 1999.

*——. *Generals In Gray*. Baton Rouge: Louisiana State University Press, 2000.

Wartenburg, Yorck von. *Napoleon as a General*. 2 vols. London: Wolseley Series, 1955.

Weigley, Russell F. *The American Way of War*. Bloomington: Indiana University Press, 1977.

——. *Eisenhower's Lieutenants*. Bloomington: Indiana University Press, 1990.

——. *A Great Civil War*. Bloomington: Indiana University Press, 2000.

Weinberg, Gerhard L. *A World at Arms*. Cambridge, Mass.: Cambridge University, 1994.

Weller, Jac. *Wellington at Waterloo*. London: Greenhill, 1992.

———. *Wellington in the Peninsula*. London: Greenhill, 1992.

———. *Wellington in India*. London: Greenhill, 1993.

*Wellman, Paul I. *The Indian Wars of the West*. 2 vols. New York: Pyramid, 1963.

Werth, Alexander. *Russia at War*. New York: Avon, 1970.

Wise, James E., and Ann Rehill. *Stars in Blue*. Annapolis, Md.: Naval Institute Press, 1997.

———. *Stars in the Corps*. Annapolis, Md.: Naval Institute Press, 1999.

Wise, James E., and Paul W. Wilderson. *Stars in Khaki*. Annapolis, Md.: Naval Institute Press, 2000.

Wolff, Leon. *In Flanders Fields*. New York: Viking, 1980.

Woodham-Smith, Cecil. *The Charge of the Light Brigade*. New York: Signet, 1968.

Young, Desmond. *Rommel: The Desert Fox*. New York: Berkeley Medallion, 1962.

Young, Peter, ed. *Atlas of the Second World War*. New York: G. P. Putnam, 1974.

Young, Peter, and Richard Holmes. *The English Civil War*. London: Wordsworth, 2000.

Younger, Carlton. *Ireland's Civil War*. London: Fontana, 1979.

Ziemke, Earl F. *Stalingrad to Berlin*. Washington, D.C.: Center of Military History, 1968.

Ziemke, Earl F., and Magna E. Bauer. *Moscow to Stalingrad*. Washington, D.C.: Center of Military History, 1985.

Zhukov, Georgi et al. *Battles Hitler Lost*. New York: Jove, 1988.

Index

Page numbers in bold refer to photographic inserts.

About the Author

M. Evan Brooks served for 31 years in the Army Reserve (retiring as a lieutenant colonel in 2001), including participation in Desert Shield/ Desert Storm, where he was the military liaison to the Kuwaiti Red

LTC M. Evan Brooks at Subhan, Kuwait City, Kuwait (April 1991)

Crescent Society. He is a graduate of the Naval War College, Command & General Staff College, and nine branch officer courses, and served in seven different capacities during his military career (in fields ranging from infantry to staff judge advocate to military police). He has written extensively in the computer simulation field and has been a regular contributor to many computer gaming magazines. He has also written numerous book reviews. He is a regular speaker at the U.S. Air Force's *Connections,* an annual civilian-military symposium on military gaming. An attorney for a government agency, Mr. Brooks currently resides in northern Virginia with his wife and his Samoyed, Mowgli.